Victorian Journalism:
Exotic and Domestic

To Maggie Collins
with love,
and in memory of her early
mentorship and the fifty years of
academic striving which it helped
initiate and which are too kindly
chronicled on pp 212-218 below.

Peter Edwards
London 5 July 1999

LONDON:
PUBLISHED AT THE OFFICE, 85, FLEET STREET.
AND SOLD BY ALL BOOKSELLERS.
1846.

Victorian Journalism: Exotic and Domestic

Essays in Honour of P.D. Edwards

**Edited by
Barbara Garlick and Margaret Harris**

Queensland University Press

First published 1998 by University of Queensland Press
Box 42, St Lucia, Queensland 4067 Australia

© University of Queensland Press 1998

This book is copyright. Apart from any fair dealing
for the purposes of private study, research, criticism
or review, as permitted under the Copyright Act, no
part may be reproduced by any process without written
permission. Enquiries should be made to the publisher.

Printed in Australia by The University of Queensland Printery

Distributed in the USA and Canada by
International Specialised Book Services, Inc.,
5804 N.E. Hassalo Street, Portland, Oregon 97213–3640

Cataloguing in Publication Data
National Library of Australia

ISBN 0 7022 3104 5

Contents

Preface

1   Virginia Blain   1
Anonymity and the Discourse of Amateurism: Caroline Bowles Southey negotiates *Blackwood's* 1820-1847

2   Judith Johnston   19
Anna Brownell Jameson and the *Monthly Chronicle*

3   Michael Slater   38
How Mrs Caudle Went On and On; or, The Afterlife of a Minor Victorian Classic

4   Barbara Garlick   46
'The true principle of Biographical delineation': Harriet Martineau's 'Biographical Sketches' in the *Daily News*

5   John Sutherland   62
Trollope, the *Times*, and *The Warden*

6   Christopher Kent   75
The Angry Young Gentlemen of *Tomahawk*

7   Joanne Shattock   95
Margaret Oliphant: Journalist

8	Paul Crook Benjamin Kidd: Social Prophet as Journalist	108
9	Judy McKenzie Paper Heroes: Special Correspondents and their Narratives of Empire	124
10	Chris Tiffin Literature and Politics in the Queensland Colonial Press	141
11	Meg Tasker Learning Journalism in Australia: Francis W.L. Adams, an Englishman Abroad	155
12	Sue Thomas Jean Rhys and Dominican Autoethnography	171
13	Lloyd Davis Journalism and Victorian Fiction	197
14	Margaret Harris P.D. Edwards: Victorianist	212
Notes on Contributors		219
Index		222

Preface

The interest and significance of the periodical press for the study of the era defined by the long reign of Queen Victoria (1837-1901) is now well recognised as are the challenges posed by the study of so voluminous and various a body of writing as that generally described as 'Victorian journalism'. The Victorian period saw both the rise and the demise of many fine journalistic ideas and projects. There was a rapid increase in the number of journals and newspapers catering to all groups in society, particularly after the repeal of the newspaper tax in 1836. Increasingly journalists wrote to a particular audience, creating 'the appetite which his writings satisfy', whether that audience was delineated by class, political leanings, geography or gender.

The question of readership is ever-present in the essays in this volume, along with other common and urgent issues: the gradual professionalisation of the journalist and the lingering attractions of amateurism, recognised also in the novels of the period; the continuing debate about anonymity; the status of journalism in a hierarchy of literary forms, and the conflicting demands of the higher journalism and the popular press; the negotiations that women journalists had to make across the public/private domain; nationalism, imperialism and colonialism.

While such issues and themes recur throughout the volume, *Victorian Journalism* nevertheless demonstrates the heterogeneity of its subject. A range of journals comes in for discussion: the influence of establishment newspapers like the London *Times* is an element of John Sutherland's account of 'Trollope, the *Times* and *The Warden*'; the power of *Punch* is seen both in Michael Slater's discussion of a famous figure created in its pages, and Christopher Kent's of the shortlived challenge to *Punch* by 'The Angry Young Gentlemen of *Tomahawk*'; the particular character of the *Daily News* is a consideration in Barbara Garlick's presentation of Harriet Martineau as obituarist. A number of the essays explore the role of journals in political and literary debate and in topical social commentary, while Paul Crook depicts the idiosyncratic combination of scientific discourse and demogoguery in 'Benjamin Kidd: Social Prophet as Journalist', and Lloyd Davis explores some significant interactions between 'Journalism and Victorian Fiction'.

The essays begin with the early part of Victoria's reign and move through the years and across the globe, to the island continent of Australia, and to the island of Dominica in the West Indies in the last years of the century. While the focus is on London as the seat of Victorian journalism, the essays are not confined to this metropolitan and imperial centre. There is insight into activity in other centres in Britain, notably Edinburgh, and in particular the house of Blackwood, discussed in Virginia Blain's essay, 'Anonymity and the Discourse of Amateurism: Caroline Bowles Southey negotiates *Blackwood's*' and in Joanne Shattock's account of 'Margaret Oliphant: Journalist'. A number of the essays look at Victorian journalism in exotic places: in Judy McKenzie's discussion of the special correspondent and Meg Tasker's of 'Francis W.L. Adams, an Englishman Abroad' the journalists are still in large measure 'writing home', but as Chris Tiffin's consideration of fiction in the *Queenslander* at mid-century, and Sue Thomas's of Dominican periodicals at. the end of the century show, an orientation to England did not inhibit the development of indigenous journalism.

During the period women were becoming more numerous and more important as contributors to both journals and newspapers (though as Lloyd Davis reminds us 'the periodical press, from proprietors to readers, was a man's world'). Judith Johnston makes a case for seeing Anna Jameson as a contender with Harriet Martineau for recognition as the first professional woman journalist. Moreover the writings of both Jameson and Martineau, along with Margaret Oliphant, provide ample evidence of the extent to which women journalists did not confine themselves to issues which impinged most directly on women's lives, such as marriage and education, but also covered political, social and other national subjects.

The essays in this volume were written by colleagues and friends of Peter Edwards, Emeritus Professor of English at The University of Queensland. Former students are numbered among the contributors, most of whom work in literary studies while some are historians. All join to honour Peter Edwards's work in Victorian literature and particularly, in later years, in the field of Victorian journalism. The presence in various of the essays of Anthony Trollope, as novelist, travel-writer, or journalist, is a tribute not only to Trollope's ubiquity, but also to Peter Edwards's eminence in Trollope studies. The editors thank all the contributors both for their essays and for their patience during the editing and publishing process. Our thanks must also go to Judy McKenzie for her skill and imagination in preparing the camera-ready copy, and to Craig Munro of the University of Queensland Press for his helpful support and advice.

Barbara Garlick
Margaret Harris

1 Anonymity and the Discourse of Amateurism: Caroline Bowles Southey Negotiates Blackwoods 1820-1847

Virginia Blain

Caroline Anne Bowles, later Southey, entered the domain of literary journalism through *Blackwood's Edinburgh Magazine* (founded in 1817) during the 1820s. She was drawn to contribute her poems and prose sketches to this masculinist Tory stronghold largely because of an ideological sympathy: she too was a Tory, and she was by no means—initially at least—a feminist. However, she was also urged towards this choice by her literary mentor, Robert Southey, who had initially undertaken to introduce her work to William Blackwood (in his role of book publisher) after Longmans (who published her first books) proved unsatisfactory. Over a number of years she built up a quasi-intimate working relationship with the magazine ('Maga'), contributing regularly, including topical 'insider's' pieces on, for example, James Hogg's *Shepherd's Calendar*, and earning several friendly mentions in the ponderously jocose columns of 'Noctes Ambrosianae'.[1]

Caroline Bowles Southey[2] (1786-1854) was well regarded as a writer of both prose and poetry during her lifetime. Her poetry in particular attracted some excellent reviews, and was admired by Wordsworth and his circle, as his letters attest.[3] The affinity with Wordsworth is not surprising, since her major achievement is unquestionably her long, blank-verse narrative poem, *The Birthday* (1836), which is an autobiography of her early years. Published well before the appearance of *The Prelude* in 1850, it represents a unique achievement for a woman writer and was the first publication to which she set her name. She had already brought out two collections of poems, in 1820 and 1822, and one of mixed prose and verse (1826), as well as a pseudonymous *jeu d'esprit*, *The Cat's Tail* ('by the Baroness de Katzleben') illustrated by George Cruikshank, and a little-known verse tract of 1831, *Tales of the Factories*, which responded to Sadleir's parliamentary reports on the plight of factory children. But her most immediately popular work was undoubtedly the series of prose sketches she contributed to *Blackwood's Magazine* during the 1820s, under the title Chapters on Churchyards. These were collected into two volumes published by Blackwoods in 1829 and reprinted in one volume in 1841. Her *Poetical Works* were published posthumously in 1867, thanks largely to the efforts of Robert Southey's son-in-law, John Warter.[4]

Apart from her two earliest verse volumes, *Ellen Fitzarthur* (1820) and *The Widow's Tale* (1822), brought out by Longmans, all of her works were published by Blackwoods. Most of her writing (apart from stray pieces issued in the annuals[5]) appeared first in *Blackwood's Edinburgh Magazine*. Her 27-year relationship with the firm is well documented in the manuscript letters of the Blackwood Collection in the National Library of Scotland,[6] supplemented by the published correspondence between Caroline Bowles and Robert Southey, edited in 1881 by Edward Dowden.[7] Her long friendship with Southey, dating from the occasion of her first letter to him in April 1818, clearly grew out of shared literary tastes and sympathies (although he always objected to her liking for the ghoulish and for the heart-rendingly pathetic), as well as an enjoyment of each other's humour and forthrightness. Both were passionate, outspoken, kind, and inconsistent. Yet their friendship was never intended for a moment to culminate in marriage: Edith Southey, Robert's first wife, whom Caroline met in 1823 when she visited Southey's family at Keswick, did not die until 1837, although she had lived for many years before then in a mental institution. Yet marry they did, in 1839 when she was 52 and he was 65, already manifesting the early signs of senile decay (noticed by his son Cuthbert, but not by Caroline, whose usual communication with him was epistolary). This marriage, apparently undertaken on his side from fear of loneliness and a desire to be looked after, and on hers, from feelings of 'tender friendship'[8] while still in ignorance of his true state of health, effectively ended her writing career.

His health deteriorated rapidly over the last few years of his life, much of which were spent in his room at Keswick, unable to think, read or write (though he still loved his books), and at times becoming violent. When he died in 1843, after several years of selfless nursing by Caroline (whose own health had never been strong), it was a relief to all who loved him to see his suffering end. His son Cuthbert and daughter Kate never forgave their father for remarrying, and as soon as his eyes were closed they sent his second wife packing. She was thankful to be able to return to Buckland Cottage, near Lymington in Hampshire, which had been her childhood home, though with a greatly reduced income as the result of forfeiting her annuity upon marriage. Southey made no equivalent provision for her in his will, and she was forced to buy some of his effects at the household sale at Greta Hall, his Keswick home. Apart from a few poignant sonnets, referring to her soul-shattering experiences as wife to the shell of the man she had so warm-heartedly agreed to marry '. . . so mated, yet so desolate',[9] she wrote nothing further; although she did, in 1850, attempt to re-open negotiations with Blackwoods about further collections of her earlier work.[10]

The 1830s was a key decade in the professionalisation of the woman poet,[11] yet primary sources of evidence are all too scant. Caroline Bowles Southey is a particularly interesting case for several reasons. Firstly, being a single woman, she conducted all her negotiations on her own behalf; secondly, her financial arangements appear to have been unusual; and thirdly, she built up over the years particular discursive strategies as a means of getting what she wanted from her publishers, with whom she had an enduring but fluctuating relationship. In addition, and of especial significance to recent feminist attempts to theorise issues pertaining to female authorship, she is shown to have been keenly alive to the nuances of the various grades of anonymity and pseudonymity (ranging from complete absence of signature, through initials 'C' or 'A'—her second name was Anne—to 'by the author of . . . ') and their changing meanings for the woman writer of this period.

The Bowles correspondence, catalogued in the National Library of Scotland under Southey, consists of more than 150 letters from Bowles to Blackwoods. I have only managed to locate one or two copies from the other side, but it is often easy to guess what might have been said by Blackwood from Bowles's responses. Here is an example: 'My Pegasus is a very wayward palfrey, and will by no means go thro' his paces at my will and pleasure; I can only say that when I find him in a tractable mood, he shall do his best for Mr B's review'.[12] This spirited communication comes from the first of Caroline Bowles's surviving letters to Blackwoods, dated 30 August 1821, written to William Blackwood, senior.[13] It is evidently not the first letter she wrote to him; there is apparently an earlier letter offering him a poem which was now accepted for the Magazine.[14]

Her reference here to her writing gift as both a 'Pegasus' and 'a very wayward palfrey' is typical of her refreshingly forthright style. She was, after all, despite her diminutive size, a woman of old-fashioned Tory courage, who kept a brace of pistols primed while living as an 'unprotected' female during the agricultural riots in her Hampshire district, and she knew how to shoot them. There is no sign of false modesty—she knows she possesses a real gift—a winged horse—but nor is there any giving in to the temptation of 'Mr B's' no doubt flattering solicitation to become a contributor on a regular basis—her horse will not become anybody's hack.

Even though she began to think of publication because she needed the money (a guardian purloined funds due to her at her parents' death), she is far from allowing herself to be treated as if she wrote for a living. Her English father had been an army officer, her Jersey French maternal grandmother, herself of aristocratic background, had married into a baronet's family, and Caroline Bowles, who had inherited her father's house at Buckland, was conscious enough of her own social status to be aware of the gulf dividing the amateur from the professional. In this context, to have been viewed as 'professional' would not have been felt to be a compliment, as it would have jeopardised severely her status as a 'lady'. The same was largely true for upper-middle-class male writers of her political colour; Robert Smith Surtees, country squire born a little later than Bowles, and author of comic-satiric novels including *Jorrocks's Jaunts and Jollities* (1838) and *Mr Sponge's Sporting Tour* (1853), felt so strongly the impropriety of a gentleman dabbling in fiction that he not only concealed his writings from all who knew him, but he sacked his publisher when his much-prized anonymity was carelessly breached in an advertisement.[15]

Sacking one's publisher, however, was an extravagance that few authors could afford. Publishers needed to be treated with circumspection, at the very least. Caroline Bowles, although a lady, had only limited private means, and there were several occasions during her writing career when she felt more than usually pressed for funds, and even came close to losing her house. As a result of these fluctuating circumstances, her determination to pursue proper payment for her work tended to fluctuate also. The initial alarm over the possible loss of her home had propelled her into publishing her first narrative poem, the metrical tale *Ellen Fitzarthur*, with Longmans, having taken advice, according to custom, from the Poet Laureate and thus, incidentally, initiating the long correspondence with Southey (who notably did *not* give her the dusty answer about women's duties that poor Charlotte Brontë smarted under in later years[16]). The popular success of *Ellen Fitzarthur* (published anonymously) was followed quickly by *The Widow's Tale* in 1822 (also anonymous); hence it is with the confidence of an already-published author that she wrote to Blackwood in the manner quoted.

Her relations with William Blackwood senior soon developed into cordial liking on both sides; although the two never met, they happily swapped health reports (hers was often precarious: she never believed she would have long to live) as well as gossip about other contributors to 'Maga'. Her distress at his death in

1834 was real; it shows in the stiffness she felt with the sons, and the time it took her to settle in with them. It is not always clear exactly what her financial arrangements with the firm were at any given moment, but a certain pattern emerges. Originally she seems to have been offered the choice between a payment of ten guineas per sheet[17] and a parcel of books. Usually she appears to have accepted books in lieu of money for her verse and prose contributions, and Blackwood's payments-in-kind erred on the side of generosity; he too liked to do the gentlemanly thing. Having parcels of books sent to her home in the country was a godsend to someone as cut off as she was from any major literary centre. But in 1824, when her financial situation was again pressing, she wrote asking for the money instead: 'if [Mr B] is still disposed to accept *my literary wares* on those terms, which different considerations have of late strongly inclined me to accept'.[18] We can safely assume that 'my literary wares' is underlined by way of humorously distancing herself from the vulgar necessity of mentioning writing in terms of a trade.

Money-talk and how it is handled is one of the important keys to distinguishing professionalism from amateurism. Although she defers to William Blackwood's experience on some matters, she never actually plays the role of helpless female, preferring instead a more aristocratic flourish. For example, on 7 August 1827, she wrote returning a cheque that had been sent her: 'the accompanying order on Mr Cadell was one I neither expected nor felt myself entitled to—and I must beg you in common honesty—not again to send me *retaining fees*—for I am *not to be* depended on—nothing in the world more likely, than that I may die and cheat you—.'[19] But this grand gesture of carelessness about cash masks a determination to preserve her artistic freedom, always her first concern. Whenever she has to await an answer to some request, she writes to doubt that his 'greatly increased establishment' can have any need of authors like her.[20] This comment gets him back into line pretty quickly. If he presses her too hard, she lets him know it in no uncertain terms: once he capitulates, she instantly breathes sweetness and light. For example, a miscellany of her verse and prose pieces from 'Maga', which was eventually published anonymously under the title *Solitary Hours* in 1826, underwent some strenuous pre-publication negotiations.

On 28 April 1825 Bowles wrote with a very conscious exploitation of what I term the 'discourse of amateurism': 'I am afraid you will note me down, in the black book (which I dare say you keep) of obstinate, conceited authors, when I avow myself disinclined to adopt *all* your suggestions relative to my proposed publication—'. She then agrees to drop one piece, but wants to retain two others:

> The two other papers you propose cashiering—viz 'Beauty' & 'Thoughts on L.Wg' [i.e., Letter Writing] are by no means darlings of mine, and I would say 'let them go to the dogs too' if their condemnation did not involve the sacrifice of my whole plan—namely, either now, or to be completed at some future time, the publication of two Vols—the first containing what you have inspected—the second 'The Chaps on Churchyds' with one or two other poetical additions. Neither of my former vols (with which I wish these to be stitched up uniformly) contains more than from 200 to 220 pages (to the best of my recollection for I have them not by me). The small edn of Southey, Crabbe, Byron, etc etc—now lying by me contains I perceive from 203 to 230 pages, and I by no means wish my Vol to exceed the thickness of these—[. . . If he is] averse to both these propositions, I will for the present relinquish the scheme altogether . . . The two papers you purpose laying aside as 'least akin to the others' I am desirous of inserting for that especial reason, all the rest being in the dismal strain, which I am accused of being unmercifully given to. Now I have set before you all my *reasons* which I suppose *you* will resolve

> into one *unreasonable* argument A Woman's wile—and if I were to talk for an hour I should only subject myself to another reflection so often cast upon us—without bringing you over to my way of thinking; So leaving you to decide as shall seem most expedient to you, I shall add no more.[21]

His reply cannot have been to her liking, as it was followed by a three-month silence. On 11 November she sent a letter written in the third person, the excuse being her recent serious illness. But the use of this impersonal mode of address underscores the distance in her tone:

> Miss B was indeed much disappointed at the long postponement of her little miscellaney [sic], and would not willingly let another season slip past her so unexpectedly—but she is still very decided as to the form of publication—namely one Vol with the whole of the poetical pieces as now arranged—and the miscellaneous prose pieces—Reserving the Chapters on Churchyards, with some others in M.S. for a separate Vol to be published either at the same time with the first, or later—If Mr W Blackwood is still disinclined to this mode of publication, Miss Bowles will not of course press it on him, but will be obliged to him for a definitive answer, that she may arrange accordingly.[22]

She refused his wish to include any of her popular 'Chapters on Churchyards', having enough of them on their own, as she says, to bury a whole parish, and wanting therefore to reserve them for a separate publication. She also wins on the selection, as the two prose pieces he had wanted to exclude as 'least akin to the others' are in fact included. One on 'Beauty', the other 'Thoughts on Letter-writing', are actually two of her most pungent and quirky satires, though both written in what he would probably have thought rather doubtful taste.

Evidently she won the battle of wills; on 30 December she writes thanking him for 'indulging me in *my own* way (a woman's desideratum you know)'; i.e., for agreeing to her plan to publish the miscellaneous pieces without using the 'Chapters'. She sends a few more 'poetical trifles': she had been holding off sending any contributions to 'Maga' on plea of suspecting he has many 'more competent sources'; she is now all honey and spends the next three pages agreeing with him and flattering him: ' . . . I am exceedingly obliged to you for taking the trouble to correct my absurd mistakes in your beautiful Scottish tongue'. She expatiates on how splendid it is to compose in the Scottish: 'Together with "the Birdie", you will find another *rash venture*'—and asks him to correct this too.[23] By January 1826, she is gloating to Southey about her victory: 'The Monster is going to publish my bundle of scraps this month. Indifference and silence have fought my battle for me—brought him to terms—that is, to publish only what I stipulate for, instead of the thumping volume he wanted to make' (Dowden, *Correspondence*, p.94).

As usual, she expected Blackwood to furnish the volume with a title. On this occasion, however, it was Southey who came up with 'Solitary Hours'. Titles were never important to her, they were mere packaging, something for the marketing side to supply; such carelessness betrays either too much snobbishness or too much anxiety: perhaps it is another hallmark of amateurism. However, this apparent carelessness is at odds with the care she took over other aspects of her published work.

Apart from the key issue of payment, another important pointer to a writer's degree of professionalism must be the amount of attention paid to matters of presentation, including printing and typeface. Given her peculiar disdain for titles, and given her constant self-deprecating reference to her own magazine contributions as 'trifles, scraps, idle verses, bundles of fragments', one might have expected that she would leave *all* matters of material production to her publisher's editor. Far from it.

Except on the occasions when David Moir's services as editor were offered her,[24] she insisted on correcting proof herself with great minuteness, becoming exceedingly cross if her instructions were neglected. Part of the reason why details of visual presentation engaged her so strongly, was that she was artist as well as writer. She painted in both watercolour and oils, provided illustrations for her own work, and had a number of her paintings engraved and circulated as popular prints, with subjects such as 'A Country Ball', 'Packing Up After the Ball'.[25]

Her satiric poem (or 'burlesque epic', as she called it), *The Cat's Tail, being the history of Childe Merlin*, published separately in 1831, was illustrated with engravings by George Cruikshank from Bowles's own sketches. When she offered Blackwood this poem, she told him to publish only if he thought it would cover its own cost, as it was merely part of a joke she had with friends: 'of course you are not to run any risk, for my jest's sake, nor can I afford to publish on my own account . . .' Nonetheless, she pressed him to illustrate it: '[P.S.] I should imagine coarse woodcuts, from the designs would not be very costly—& you know—*effect* is everything'.[26]

Blackwood went ahead with such enthusiasm that he even ran to *coloured* engravings. However, a small crisis arose during the book's preparation for the press when two of her sketches were apparently rejected. She lost the battle to include them, and wrote later:

> My dear Sir/ I hasten to tell you that I have received the consignment of *Cats Tails*—I think that sublime poem beautifully got up—save and excepting that mutilated passage—where the 4th illustration is substracted [sic]—It would have been better to leave the lines as they were—leaving the reader to account as he could, for the absence of the picture, & I should have written to request it, on receiving your last letter, but thought my protest would be too late—Except this unlucky passage, which is now

> *un*intelligible, instead of *in*telligible nonsense—I cannot but be pleased with the manner in which you have sent out the little oddity—, & Mr.G.Cruikshanks [sic] has done his part excellently—In the copies sent me, I have scratched out the faulty line & substituted two others.²⁷

It would be most unladylike to show any direct resentment over this issue, yet her letter ensures that her feelings are made known: a key feature of the 'discourse of amateurism'.

Another feature is the reliance on anonymity, the refusal to associate the private and social self with the public, published self. On this occasion Bowles was particularly adamant that no hint of her authorship should be made known. The book had first been offered, anonymously and with a theatrical flourish of secrecy, to John Murray, who unfortunately declined it.²⁸ She then had to approach the publisher who knew her, but swore him to secrecy: '—One thing, & *the principal* in my account—I had forgotten to state—that I wish (in case of publication)—to keep the *strictest incognita*—*Not* "by the Author of E.F. etcetera"—for the world—People expect *pathetic Poetesses* to be "like Niobe, all tears"'.²⁹

Sadly, despite its delightfully sardonic portrait of Anglo-French relations by way of a mangy tabby and a tomcat, the volume failed after all to cover its costs and, what was more unfortunate, became separated over time by the very effectiveness of its pseudonym, from the rest of its author's *oeuvre*. Fewer than two hundred copies were sold,³⁰ and it is now even harder to find owing precisely to its quirky pseudonym, which has generally led libraries to catalogue it under its title alone (as in the British Library) or under 'Katzleben', with no cross-reference to either 'Bowles' or 'Southey'.

Probably the major penalty for any author pursuing this kind of dilettantish anonymity is the posthumous confusion surrounding her or his actual publications and, hence, reputation. Just as some of Caroline Bowles Southey's works have almost vanished, she has also been wrongly credited with works by other writers. The *New Cambridge Bibliography of English Literature* (1969) gives her almost all the indifferent prose writings of one Mrs Amelia Gillespie Smyth, for example. And while she was alive, she objected on several occasions to the way in which anonymously published verse of hers was lifted straight from *Blackwood's Magazine* and reprinted elsewhere over someone else's signature.[31]

Her magazine contributions were generally signed with either her first or second initial ('C' or 'A'), and she was very upset whenever one of the Annuals published her name. In 1833 she wrote to Blackwood:

> ... above all do not affix *my signature* to anything of mine—the example of fine company is no encouragement to me—on the contrary, I am but the more disposed to shrink into my anonymous corner, from the blazonry of names—I have lately— shunned the Annuals on that account—when I was *affichée malgré moi*—I have no such objection to affix my name to an addition [sic] of my little works—collected should that ever be—but no name less distinguished than that of Mrs Hemans—no female name I should say—bears being perpetually placarded—.[32]

However, as early as 1829 she had shown a certain pride in authorship in her request that the title page of *Chapters on Churchyards* should carry the notice 'By the author of . . .' to include *all* of her previous titles: 'as it oddly happens—I now get addressed as two *separate persons* relative to these little works'.[33]

It is an index of the importance her blank verse autobiography, *The Birth-day* (1836) held for her, that it was the first work to which she set her own name, Caroline Bowles. She had come to realise, she said, that 'The Author's name sometimes . . . forwards a work—tho' the name itself be of no considerable note'.[34] It is also significant that she took this step long before her marriage to Southey improved the commercial value of her name (an event Blackwoods were not slow to capitalise on with reprints), although she did believe that the association of her patronymic with that of 'my good friend and namesake W.L. Bowles' might reflect some borrowed light, as they were often mistaken in the literary world for relatives.[35] After *The Birth-day*'s success in attracting some excellent reviews, Caroline Bowles was evidently emboldened to emerge from her previous genteel discretion about money and demand in a very business-like tone a full and complete set of up-to-date accounts.[36]

The account then prepared for her is extant, and provides an informative record of all her Blackwoods publications over the years to 1838, with numbers printed and sold and all costs included.[37] Although sales of *The Birth-day* were not so large as she had evidently hoped, she was sufficiently pleased by a cheque for £60 (including some overdue payments for previous works, which she had enquired about) to fall back easily into ladylike discourse:

> Dec 19th 1838 [to Alexander Blackwood]
>
> I have to acknowledge & thank you for the bill for £60—That 'The Birthday' has been so unsuccessful, is of course a matter of regret to me, as it must be to you—but far better things in the way of Poetry fail of success now-a day, and others seem more sanguine with regard to my little Poem, than I ever was myself—...

She goes on to say, she believes she has had more verses in 'Maga' than she has been paid for, but never mind, since it has been sent to her regularly 'of late', she will consider that sufficient.[38]

After her marriage to Southey in 1839, Blackwoods evidently believed that her new and most interesting literary connection would bring them increased sales if they reissued her works under her married name. Accordingly, they brought out a second edition of her popular *Chapters on Churchyards* in 1841. Caroline Southey obligingly provided a sketch of picturesque Boldre Church on the edge of the New Forest in Hampshire (where she and Robert Southey were married) for an engraved frontispiece. This was not her only venture into illustration. Southey's house Greta Hall at Keswick, where their all-too-brief married life was spent until his death in 1843, was the subject of her painting used for the frontispiece to Longmans' popular posthumous edition of his collected poems in 1844.[39] After its appearance, Caroline Southey wrote to Blackwoods with a request for some professional advice—albeit in the name of amateurism. Longmans had omitted her signature from the engraving, and she wanted to know: 'is it usual in such cases to wholly omit the name of the designer and substitute the name of the intermediate artist'? In her next letter she thanks Blackwood for his information 'about the usual mode of engraving from Amateur drawing'.[40] Longmans have now assured her her name was omitted in error and this will be rectified in future editions (which it was).

What is notable here is firstly, how assertive she has become about precisely the issue which caused her such distress at the beginning of her career: her signature. Secondly, however, she still milks the udder of amateurism for its last drops of sustenance. She carefully dissociates herself from any appearance of professional knowledge; yet this is what she wants (and gets). As was so often the case, Blackwoods behaved generously towards her, providing all the information she needed. In fact the generosity with which Blackwoods usually did behave towards her was clearly taken by her as no more than what was due to a lady, in the spirit of a continuing game of gentlemanly amateurism. Such usage of the discourse of amateurism was facesaving for an author who was never more than moderately successful in a financial sense.

What is especially interesting in Bowles's case, however, is the way she can exploit ladylike conventions of politeness intermixed with a more dashing gentlemanliness (or aristocratic ladyhood?) to get exactly what she wants. But when questions of money are involved, and at a stage in her career when she has gained some confidence in her reception, this discourse breaks down and she resorts to more direct methods, thus denoting, almost despite herself, her own underlying professionalism. Yet because her career was cut off in its prime, as it were, by the disastrous consequences of her marriage, she was never able to build on the base she had finally established for herself. Her literary reputation too remained fragmented as a direct result of her early efforts to avoid any construction of herself as 'author'. By the time she had admitted her mistake, it was too late. Her posthumous reputation, however, can still be redeemed, once the apparent fragmentariness of her output is reassembled into a whole. It is important that her Blackwoods correspondence be recognised as a significant part of that whole.

Notes

[1] James Hogg's *The Shepherd's Calendar*, which began its serialisation in *Blackwood's Magazine*, 5 (April 1819)—the same year that Mary Russell Mitford began to publish *Our Village* in *The Lady's Magazine*—was, like Mitford's, a series of character sketches based on different aspects of rural life. John Galt's *Annals of the Parish* picked up the genre in 1821, and Caroline Bowles Southey did it her way in *Chapters on Churchyards*, from 1824. Her letter 'To the Author of "The Shepherd's Calendar"' was published in *Blackwood's*, 15 (June 1824). The 'Noctes Ambrosianae' was a regular feature in the magazine from 1822 to 1835, in the form of imaginary conversations written by several hands, including Hogg and J.G.Lockhart, also William Maginn; but mainly John Wilson ('Christopher North'), an early champion of Wordsworth who also admired Caroline Bowles's work.
[2] It is useful to call her this; but she was known in her lifetime first as Caroline Bowles, then, after her marriage in 1839, as Caroline Southey.
[3] Her poems were 'read with very much pleasure' in the Wordsworth household in September 1836 (*The Letters of William and Dorothy Wordsworth*, edited by E. de Selincourt [Oxford: Oxford UP, 1967], 6, 3, p.296).
[4] The Reverend John Wood Warter was husband to Edith Southey, the only one of Robert's children who welcomed his second wife. Edith died before

Caroline, who made John Warter her literary executor. Although his name does not appear on her *Poetical Works*, he was editor of the volume.

[5] See Andrew Boyle, *An Index to the Annuals* (Worcester: Boyle, 1966), pp.33-35: however, he is mistaken in some attributions.

[6] My primary source for this paper is the Blackwood Collection containing around 150 of her letters written between 1820 and 1847. I gratefully acknowledge the courteous assistance of the staff of the National Library of Scotland in late 1994. My special thanks to Lalla Rees for her excellent research assistance.

[7] *The Correspondence of Robert Southey with Caroline Bowles*, edited by Edward Dowden (Dublin and London: Hodges, Figgis, 1881). Dowden was given the collection of Caroline Bowles letters by John Warter's daughter, after her father's death. Further references to this work are given after quotations in the text.

[8] This phrase is used by Alaric Watts in a letter to W.H. Dixon (n.d.) deposited in the Beinecke Rare Book and Manuscript Library, Yale University.

[9] From 'To an old family portrait', published in *Robin Hood: a fragment, by the late Robert Southey and Caroline Southey* (Edinburgh, 1847), p.246.

[10] See the letter of 15 October 1850 in the Blackwood Collection, National Library of Scotland, MSS 4091 ff.122-25. All subsequent MS references in the notes are to this collection, unless stated otherwise.

[11] Felicia Hemans (1793-1835) and Letitia Landon (1802-1838) were both remarkable pioneers in the nineteenth-century literary woman's struggle to support herself by writing (and marketing) poetry. Dorothy Mermin's pertinent study *Godiva's Ride: Women of Letters in England, 1830-1880* (Bloomington: Indiana UP, 1993) begins with this decade.

[12] MSS 4007 ff.236-37.

[13] William Blackwood (1776-1834) was the founding father of both the publishing house and the magazine, which he set up as a rival to the *Edinburgh Review*. Genial as well as shrewd, he became a great favourite with many of his authors.

[14] Confusingly, there *is* an 1820 letter listed in the catalogue, but this is an error: the date proves to be 1830. This mistake between a 2 and a 3 occurs a number of times in the catalogue, owing to a peculiarity of her handwriting, and sorting it out has led me to some reshufflings in their order, with enlightening results.

[15] Surtees's novel *Young Tom Hall's Heart-Aches and Horses* was published serially in Harrison Ainsworth's *New Monthly Magazine* from October 1851 until January 1853, when it abruptly terminated as a result of

Ainsworth's careless inclusion of Surtees's name in an advertisement. See E.D. Cuming, *Robert Smith Surtees* (1924), pp.358-59, for a transcription of the correspondence.

[16] See his gracious reply to her first letter to him of 1818: 'I write to you without the delay of a single post, and with sincere pleasure' (Dowden, *Correspondence*, p.5). By contrast, in 1837 he writes to Bowles about Charlotte Brontë: 'I sent a dose of cooling admonition to the poor girl whose flighty letter reached me at Buckland. It was well taken, and she thanked me for it . . . probably she will think kindly of me as long as she lives' (p.348). Caroline Bowles's comment on this exchange does not survive.

[17] 9 November 1824, MSS 4013 ff.120-21. By comparison, Felicia Hemans received 24 guineas a sheet in 1827. See Paula Feldman, 'The Poet and the Profits: Felicia Hemans and the Literary Marketplace' in *Women's Poetry, Late Romantic to Late Victorian: Gender and Genre 1830-1900*, edited by I. Armstrong and V. Blain (London: Macmillan, 1998).

[18] 9 November 1824, MSS 4013 ff.120-21.

[19] MSS 4020 f.189.

[20] 6 January 1842, MSS 4062 ff.182-91.

[21] MSS 4015 ff.229-30.

[22] MSS 4015 ff.231-32.

[23] MSS 4015 f.233.

[24] David Macbeth Moir (1798-1851) had earned her respect not only for the wit and liveliness of his own contributions to 'Maga', but for his tact and skill as an editor.

[25] See [Eleanor Orlebar] 'E.O.', 'Robert Southey's Second Wife', *Cornhill Magazine*, 30 (July-December 1874), 221.

[26] MSS 4727 ff.97-98.

[27] 23 April 1831, MSS 4727 ff.133-34.

[28] Bowles arranged for a 'friend' to drive up to Murray's in Albemarle Street, in an aristocratically emblazoned carriage, believing that Murray's snobbery would induce him to accept the piece from such a source: 'the most likely gudgeon in the world to bite at any hook baited with rank and fashion, and half my sport was the idea of getting him to bring out my nonsense' (Dowden, *Correspondence*, p.196).

[29] MSS 4727 ff. 97-98.

[30] Of 1000 copies printed, only 152 were sold by 1838, compared with 846 of Chapters on Churchyards (see Blackwoods' records of sale, MS 30 302 ff.576-77).

[31] On 26 February 1831 she mentioned in a postscript to Blackwood: 'I am told that a Miss Bowles is advertising a forthcoming work called "Fortunes Reverses"—As I have never put my name to any of my own books—this rather annoys me—much less on account of their being ascribed to another—than that the works of others—good or bad—should be ascribed to me—' (MSS 4031 f.132).

[32] 15 July 1833, MSS 4037 ff.134-45.

[33] 26 February 1829, MSS 4026 ff.156-57.

[34] 20 April 1836 (misfiled under 1826), MSS 4018 f.192.

[35] As above. William Lisle Bowles (1762-1850) was a poet and clergyman, whose Fourteen Sonnets of 1789 had greatly appealed to Coleridge and Southey.

[36] 3 April 1837, MSS 4045 ff.134-35. By this time her old friend William Blackwood was dead (1834) and the firm was now run by his sons, Robert and Alexander, whom she found less congenial. *The Birth-day* was reviewed in the *Spectator*, 9 (23 July 1836); the *Athenaeum* (2 July 1836); *Blackwood's*, 41 (March 1837).

[37] MS 30 302 ff.576-77.

[38] MSS 4047 ff.97-98.

[39] Two of her oil paintings were shown as part of the Romantic Women Writers exhibition shown in 1994 at the Dove Cottage museum at Grasmere, under the auspices of the Wordsworth Trust. One was this view of the entrance to Greta Hall (from outside), the other was a view of Southey's study window (from inside). She bequeathed them both to Southey's daughter, Edith Warter; they are now owned by the Keswick School.

[40] 23 May 1844 and 8 June 1844, MSS 4072 ff.140-43.

2 Anna Brownell Jameson and the *Monthly Chronicle*

Judith Johnston

The *Monthly Chronicle* ran only from 1838 to 1843, years which saw an upsurge in the vitality of British national industry and the arts, and which gave definition to the era that would come to be called 'Victorian'. Alexandrina Victoria came to the throne in 1837. Following her marriage to a German prince of considerable energy and influence, the young British Queen Victoria was depicted in the domestic roles of wife and mother, but as a monarch whe was also a working woman and in this role may have inadvertently bestowed respectability on the presence of women in the public sphere. The *Monthly Chronicle* held no especial brief for women. A review of the new periodical refers to an unusual pretension in its favour, that 'of its being conducted by men of the highest distinction in letters and science'.[1] In the event a *woman* of letters—Anna Brownell Jameson (1794-1860)—was enabled to establish her credentials in the *Chronicle*'s pages, not only as a professional art critic, but also as a journalist.

In 1837 Dionysius Lardner, a minor figure in early Victorian journalism, persuaded Edward Lytton (later Bulwer-Lytton), whose career as novelist and journalist was flourishing, to join with him in introducing a new journal to the London scene. As Houghton points out, although Bulwer was a founder, the project 'was first conceived and mainly edited by Lardner' (Houghton, 3, p.109). On 3 February 1838 a full-page advertisement appeared in the *Athenaeum*; it was a prospectus for the first number of the *Monthly Chronicle*. The new periodical was described as 'A National Journal of Politics, Literature, Science and Art', revealing a specific emphasis on nationalism, an intense awareness of a new historical era. Under 'History', for instance, the editors offered prospective readers 'a record of our own times' commencing with the 'accession of Victoria I'.[2] The editors claimed that such a project 'has long been felt to be a desideratum in our national literature', yet Victoria had been on the throne at this point for less than a year. Under the heading 'Literature and Criticism', the *Chronicle* also offered 'articles of standard value, illustrative of the Philosophy of Criticism or the History of Letters—supplying the place of those ORAL LECTURES which have enriched the literature of the Continent with the most celebrated compositions of Schlegel, Villemain, Guizot and Cousin'. In addition a discussion of progress in the 'Fine Arts' would be designed to 'illustrate the spirit and changes of National Manners'.[3] It is apparent that for the editors, but more particularly for Lardner who wrote the prospectus (Houghton, 3, p.109), the emphasis on nationalism could most effectively be constructed by comparison to, and in competition with, European literature and art.

The only woman mentioned in the prospectus is 'Victoria I'. Otherwise the advertisement is directed at male readers: 'the Tradesman, the Manufacturer, the Agriculturist, and the Mechanic, . . . the Statesman and the Man of Letters', offering that male reading public, male writers: 'our most eminent men of letters', and 'our most acknowledged authorities in science'. However, despite the emphasis on male readers and male writers, Dionysius Lardner appears to have been happy to employ women on his literary projects. Lardner contacted the writer Anna Brownell Jameson in early April 1838 to suggest she write for the new *Monthly Chronicle*. While Jameson had a steadily rising literary reputation based for the most part on the favourable reception of her *Characterisitics of Women*, published in 1832, she had only recently returned from Canada, where she had been formalising a separation from her husband, and she had published nothing substantial since 1834. Lardner's pursuit of Jameson as a contributor must therefore have been based on criteria other than her various books on women, which included *Loves of the Poets* (1829), *Memoirs of the Celebrated Female Sovereigns* (1831), and *Characteristics of Women* (1832). Her response to Lardner's approach makes no claim to a reputation for journalism: 'Mrs. Jameson presents her compliments to Dr Lardner—& if convenient would be happy to see him on Thursday morning at 11 o'clock—She has hitherto declined writing in any periodical work—but will not finally decide till she has had the pleasure of speaking with Dr Lardner.'[4]

It was not altogether the case that she had 'hitherto declined' contributing to periodicals. Her formal essays 'Althorpe' and 'Mrs. Siddons' had appeared in *New Monthly Magazine* in 1829 and 1831 respectively, and earlier still in 1826 the same journal had published 'The Windsor Beauties' and 'The Hampton Court Beauties', forerunners to her book *The Beauties of the Court of King Charles the Second* (1833). This book was basically a showcase for the etched copies done by her father, Denis Murphy, of the famous paintings of women at Windsor Castle and Hampton Court Palace. But Jameson, on the edge of success as a published writer, was being careful. None of these earlier contributions could be considered cutting-edge journalism, that is, formal criticism in which the opinions of the writer are as important as the work being discussed.

In the four-year period between the publication of her highly successful *Characteristics of Women* in 1832 and her journey to Canada in late 1836, Jameson had published only one major and two very minor books. The major work was *Visits and Sketches at Home and Abroad*, first reviewed in July 1834. John Steegman cites *Visits and Sketches* as 'historically important' and claims Jameson as 'one of the first interpreters of the world of contemporary German thought' to her English readership.[5] Volumes 1 and 2 of *Visits and Sketches* comprise various discussions in diverse forms of the current state of art and literature in Germany in relation to the condition of the arts in England. Thus Jameson's work from this period mediates impressions of Germany to the British reader while at the same time maintaining a distinct British nationalism. This background specifically qualified her as a writer able to fulfil Lardner's nationalist ambitions for his new journal.

The *Athenaeum* obituary of Jameson noted that after the publication of *Characteristics of Women*, 'the Germanism so prevalent five-and-twenty years ago, and somewhat gone by, possessed itself of the authoress, and she published her reminiscences of Munich, the imitative art of which was new, and esteemed as almost a revelation'.[6] Jameson's 'Germanism', however, while enthusiastic, was never of the same proselytising style as that of, say, Carlyle. In March 1838 Carlyle comments in a letter to John Stuart Mill that the *Examiner*, in reviewing the prospectus for his forthcoming lecture series, had described his 'syllabus' as being about 'the four great periods of Paganism, Christianity, Scepticism, and what, . . . we suppose we are to call Germanism or *Goetheism*'.[7] As Rosemary Ashton explains in *Little Germany: Exile and Asylum in Victorian England*, Carlyle had enthusiastically endorsed Germany's idealism by opposing it to British materialism,[8] a process which had begun with his translations of, and friendship with, Goethe. In his review of William Taylor's *Historic Survey of German Poetry* for the *Edinburgh Review* in 1831, Carlyle comments:

> In the present fallow state of our English Literature, when no Poet cultivates his own poetic field, but all are harnessed into Editorial teams, and ploughing in concert, for Useful Knowledge, or Bibliopolic Profit, we regard this renewal of our intercourse with poetic Germany, after twenty years of languor or suspension, as among the most remarkable and even promising features of our recent intellectual history.[9]

Jameson did have considerable knowledge of Germany, nevertheless. Accompanied for several months by her sister Charlotte Murphy, she spent much of 1833 travelling and working independently there, that is they had no male cicerone. Jameson had earlier travelled extensively in Germany when she and her father, probably as paid companions and guides, had accompanied Sir Gerard Noel and his daughter to the Continent. In a letter dated 27 June 1833 from Weimar, Charlotte Murphy reported to the family: 'the first news we learnt at Weimar was that a German translation of the "Characteristics of Women" will appear soon. It is published at Leipsick, unfortunately from the first edition'. Jameson herself, in the same letter, adds that, 'fortunately I have just arrived in time to have some alterations made —& to send the translator a copy of the last edition', revealing with what acumen and dispatch she handled matters of business.[10]

In *Visits and Sketches at Home and Abroad* (1834), based on her travels in Germany, Jameson reports on German intellectual life and culture to her readers back home, writing for instance of the veneration of the Germans for the British sculptor Flaxman which 'like their veneration for Shakespeare, is a sort of enthusiasm all over Germany'.[11] As G.H. Needler points out, this was also the period in which German scholarship was focused on Shakespeare, and Jameson's *Characteristics of Women*, based on a discussion of the women in Shakespeare's plays, won for her a considerable reputation in Germany.[12] F.D. Maurice in an article for *Macmillan's Magazine* in 1860 notes the presence of the German writer Ludwig Tieck's annotated copy of *Characteristics* in the British Museum and writes 'I can suppose that that accomplished man may have learnt from an Englishwoman some lessons which all his studies in Shakespeare and in art had not imparted to him'.[13]

In 1833 Jameson also met and quickly formed a close friendship with the daughter-in-law of Goethe, Ottilie von Goethe. This friendship was to last throughout Jameson's life. She told her family that 'Madame de Goethe is a charming little woman full of talent and vivacity' (Erskine, p.99). Ottilie invited them to accompany her to Frankfurt and the Rhine and Jameson accepted, she discloses quite openly to her family, 'partly to improve my acquaintance with her and partly to be introduced under her auspices to the best society at Frankfort [sic] and Bonn which is of great consequence to me'.[14] In a letter only a month later dated 30 July 1833 Jameson tells her father that she has left her new friend and travelled to Bonn 'to be very quiet and studious for three weeks—I have an excellent German [sic] and work sometimes four or six hours a day—till I have mastered my German Grammar I could do nothing—& I am determined not to be repelled or diverted from my German studies' (Erskine, p.102). Despite this detemination, in her letter of 20 August 1833 she begs Ottilie '*pray* do not write to me in German yet'.[15] And in the event she never achieved that facility with the language for which she had hoped. Apart from occasional throwaway lines, her letters to Ottilie von Goethe throughout their life-long friendship are almost always written in English.

Given the list of articles and contributors to the short-lived *Monthly Chronicle*, it is likely that the combination of Jameson's connections to and knowledge of German intellectual and social life, with her expertise in matters of art and her skill as a writer, caused Lardner to seek her out. As I have indicated, Lardner's ambition for the *Chronicle* was primarily that it be a national journal, thoroughly modern and wide-ranging, featuring art, architecture, politics, science, literature, theatre. The earliest numbers are dominated by topics of national interest, 'The Irish Church' and 'Manners' in May 1838; 'Review of the British Army' and 'Letters by an English Member of Parliament' in June 1838; 'Speeches of Lord Brougham' and 'The Duke of Wellington' in August 1838. Later numbers reveal a steady increase in articles *about* Germany like 'Characteristics of the German Universities' in the December 1838 issue. At the same time there is an increasing national English consciousness of Germany, with comparisons reflected in such articles as 'German manufacturers and English Corn Laws' and 'Commercial Policy of England; the German commercial league; the English Corn Laws' both of which appeared in 1839, and more and more translations from Goethe, Schiller and Richter, and even the lesser known poet Uhland, who appears in the very last number for June 1841. This upsurge of interest in German literature and culture may be in part attributable to Victoria's marriage to the German Prince Albert on 10 February 1840. Victoria's engagement to Albert in late 1839 also triggered a particular anxiety about exactly where his national loyalties would lie, reflected in cartoons showing Albert trying on Victoria's crown,[16] and perhaps also in such articles as 'The Foreign Policy of England' which appeared in the *Chronicle* in December 1839.

Jameson is also distinguished as the only woman, apart from Mary Shelley,[17] to be mentioned in an advertisement which appeared in the *Athenaeum* on 7 March 1840 listing the *Monthly Chronicle*'s twenty-four major contributors to the first four volumes which ran from March 1838 to December 1839. Some of the men listed are experts in at least one field, for instance, J. C. Loudon, noted for his books on landscape gardening, or the Italian exile Joseph Mazzini, writing on French literature and the political condition of Italy. Apart from Bulwer, the other male journalists have sound, long-established literary careers. The list includes writers like Lardner himself, Thomas Moore, Leigh Hunt, and R. H. Horne. Some of them (including Moore, Baden Powell, De Morgan and Phillips) had worked for Lardner before on the *Cabinet Cyclopaedia*. Many on the *Monthly Chronicle* list had some link with European literature and culture. Jameson herself in *Visits and Sketches*, writing of the reception of modern English literature in Germany, notes that 'Bulwer is exceedingly popular with the women; so is Moore. Some of those who most admired the latter, gave as one reason that his English style was so easy' (*Visits and Sketches*, 1, p.196).

Even if Jameson had been recommended to Lardner by friends like the translator Sarah Austin,[18] who writes to Jameson from Boulogne in September 1835 that she has been approached by Lardner to write German literary biographies for his *Cyclopaedia*,[19] the reviews of Jameson's *Visits and Sketches at Home and Abroad* (1834) may well have attracted Lardner's attention to her work in the first place. The *Spectator*, for instance, comments that it is her 'view of the state of the Fine Arts in Germany [that] is particularly interesting'.[20] In expressing some of those views Jameson makes pertinent comparisons with England. For instance she recalls that the plans for the new National Gallery in London were exciting some attention just before she left England in 1833 and 'the merits of different designs . . . violently discussed in public and in private'. She therefore visits the new national gallery (the Pinakothek opened in 1830) in Munich, 'anxious to comprehend both the general design and the nature of the arrangements in detail' (*Visits and Sketches* 2, p.79). Jameson acknowledges the 'mutual esteem and understanding' established between the two nations on literary matters, while remarking on 'the singular and mutual ignorance in all matters appertaining to art, and consequently, a good deal of injustice and prejudice on both sides' (2, 197). She determines that the difference is a difference of taste 'which I will not call natural but national' (2, p.201).

The *Athenaeum* bestowed three notices on Jameson's *Visits and Sketches*, a preliminary announcement, then a first and a second notice. The work was also reviewed in *Tait's Edinburgh Magazine*, and in *New Monthly Magazine*, a notice which begins with the pronouncement that this 'may be termed the intellectual age of woman'.[21] The *Athenaeum* reviewer, in the short preliminary announcement of 28 June 1834, draws the reader's attention to two main issues. First the review suggests that Jameson's work evidences 'the strength and reach of the female talent of the present day' betraying 'little or no deficiency of the strength upon the presumed exclusive possession of which, man has been so long used to crest himself'.[22] This comment may well have been prompted by a discussion in *Visits and Sketches* about the 'strong prejudice against female authorship, which still exists in Germany' (1, p.169), and while Jameson disclaims any political intent, claiming she is 'no vulgar, vehement arguer' about the 'rights of women' (1, p.174), she quickly produces valid reasons for women to become writers, including money, independence, parental support, supplementing the family income, fame, 'energy of intellect and will', the wish to do good and to add to 'the progress of thought' (1, p.176).

The *Athenaeum* reviewer's second point is that Jameson's writing illustrates 'the more generous and poetical style of criticism which is now extended to art' ('Visits and Sketches', p.489). In the notice of 26 July 1834 the reviewer particularly cites as an illustration of that second point the following passage:

> Rubens is just such a painter as Dryden is a poet, and *vice versa*: his women are just like Dryden's women, gross, exaggerated, unrefined animals; his men, like Dryden's men, grand, thinking, acting animals. Like Dryden, he could clothe his genius in thunder, dip his pencil in the lightning and the sunbeams of heaven, and rush fearlessly upon a subject which others had trembled to approach. In both we see a singular and extraordinary combination of the plainest, coarsest realities of life, with the loftiest imagery, the most luxurious tints of poetry. Both had the same passion for allegory, and managed it with equal success. 'The thoughts that breathe and words that burn' of Dryden, may be compared to the living, moving forms, the glowing, melting, dazzling hues of Rubens (*Visits and Sketches*, 1, p.296, quoted *Athenaeum*, p.547).

The reviewer did not, however, quote Jameson's comment on Rubens's 'Slaughter of the Innocents' which she said 'makes me sick—it has absolutely polluted my imagination' (1, p.295).

Jameson's prose often shifts between two extremes of discourse, one a powerful, but nevertheless objective, style that comes into its own in her major essay 'The House of Titian' published in *Memoirs and Essays Illustrative of Art, Literature and Social Morals* (1846); the other an idiosyncratic, forthright response, which often surprises with its honesty and its validity, a response Hilary Fraser describes as 'horrified admiration'.[23] There is evidence that the combination of these two styles inspired Felicia Hemans's poem 'On Retzch's Design of the Angel of Death', published in *New Monthly Magazine* in 1835 under the title 'Thoughts During Sickness'. Hemans, in a note, states this poem was suggested 'by the beautiful and remarkable description in Mrs. Jameson's "Visits and Sketches"'.[24] Jameson had written of a 'wondrous' face, which had made her 'shrink back': a melodramatic, almost gothic evocation of Retzch's portrait (*Visits and Sketches,* 2, p.189). Such positive enthusiasm for Jameson's work on German art and culture, in which the beauty of her prose style is so often noted, offsets the slight, dismissive notices in *Tait's* and the *Westminster Review*. Both journals were to react far more strongly, and in very positive ways, to her *Winter Studies and Summer Rambles in Canada* published in 1838.

Jameson's first article for the *Monthly Chronicle*, 'The Exhibition of the Royal Academy. English Art and Artists', was published in the fourth number (June 1838) and fulfils the offer of the Prospectus to locate in the progress of the fine arts a nationalist spirit. It opens, however, with a German epigraph: some lines of address to the artist by Goethe.[25] For Jameson, Goethe's lines surely focus on the issue of praise and criticism, but she begins her review proper with another quotation, this time with greater nationalist bearing, from Walter Scott, who told his private diary that a painting could only be excellent if it appealed to 'the mind of a man like myself', that is an educated mind susceptible to natural emotions. Jameson agrees but qualifies her acquiescence by suggesting that a work of art should also appeal to the imagination and 'satisfy the judgment'. By quoting from the two most prominent men of letters of the age, Jameson carefully authorises the practice of criticism and defines her own role as an art critic. At the same time she manages to shift the focus away from herself and onto her readers. This she achieves by disclaimer, stating that her criticisms are merely 'thrown together' to enlarge the 'sphere of enjoyment' of those who are amateurs, who are not 'connoisseurs in painting'.[26]

This deferential style is consistent throughout the introductions to her various works on art, as Jameson eschews the didactic in favour of a more companionate role. As she later writes in the General Introduction to her *Companion to the Most Celebrated Private Galleries of Art in London* (1844): 'I call this book a Companion, not a Guide to the galleries of art; . . . the reader, in turning over these pages, will find that I have here endeavoured to unite the attractions of a pleasant companion and a safe guide; to arrange information methodically, for immediate reference, like plants in a botanic garden'.[27] 'Safe' seems today a peculiar term to use in this context but is very Victorian in its moral intention.

Jameson's *Handbook to the Public Galleries of Art* (1842) defines the five major classes of painting as history; portrait; landscape; genre, or 'Familiar Life'; and natural history and still life,[28] and she chooses representative examples of these classes from the 1382 works on exhibition at the 1838 Royal Academy. She begins with 'History' painting, 'the grandest department of art' and bemoans British deficiency in this class because of a lack of patronage and Government interest. She compares this failure to the 'magnificent temple of art, the Glyphothek at Munich' and adds that it 'remains for our young queen, Victoria, to make her reign a new and a glorious era in the annals of English art' ('Exhibition', pp.348, 349).

This 'new and glorious era' is not achieved with Wilkie's 'Queen Victoria presiding at her first Privy Council' which Jameson considers a failure historically because it does not centre around 'the young queen' who instead 'sits on the edge of her chair like a timid country girl, and holds her "most gracious declaration" as if it were a petition for mercy' (p.350). What Jameson observes in Wilkie's painting is a manifestation of anxiety about an unmarried queen. Victoria must be no threateningly princely monarch like the last virgin queen, Elizabeth I, but an ordinary, preferably submissive, woman. Yet as Margaret Homans points out, 'she was unique, a woman whose life was related to ordinary female domesticity only by analogy and masterful tricks of representation', what Homans later terms 'monarchy's middle-class imposture' (pp.5, 7). Jameson's criticism provides us with an early example of the misrepresentation of Victoria's position as Queen of England, which Jameson explicitly registers as a failure in artistic representation. Implicitly the failure rests in diminishing legitimate female power. Jameson, always a moderate feminist, argues that she sees no reason to give Victoria 'the imperious airs of an Elizabeth', but she also saw no reason to deny her majesty.

Because of the popularity of the form, Jameson devotes considerable space in her review to genre painting, selecting Mulready's 'All the World's a Stage'[29] which she praises for its originality, its charm and its 'beautiful moral touch'. Artist-like, however, she places Edwin Landseer at the centre of her discussion of genre painting, designating him not only a *'poet painter'* but more significantly as 'our *national* painter', a term she explicates as:

> national in the turn of his mind, in his habits of thought, in his pursuits and sympathies as an artist: peculiarly national in the quaint yet earnest significance of his humour: he is homebred—English—owing nothing to foreign inspiration or education. . . . We regard him as decidedly the finest painter in his own department in all Europe—the boast of our English School of Art—of his brother artists the delight, the wonder, the despair. ('Exhibition', p.351)

Jameson's sentiments here are very similar to Ruskin's about the artist Turner in *Modern Painters* 1 (1843), when he suggests that Turner's great power rests in his Englishness. Moreover, despite her 'Germanism', Jameson in *Visits and Sketches* writes: 'If I should whisper that since I came to Germany I have not seen one really fine modern portrait, the Germans would never forgive me; they would fall upon me with a score of great names—Wach, Stieler, Vogel, Schadow—. . . But before they are angry and absolutely condemn me, I wish . . . they could come to England and look upon our school of portraiture here! I think they would allow, that with all their merits, they are in the wrong road'. Her complaint is that the German artists think too much of accessories and she adds that 'the vulgar eye alone is caught by such misplaced skill—the vulgar artist only ought to seek to captivate by such means' (2, p.63).

Some well-known Academicians of the period are summarily dismissed in Jameson's review. Howard[30] is criticised for his '*fades* common-places of mythology and allegory', and of Ward[31] Jameson asks 'is he quite mad? His pictures . . . are the most perversely atrocious things which we have seen for this long time' (p.353). Turner too 'has turned Bedlamite. Since he has been afflicted with this incurable prismatic madness, we have avoided speaking of him' (p.354). Jameson ends this first review by noting that the subject of sculpture requires some serious consideration, in a separate essay, and by appealing to the nationalism of her readers in fine rhetorical form:

> Do we find here the material on which to build great exulting prophecies of what may yet be performed by our English artists, when themes grand enough, and space wide enough, are allotted to them,—when they can command not only the patronage of the great, but the sympathy of the people? Look around, and say—
> 'What consolation may be gained from Hope?
> If not, what resolution from Despair?' (p.355)

Jameson's promise of an essay on sculpture was not realised until a year later in June 1839. 'Sculpture in England' is a review essay built around particular publications: Flaxman's *Lectures on Sculpture* (1838); the *Catalogue of the Seventy-first Exhibition of* the Royal Academy London 1839; The Elgin Marbles (1839); and 'The Nelson Testimonial' by William Behnes (1839). Jameson recounts a glorious national past in the history of British sculpture by pointing to Wells Cathedral and its 'magnificent and tasteful' sculptures of the twelfth century, and to the reigns of Henry III to Henry VIII, designated by her 'the period of English sculpture', and she blames the Reformation for the decline of British sculpture.[32]

Sculpture's more immediate history is not so triumphant. George III is dismissed as having 'no idea of sculpture' and his successor as 'miserably devoid of taste'. In St Paul's 'the want of pre-arrangement and general design has reduced the monuments to a multitude of unconnected statues and incongruous ideas' ('Sculpture', p.528) and she concludes, with some patriotic fervour still intact, that 'mediocrity is the mark of our time rather than of our country: a fact the more remarkable, as this may be considered the peculiar period of science' (p. 529). It is in her scathing accounts of petty squabbles and intrigues over the Nelson and Wellington monuments, to celebrate the achievements of those grand national heroes who represent 'English valour and sagacity' (p.534), that Jameson's article comes into its own as a powerful indictment of national art and politics. She drily notes of the Wellington monument debacle that 'as on all such occasions, a great number of noblemen and gentlemen who had consented to be of the committee had carefully abstained from taking any share in its labours, or encountering any part of its responsibilities' (p. 534). Of the competition for a Nelson memorial she concludes that among 'the multitude of designs, few indeed were fitted to be the monument of any thing but the dulness of him who had conceived it' (p.535). In conclusion she sees only that the nation must be educated as a whole 'to an understanding of art' and perhaps then a Nelson monument might 'mark the commencement of a new era in English art' (p.536).

Jameson's final article for the Chronicle, 'On Albert Durer, and the Modern German and English Schools of Painting' appeared in July 1839. In this article she offers specific comparisons between German and English painting in which nationalism apparently gives way to Germanism. Where a year previously she had celebrated Landseer as 'homebred—English—owing nothing to foreign inspiration or education' ('Exhibition', p.351), she now claims that England 'has never produced an original painter'. She writes that recent criticisms drawing the notice of the English public to the inferiority of English artists in comparison to those from Germany, were received as 'ignorant paradoxes' by English writers and English artists, stigmatised as 'that irritable race'. She denounces the state of English art as 'stationary', 'retrograde', 'barren' and 'null'. As a nation, England must 'yield the palm of superiority to our rivals'.[33] The chief rival, as suggested by the focus of the article on Dürer, is Germany. Jameson describes Germany as a 'land of dreaming sentiment and ideal beauty' that has 'awoke from her lethargy of ages, and in the imitation of her ancient greatness, sought the inspiration which created such marvels' (p.42), a reference to the Nazarene school, soon to emerge in England as Pre-Raphaelitism.

Rosemary Ashton comments that 'the British view of Germany in the 1840s was of a country of philosophy, of idealism, even of mysticism' (p.10), and certainly Jameson's article occurs at precisely the moment to promote that view, although in the event some nationalist sentiment prevails, and Jameson roundly rejects German mysticism, in literature at least:

> [A]n imitation or infusion of this school of design might, like the infusion of their romantic literature into the spent and exhausted life of our times, create a new and copious fountain of beauty. In music and painting, this imitation might be carried to some profit, but we must ever protest against the infusion of German mysticism which some writers have poured into our literature; never shall we cease to lament, that German boars should have been

suffered to muddy the 'clear well of English undefiled'. ('On Albert Durer', 42-3)

In 1838 Anna Brownell Jameson was about to see her career as a writer and art critic flourish, and during the period 1838 to 1843 it did so. The enthusiastic reception of her travel book *Winter Studies and Summer Rambles in Canada* (1838) marks the turning-point. In 1842 she published *Handbook to the Public Galleries of Art*, a commission obtained through the offices of Sarah Austin. The exhaustive labour demanded by the *Handbook* cut short her *Chronicle* articles, but she subsequently produced the series 'Essays on the Lives of Remarkable Painters' for the *Penny Magazine* (1843-45). In 1843 Jameson was invited to write for the *Athenaeum*, the most influential of the Victorian literary reviews because the most independent under Dilke's editorship (1830-46). During 1844 the *Athenaeum* published her articles 'Washington Allston', 'The Spanish School of Painting', 'Dutch Landscape Painters' and 'The Xanthian Marbles', and in 1845-46 the first seventeen parts of her major work of art criticism, *Sacred and Legendary Art* (1848).

But the first piece that Jameson ever produced for the *Athenaeum* was also her most important journalism, and it was social journalism, not art criticism. Three articles addressing the 'Reports of the Court of Commissioners on the Employment of Women and Children' appeared in the *Athenaeum* on 4, 11 and 18 March 1843. Jameson wrote the third of these articles, 'Condition of the Women and the Female Children', a forthright discussion of working women which also examined the problems of middle-class women forced to support themselves and their families.[34] The *Monthly Chronicle* had provided Jameson with a forum in which to practise the exercise of her own voice and it had given her the confidence to express her own opinions. The experience enabled her to take her place in the vanguard of a new national cause, not only women's right to retain their wages for work outside the home, but the need for their presence in the work-force to be both acknowledged and accepted.

Notes

[1] For a general overview of the *Monthly Chronicle* I am indebted to Walter E. Houghton's introductory essay in the *Wellesley Index to Victorian Periodicals 1824-1900*, 5 vols (Toronto: U of Toronto P, 1979), 3, p. 113. All subsequent references to Houghton are to this edition.
[2] The roman numeral 'I' after Victoria's name occurs during this period. It signals the way in which Victoria, as a virgin queen, was being linked in the minds of the English to Elizabeth I. After Victoria's marriage to Albert the 'I' disappears.
[3] 'Monthly Chronicle Prospectus', *Athenaeum* (3 February 1838), 95.
[4] MS letter, 3 April 1838, Ch.H.9.36, by courtesy of the Trustees of the Boston Public Library.
[5] John Steegman, *Consort of Taste 1830-1870* (London: Sidgwick & Jackson, 1950), pp. 186-87.
[6] 'Mrs. Jameson' (Obituary), 24 March 1860, p.408.
[7] *Collected Letters of Thomas and Jane Welsh Carlyle*, edited by Clyde de L. Ryals *et al.* (Durham: Duke UP, 1987-), 10, p.48n.
[8] *Little Germany: Exile and Asylum in Victorian England*, (Oxford: Oxford UP, 1986), p. 10.
[9] 'Historic Survey of German Poetry', in *The Works of Thomas Carlyle*, 30 vols (London: Chapman & Hall, 1899), 27, p.337.
[10] Beatrice Steuart Erskine, *Anna Jameson: Letters and Friendships, 1812-1860* (London: Fisher Unwin, 1915), pp. 98, 99.
[11] *Visits and Sketches at Home and Abroad*, 3 vols (London: Saunders and Otley, 1835), 2, p.198. All subsequent references are to this edition.
[12] *Letters of Anna Jameson to Ottilie von Goethe* (London: Oxford UP, 1939), p. xii.
[13] 'Female School of Art; Mrs. Jameson', *Macmillan's Magazine*, 2 (1860), 231. Tieck, critic and writer of the Romantic school, along with Novalis and the Schlegel brothers, was noted for his essays on Shakespeare (1823-29), and was included in Thomas Carlyle's *German Romance: Specimens of its Chief Authors; with Biographical and Critical Notes* (1827).
[14] MS letter, 27 June 1833, J23b M833 6:27, Beinecke Rare Book and Manuscript Library, Yale University. Beatrice Erskine cuts this frank avowal from her biography of Jameson.
[15] Goethe & Schiller Archiv, Weimar, MS272.

[16] Margaret Homans, '"To the Queen's Private Apartments": Royal Family Portraiture and the Construction of Victoria's Sovereign Obedience', *Victorian Studies*, 37 (1993), 11.

[17] In his *Wellesley* introduction Houghton notes that he and his editors were unable to attribute any articles to Mary Shelley (3, p.115). Betty T. Bennett, editor of *The Letters of Mary Wollstonecraft Shelley*, 3 vols (London: Johns Hopkins UP, 1983), notes the *Monthly Chronicle* advertisement but comments no further on whether in fact Mary Shelley ever contributed to it (3, p.95). Mary Shelley wrote the lives of Petrarch, Boccaccio, and Machiavelli for the volume of Lardner's *Cyclopaedia* which appeared around February 1835, and of Metastasio, Goldoni, Alfieri, Monti, and Foscolo for the volume which appeared September/October 1835. She also worked on Spanish literary lives (Bennett 2, pp.202, 255).

[18] Austin was noted especially for her translation of Cousin's *The State of Public Instruction in Prussia* (1834), in the preface to which she 'argues the case for a national system of education' (Joanne Shattock, *The Oxford Guide to Women Writers* [Oxford: Oxford UP, 1993], p.16), and later for her translations from the work of Guizot, Goethe, Ranke and Raumer.

[19] Probably his *Cabinet Cyclopaedia*, 133 volumes of which appeared between 1829 and 1846 (Houghton, 3, 110).

[20] 'Visits and Sketches', *Spectator*, 7 (1834), 616.

[21] 'Visits and Sketches', *New Monthly Magazine*, n.s. 41 (1834), 372.

[22] 'Visits and Sketches', *Athenaeum* (28 June 1834), 489. Two later reviews appeared on pp.515-16 and 547-48. The reviewer's name is unfortunately not marked on the *Athenaeum* ledger held by the *Athenaeum* Indexing Project at City University, London.

[23] *The Victorians and Renaissance Italy* (Oxford: Blackwell, 1992), p. 24.

[24] 'Thoughts During Sickness', *New Monthly Magazine*, n.s. 43 (1835), 329.

[25] I am obliged to Dr Peter Morgan, School of European Languages, University of Western Australia, who translates the epigraph as: 'Artist! in order to ennoble yourself / You must vaunt yourself with modesty:/ Let yourself be praised today, criticised tomorrow,/—And paid always!' Dr Morgan suggests this may be a sample of impromptu occasional verse for a visitors' or a commonplace book.

[26] 'The Exhibition of the Royal Academy. English Art and Artists', *Monthly Chronicle*, 1 (1838), 348.

[27] *Companion to the Most Celebrated Private Galleries of Art in London* (London: Saunders and Otley, 1844), p. xvii.

[28] *Handbook to the Public Galleries of Art in and near London* (London: John Murray, 1842), p. xvii.
[29] My survey of several volumes of the *Art-Union* journal, 1839-1841, reveals that across the English exhibitions generally scenes from Shakespeare, Scott, *Gil Blas* and Dickens tend to recur with remarkable frequency.
[30] Henry Howard (1769-1847), Academician from 1808 and Secretary of the Royal Academy 1811-1833.
[31] James Ward (1769-1859), Academician from 1811.
[32] 'Sculpture in England', *Monthly Chronicle*, 3 (1839), 526.
[33] 'On Albert Durer, and the Modern German and English Schools of Painting', *Monthly Chronicle*, 4 (1839), 41.
[34] 'Condition of the Women and the Female Children' *Athenaeum* (18 March 1843), 257-59.

3 How Mrs Caudle Went On and On; or, The Afterlife of a Minor Victorian Classic

Michael Slater

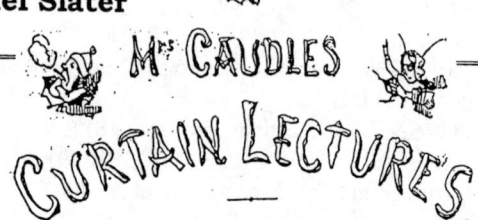

There can be few comic characters in nineteenth-century British literature, apart from Dickens's, who made as big a splash on their first appearance as Douglas Jerrold's Mrs Caudle. She delivered the first of her 'Curtain lectures', or nightly matrimonial harangues on the day's domestic events, to her hapless husband and bedmate, the toy manufacturer Job Caudle, in the pages of *Punch* on 11 January 1845; the series continued, with occasional gaps, until 8 November when Jerrold killed her off (the last episode was entitled 'The Tragedy of the Thin Shoes'). Mrs Caudle (her name means a hot sweet drink made of sherry or brandy and milk, much favoured as a nightcap by the Victorians) 'created a national furore', according to Spielmann, 'and set the whole country laughing and talking . . . [she] passed into the popular mind and took a permanent place in the language in an incredibly short space of time'.[1] There were the usual manifestations in popular culture of a Victorian literary success: three London theatres staged the Lectures with popular comic actors (Oxberry, Keeley) enacting Mrs Caudle; there were street ballads like 'Victoria's Caudle Lectures'; crude plagiarisms like *Mrs. Cuddle's Bedroom Lectures*; ceramic objects with a Caudle motif; and a hit song at Vauxhall Gardens 'sung by Mr. J.W. Sharp 50 nights' to the tune of 'The Good Old Days of Adam and Eve'.[2] At the end of the year, after the lectures had appeared in volume form in time for the Christmas market, Thackeray commented in the *Morning Chronicle*: 'Though Mrs. Caudle had her faults, perhaps there was no woman who died more universally lamented than she. The want of her weekly discourse was felt all over the kingdom'.[3]

Thackeray goes on to praise the work for giving in caricature form 'the most queer, minute, and amusing picture of middle-class English life'. Like most of his contemporaries (the critic of the *Saturday Review* being a notable exception[4]), Thackeray took it for granted that Jerrold had created in *Mrs Caudle's Curtain Lectures* an enduring popular classic as well as a unique social record—just what the Grossmith brothers were, in fact, to produce with another *Punch* series some forty-five years later, *The Diary of a Nobody*. The Caudles, Thackeray declared, 'have become real living personages in history, like Queen Elizabeth, or Sancho Panza, or Parson Adams, or any other character, who, false or real once, is only imaginary now'. Certainly they had become so established in the public mind by 1851 that an exhibitor of birds and mice, one of the interviewees of Jerrold's son-in-law Henry Mayhew, found it profitable to show two canaries dressed as the Caudles: '. . . they quarrel at times, and that's self-taught with them. Mrs Caudle is not noisy, and is quite amusing. They ride out in a chariot drawn by another bird, a goldfinch mule. . . . Mr and Mrs Caudle and the mule is very much admired by people of taste'.[5]

For people of even more taste, presumably, Bradbury and Evans brought out in 1866 a very handsome edition of the Lectures, printed on tinted paper and magnificently illustrated by Charles Keene (the original illustrations in *Punch* were by John Leech and are excellent caricatures in his best style). And during the latter half of the nineteenth century a variety of other editions of the work appeared in England, as well as translations into German, French, Hungarian, Swedish and other languages. Although their creator's fame began to fade (in 1903 an essay on Jerrold in *Macmillan's* is headed 'A Forgotten Jester'), that of the Caudles did not. In the early years of the twentieth century, for example, they provided much inspiration for the comic postcard industry:

> A favourite butt of the cartoonist was the hen-pecked husband, typified in many cartoons by a certain Mr Caudle and his wife. . . . 'A.L'. and Tom Brown both used the Characters on Davidson's cards around 1906, and later Tuck's produced an amusing series. . . . The Tuck's cards portray Mr and Mrs Caudle as different animals—a duck and drake, a cock and a hen or a pair of dogs.[6]

A more sombre view of the Caudles had, however, appeared in 1893 at the other end of the cultural spectrum in Sarah Grand's feminist novel *The Heavenly Twins*. Evadne, her serious young heroine ('When other people were laughing she would be gravely observant, as if she were solving a problem'), sees in Mrs Caudle a type of oppressed petty-bourgeois womanhood:

> The rule of her life is weariness and worry from morning till night, and for relaxation in the evening she must sit down and mend the children's clothes; and even when that is done she goes to bed with the certainty of being roused from her hard-earned rest by a husband who brings a sickening odour of bad tobacco and spirits home with him, and naturally her temper suffers. She knows nothing of love and sympathy; she has no pleasure in life. Fatigue and worry are succeeded by profound disheartenment. . . . the woman was thoroughly embittered, and the man had to pay the penalty. Whatever pleasure there might have been in their joint lives he had secured for himself, leaving her to stagnate for want of a little variety .[7]

This pathetic and embittered figure is hardly recognisable as the vigorous organiser of wedding-anniversary celebrations with real turtle soup and 'a nice haunch of venison'; of trips to Margate, and to France (involving a little agreeable smuggling of lace, velvet and silk stockings); or the woman who successfully campaigns for a country cottage ('The Turtle-Dovery') and a gig, but perhaps Evadne did not read as far as the later episodes in which these elements occur. She was, however, not the last reader to find a darker meaning in the Caudles.

During the first quarter of the twentieth century the continuing popularity of Jerrold's book found occasional echoes in the higher culture. For Dorothy Richardson's heroine Miriam the book was simply an expression of repugnant male chauvinism: 'What could she have to say to anyone who thought that *Mrs Caudle's Curtain Lectures*, even a nice edition bound in calf, or *How to be Happy Though Married*, suitable for a wedding present for Harriet, or for anybody?'[8] And for Joyce, Mrs Caudle took her place with the great shrews of history like Socrates's Xanthippe from whom, Stephen Dedalus asserts, Socrates learned dialectic as he learned female wisdom from his second wife: 'But neither the midwife's lore nor the caudlectures saved him from the archons of Sinn Fein and the noggin of hemlock'.[9]

After about 1930, however, the Caudle Lectures seem to drop out of sight. There are no more reprints of the little book nor references to it in other texts. No doubt this was partly owing to the general lack of interest in, or positive hostility towards, things Victorian that was part of the English cultural climate during the years 1920 to 1950. There is some anecdotal evidence, however, that the book continued to be read and chuckled over by middle-class fathers. And it was perhaps with an eye to that market that the Moray Press of Edinburgh decided on a reprint in 1950, although the blurb expressed the belief that the Lectures 'will be "enjoyed" by husbands and wives alike', adding, 'And for those about to be married [they] may prove a warning!' In a brief Foreword *Punch* writer H.F. Ellis sees Mrs Caudle as 'for all time, the archetype of the nagging wife'. He seems, the blurb notwithstanding, to be addressing an exclusively male (and married) readership as he writes in comic admiration of Mr Caudle:

> ... he declined, in the face of most determined and insidious attack, to entertain Mrs Caudle's mother as a permanent guest; and—let this never be forgotten—if he did not himself actually perpetrate the enormity, he at least connived at the corking of whiskers on her dear aunt's picture. Which of us, similarly placed, would have dared as much?[10]

When the Lectures were next reprinted twenty-four years later such an 'innocently' sexist approach to Jerrold's work was no longer possible. Anthony Burgess in his Foreword (a good deal longer than Ellis's) was only too happy to provoke feminists with his reading of what he claimed to find 'one of the funniest books in the language'. He begins with a reference to 'the forces of Woman's Liberation howling and clashing around me' and continues gleefully: 'I must say at once that what has appealed to me for the last forty years about *Mrs Caudle's Curtain Lectures* is the skill with which ... Jerrold has recorded the Eternal Sound of Woman, especially In Bed'.[11] Burgess was essentially still reading the book as a middle-class Victorian paterfamilias, the kind who, according to Jerrold's son, 'poked the points [of the Lectures] at their wives'.[12] One male reviewer of the reprint Burgess introduced, however, was very definitely not amused. Robertson Davies, recalling that he had had the book urged upon him by his grandfather as 'hilariously funny', commented that he had not been at all amused but had remained fascinated by it in that it dealt with an area of Victorian life discussed by 'serious' novelists but not usually handled directly by humorists, that is 'the region of the marriage of incompatibles, a welter of jealousy, suspicion and cruelty'.[13] The wonderful verbal arabesques created by Mrs Caudle as she prophesies the utter ruin of the household because Mr Caudle has lent five pounds to a friend or taken to an occasional game of billiards struck Mr Davies as 'dark stuff and darkly set forth' (almost as dark, one is tempted to add, as that well-known englooming figure of Chaucer's, the Wife of Bath, seen by Anthony Burgess as a mighty forerunner of Mrs Caudle's).

The fullest and most sympathetic critique of the Caudle Lectures to appear in recent years may be found in R.B. Henkle's *Comedy and Culture in England 1820-1900*.[14] But for Henkle too, the Caudles seem primarily to be victims, and he praises Jerrold for so unerringly registering their 'psychic desperation' as, in their increasing prosperity, they struggle with 'the advent of our modern economy of mass production and mass consumption'; like Sarah Grand's Evadne in 1893, he sees Mrs Caudle as essentially pathetic: 'hers is the terrible isolation of the circumscribed experience and dulled relationships that characterises small, ordinary lives'. Even Frank Muir, including one of the Lectures (the classic 'Mr Caudle has lent five pounds to a friend') in his *Oxford Book of Humorous Prose* writes of Jerrold's compassion in depicting 'the lack of self-confidence of a lower middle-class wife in the status-conscious, materialistic London of the 1840s'.[15] It is almost as hard to recognise Jerrold's exceedingly robust 'arch-wife' (to borrow a useful Chaucerian term) in this shrinking violet as it is to do so in the joyless embittered drudge imagined by Sarah Grand's Evadne.

Now that most intelligent readers are (fortunately) no longer likely to have the sort of simplified gendered reaction to the Caudle Lectures exemplified by H.F. Ellis and, more rumbustiously, by Anthony Burgess, responding to Jerrold's comic masterpiece is more problematic. We seem compelled to psychologise or sociologise it and, like Grand, find in the abundant wit and humour a darker strand—which takes us all the way back to the critic of the *Saturday Review* who, while scouting the idea that Jerrold might be deliberately seeking to discredit the institution of marriage, nevertheless thought the book made 'very unwholesome reading'. Mrs Caudle, supreme comic exponent of that quintessential Victorian literary form the dramatic monologue, still, it would seem, awaits a critic who can, in the right spirit, rise to the 'highth' of her great argument.

LECTURE VIII.
CAUDLE HAS BEEN MADE A MASON.—MRS. CAUDLE INDIGNANT AND CURIOUS.

(*Punch* 8 [January-June 1845], 135)

Notes

[1] M.H. Spielmann, *The History of 'Punch'*, (London: Cassell, 1895), p.291. Elizabeth Webby notes that the Caudle Lectures were 'reprinted in nearly every newspaper in Australia' ('English Literature in Early Australia 1840-1849', *Southerly*, 36 (1976), 300-01).

[2] *Sharp's Vauxhall Comic Song Book, First Series*, n.d. ('Second Series' dated 1847), p.97ff.

[3] W.M. Thackeray, *Contributions to the Morning Chronicle*, edited by Gordon N. Ray (Urbana: U of Illinois P, 1955), pp.93-94. See also Richard D. Altick, *Punch. The Lively Youth of a British Institution 1841-1851* (Columbus: Ohio State UP, 1997), pp.13-16, for further examples of the great contemporary popularity of the Caudle lectures.

[4] Reviewing an 1856 reissue of the Curtain Lectures, the critic of the *Saturday Review* commented, 'We rise from reading them with the sensation of having dined for a week on mouldy wedding cake' (1 November 1856, p.597).

[5] *Mayhew's London*, edited by Peter Quennell (London: Pilot, 1949), p.545.
[6] T. and V. Holt, *Picture Postcards of the Golden Age* (London: MacGibbon, 1971), pp.98-99. I also recently found a Valentine's postcard from the same period showing the Caudles in bed enacted by very small children (a photograph afterwards coloured).
[7] Sarah Grand, *The Heavenly Twins* (1893; London: Heinemann, 1901), p.18. I am indebted to Professor Isobel Armstrong for this reference.
[8] *Honeycomb* (1917), ch.5. I am indebted to Dr Carol Watts for this reference.
[9] *Ulysses* (1922), the 'Library Scene'. Anthony Burgess noted in his Introduction to a 1974 reprint of the Curtain Lectures (see note 11) that 'Joyce, in *Finnegans Wake*, makes it clear what prototype he has in mind for Anna Livia Plurabelle—our geomater or earth-mother—when Henry Chimpden Earwicker is invited to "list to her caudle"'. Professor Steven Connor has pointed out to me several other apparent allusions to the Caudle Lectures in the *Wake*.
[10] *Mrs Caudle's Curtain Lectures* (Edinburgh: Moray, 1950), p.2.
[11] *Mrs Caudle's Curtain Lectures*, edited by Anthony Burgess (London: Harvill, 1974), p.11.
[12] W. Blanchard Jerrold, *The Life of Douglas Jerrold* (London: Bradbury, Evans, n.d. [1869]), p.210.
[13] *Victorian Periodicals Newsletter*, 9.3 (September 1976), 97.
[14] *Comedy and Culture in England 1820-1900* (Princeton: Princeton UP, 1980), pp.222-26.
[15] *Oxford Book of Humorous Prose* (Oxford: Oxford UP, 1992), p.291.

4 'The true principle of Biographical delineation': Harriet Martineau's 'Biographical Sketches' in the *Daily News*

Barbara Garlick

Harriet Martineau's assertive comments on the role of the obituarist and biographer in the Preface to the 1869 Second Edition of her *Biographical Sketches*, the collection of obituaries she had originally contributed to the *Daily News*, anticipate by almost fifty years the great debate about biography which attended the publication of Lytton Strachey's *Eminent Victorians* in 1918, a debate moreover which had taken many turns since the furore unleashed by Froude's multi-volume work on the life of Carlyle (1881-1884). The 'Sketches' or 'Memoirs', terms which Martineau uses interchangeably, consist of obituaries which she wrote anonymously for the *Daily News* from her first connection with the paper in 1852 to 1868, with the addition of four new 'sketches' for the fourth edition in 1876. Moreover when the collection first appeared she was at pains to stress that the contents were unaltered from their original appearance in the newspaper, 'making no other change than in the headings announcing the death, in each case. For convenience of reference, and for the sake of something like order in the presentment of materials so various, the personages are classified. In each group, however, there is no other precedence than the date of departure.'[1] These classifications were fairly standard divisions of Royal, Politicians, Professional, Scientific, Social, and Literary, with the 1876 additions as a separate final classification. The 1876 edition also contained the 'Autobiographical Sketch of Harriet Martineau', that strange third-person account which Martineau had written herself and given to the proprietors of the *Daily News* in 1855 for publication on her death, the writing of it preceding that event by twenty-one years: 'We leave this memoir precisely as it was written, not even qualifying the curious foreboding of approaching death with which it concludes, and which twenty-one years of subsequent life contradicted' (p.xxxiv).

The collection has been little regarded as a significant contribution to the developing practice of biography in the nineteenth century which was to culminate, from 1884 onwards, in the 'monumental *Dictionary of National Biography*, a fitting climax to a hundred years of incessant biographical writing'.[2] Popular in its own day,[3] running into at least five editions by the end of the century (including a Colonial Library edition), the *Biographical Sketches* nevertheless did not fit the accepted pattern of biographical writing: Martineau deliberately eschewed the contemporary passion for hero-worship, epitomised most clearly by Carlyle, at least in his own writings,[4] and instead chose to write 'honest portraiture' (p.viii) in a spirit of 'thorough sincerity' (p.vii). She justifies this approach by an insistence on integrity and the necessity to be socially responsible: 'To tell what a man did, and to conceal or falsify what he was, is to play false with society' (p.viii).[5] In many ways the medium in which she was publishing allowed her the licence to be quite explicit in her 'thorough sincerity': her obituaries were concise and immediate responses to a death as well as being ephemera eventually to be 'hidden in the files of a newspaper' (p.x). Their much later collection into book form thus allows such ephemera to metamorphose into a more easily accessible historical record which yet retains the directness of personal comment and the immediacy of contemporary assessment rather than the supposed objectivity of historical consideration.

Biography, particularly through the obituarising moment, becomes for Martineau another branch of the nascent sociology of *Society in America* and, on a more personal level, of *Retrospect of Western Travel*. Biography becomes a method of anatomising her society, not with hindsight, but at that point when a notable person dies: the contribution of the person to the life of that society crystallises its essence, either by epitome or by reaction. Reaction is frequently seen in terms of her subject having outlived her/his time, the life thereby making a comment on her own contemporary world. While Martineau avowed in her obituary of Albert Smith, journalist, that the 'office of necrologist to a daily journal is not one to be desired' (*Daily News*, 24 May 1860, p.2), she more often than not seized on a death as the excuse to explain, to reinstate, to memorialise her subject, particularly if there had been what she saw as unjust neglect or criticism, at the same time as she applied that 'sincerity' or integrity she announces is her guiding rule. Her terminology is interesting in this regard: this self-styled 'necrologist' nevertheless speaks always in terms of the 'Sketch', the 'Memoir', or 'portraiture', as if the death itself has liberated her to talk about the life within the larger context of her time, rather than forcing her into fashionable eulogy.

The obituary for Thomas De Quincey (†8 December 1859) may serve as a model for her method. She begins by setting out clearly what she sees as her own role, the recording and analysis of a state of mind from a point in time—her contemporary world when there is little sympathy for the type of excesses he displayed. Moreover his own autobiographical confessions have liberated the obituarist from 'the doubt and hesitation . . . which render the task generally embarrassing as to what to communicate to the public and what to suppress':

> . . . in sketching the events of his life, the recorder has little more to do than to indicate facts which may be found fully expanded in Mr. De Quincey's 'Confessions of an Opium Eater,' and 'Autobiographic Sketches.' The business which he has in fact left for others to do is that which, in spite of obvious impossibility, he was incessantly endeavouring to do himself; that of analysing and forming a representation and judgment of his mind, and of his life as moulded by his mind. The most intense metaphysician of a time remarkable for the predominance of metaphysical

modes of thought, he was as completely unaware as smaller men of his mental habits that in his perpetual self-study and analysis he was never approaching the truth, for the simple reason that he was not even within ken of the necessary point of view. (p.409)

The short indication of 'facts' which follows is notable for the doubt she throws on De Quincey's ability to recall events that happened when he was only eighteen months old, and this in turn highlights both the unstable nature of memory itself and the autobiographical propensity to narrate creatively, to describe the emotions of the child through the consciousness and in the words of the adult:

The impression was undoubtedly genuine; but it is impossible to read the 'Autobiographical Sketch' in which the death and funeral of the child are described without perceiving that the writer referred back to the period he was describing with emotions and reflex sensations which arose in him, and fell from the pen, at the moment. (p.411)

In addition she takes advantage of the insights of the fashionable, developing science of psychology, which she had first begun to explore in her early essay on 'Characteristics of the Genius of Scott',[5] and in which the psychology of the adult is viewed in terms of the experiences of the child: in the case of De Quincey, the absent father, the poor role model of the older brother, the many different schools, concluding that 'the Opium Eater entered life under peculiar and unfavourable conditions' (p.411).

It is at this point that Martineau makes clear her concern with the deleterious effect reading De Quincey might have on an impressionable young mind: 'It is to be feared that the description given in those extraordinary "Confessions" has acted more strongly in tempting young people to seek the eight years' pleasures he derived from laudanum than that of his subsequent torments in deterring them' (p.412). There is more than a touch of personal understanding here in her description of the pain and the guilt experienced by opium addicts:

> . . . there is no doubt of the miserable pain by which men of all constitutions have to expiate an habitual indulgence in opium . . . it is certain that every one must expiate his offence against the laws of the human frame . . . there can hardly have been one whose stomach had been well-nigh destroyed by months of incessant, cruel hunger. (pp.412-13)

Finally in the conclusion her moralising focuses on the waste of 'genius', his living on beyond his time, and the cause of his failure, 'the curse which neutralized their [such gifts] influence and corrupted its source' (p.417). Martineau consciously takes on the task of 'wiser interpretation' (p.416), that is, a retrospective analysis of genius corrupted by a social evil which she has known at firsthand. But a further motivation appears in the extended tale of De Quincey's poor behaviour to Wordsworth and his family. To her this act of ingratitude is the ultimate example of weakness compounded by his addiction, which in old age becomes a habit of 'malignant gossip, virulent and base, but delivered with an air and a voice of philosophical calmness and intellectual commentary such as caused the disgust of the listener to be largely qualified with amusement and surprise' (p.416). Rather therefore than defer to the more conventional mode of memorialising the man of letters, that is, by remembering his works and his associates, Martineau indulges her principled antipathy both to the psychology of a fatally flawed genius and to the major exacerbating factor in that flawed personality. She contextualises her sketch moreover by seeing De Quincey as the symbol of the dark side of an earlier time which encouraged the expression of 'metaphysical modes of thought' and extreme introspection, and which was no longer socially healthy. It only remained for her to issue the warning to the young of her own age. For Martineau De Quincey's death was the occasion to remedy the past rather than to exalt it.

Dying in the same month as De Quincey, Macaulay (†28 December 1859) was also seen by Martineau as not fulfilling early promise. While she gives full praise to his eloquence and skill as essayist, she sees his time as a Parliamentarian as focusing all those defects of character which were overlooked by those who only saw him as a charismatic orator. The defects were highlighted by the duties required of him in the parliamentary years: he plagiarised material; he was inaccurate in historical detail; the Code of Law for India which he framed was unusable, 'there is scarcely a definition that will stand the examination of lawyer or layman for an instant' (p.423); and finally his *History of England* was more historical romance than history proper.[6] Once again Martineau demonstrates that blend of personal animus and its justification by a protopsychological reference to childhood influence:

> Very early in life he heard more than boyhood can endure of sentiment and philanthropy; the sensibilities of the Clapham set of religionists proved too much for 'the thinking, thoughtless schoolboy;' and we have no doubt that it was the reaction from all this that made him a conventionalist in morals, an insolent and inconsistent Whig in politics, a shallow and inaccurate historian, a poet pouring out all light and no warmth, and, for an able man, the most unsound reasoner of his time. . . . For a moment, the genuine reformers believed that they had gained the most eloquent man in Parliament to their cause; but it was not for long. They soon found how thoroughly deficient he was in moral earnestness, and how impressible when the interest or impulse of the hour set any particular view, or even principle, brightly before him. (pp. 420, 423)

Martineau's liveliest obituaries are certainly those which deal with literary and scientific figures, many of whom she knew either as acquaintances or as correspondents. In many instances she attempts to redress popular misconceptions, as with Landor (†17 September 1864) in whom she perceives a deep-seated paradox between the 'contempt and bitterness', which were the external manifestation of his egoism, and 'a strong faculty of admiration; and a deep, pure, fresh current of tenderness and sweetness' (p.437). Paradox thus becomes the theme of this sketch, seen both in Landor's physical features and in the inconsistencies within his major work, the *Imaginary Conversations*: 'a writer who is too much of an egotist and a mannerist to have genuine dramatic power, must be simply Landor himself, cramped and debilitated by the restraints of his disguise' (p.440). Furthermore she makes clear the reasons why she is able to accept these paradoxes and why she finds him a congenial subject—and why, incidentally, his death justifies a sympathetic and honest obituary in the *Daily News*:

> Yet there is so genuine a force of Liberalism in his writings, so constant a vigilance against the encroachments of tyranny, as may neutralize a large admixture of self-love and self-will; and it really is so rare to see the claims of the democracy so presented, amidst the music and the lights reverberated and reflected from the classic ages, that the man who has done that service may be fairly considered an original of high mark, even if he be too paradoxical, and too measured an egotist, to be entitled to the high honours of genius. (p.440)

She supports Landor's political importance—'passionate and prejudiced, but usually in some great cause, and on the right side of it' (p.444)—through a telling comparison with Byron: 'Where Byron moaned, Landor scolded. Landor had no patience with Royalty, or any rule but the popular, because it stood between men and their happiness; whereas Byron looked upon tyranny as a mere symptom of human corruptness and misery, and saw no happiness on the other side of it' (p.439).

Byron looms again as a less than admirable figure in her piece on Barry Cornwall (†5 October 1874, nom de plume of Bryan Procter). Here Byron is the 'great poet' whose malign influence overshadowed the age in which Cornwall 'dwelt upon whatever was brightest and loveliest in nature, and kindliest, sweetest, and most heroic in man or woman. This tendency constituted his function as poet at a period when Byron ruled supreme, and the world was tempest-tossed in all directions' (p.476). Martineau's antipathy towards Byron is most evident though in the obituary of Lady Noel Byron (†16 May 1860) where he is a dark presence blighting Lady Byron's life, making public her supposed faults and encouraging the malice of his friends towards her. The absorbing narrative is framed like a pilgrim's progress: it traces the idyllic childhood of Annabella Milbank as the only child of devoted parents, the turbulent course of the marriage, the betrayals, and the abiding love she had for her husband to the extent of maintaining his life abroad: 'He spent the utmost shilling of her property that the law gave him while he lived; and he left away from her every shilling that he could deprive her of by his will' (p.322). It concludes with her largely secret work for the poor, 'the silent promotion of public morality' (p.323), particularly in the field of popular education—'Lady Byron's schools were turning the children of the poorest into agriculturists, artisans, sempstresses, and good poor men's wives' (p.323)—and finally righteousness rewarded in death. Martineau's personal interest in the plight of women in marriage and in the value of education makes this a profoundly moving memorial to a neglected figure.

For Martineau a proper regard for learning mitigates the force of other failings; a sound education is seen as a sound preparation for life and for the understanding of one's place in the world, as is seen in her sketch of Sir John Herschel (†29

November 1871): 'He was not made for office [president of the Astronomical Society], however . . . Nature wanted him as an interpreter, and inferior men may serve for official life' (p.466). By contrast Mrs Somerville (†29 November 1875) demonstrated in her work and her life what Martineau saw as the common failing forced upon women, the lack of logic and precision which a masculine education offers:

> As for Mrs. Somerville's work, while it created no small astonishment in that English public as the production of a woman, its faults were precisely those which a woman would be likely to commit, through the want of a masculine training of the faculties. She begins with full explanations, offers fewer and fewer as the difficulties increase, and ends by presenting some of the most important problems in Laplace's own forms, and without any comment. . . . Moreover, Mrs. Somerville's weakness was precisely in the point in which Laplace was all-powerful in precision of language. Her general style was flowing and clear enough; but her greatest admirers lamented that she was always supposing that her readers knew as much as herself, and that their knowledge of the quantities she was was treating of was, like her own, so thorough and familiar, that the precision of the terms by which they were expressed might take care of itself. (pp.494-95)

Martineau justifies her own seeming lack of generosity here by referring to the publisher's conviction of Somerville's 'unfitness for popularising science' (p.497), but it may yet again be associated with a difference in political views: 'When abroad, her sympathies were with the princes, and not the peoples of Italy, though she supposed herself to be a Liberal in politics, having associated with the leading Whigs in London. She was, indeed, in her later years one of the most earnest supporters of the Women's

Suffrage movement; but that cause has found as much friendship among Conservatives as amongst Liberals' (p.495).

The sketch of her friend Anna Jameson (†17 March 1860) presents a more painful example of her desire to assess honestly. Once again it begins with absorbing anecdote of her subject's youth and disastrous marriage:

> In 1836, Mrs. Jameson joined her husband at Toronto; but it was for a very short time; and they never met again. This is all that the world has any business with; and the chief interest to the world, even that far, arises from the effect produced on Mrs. Jameson's views of life and love, of persons and their experience, by her irksome and unfortunate position during a desolate wedded life of nearly thirty years. (pp.430-31)

Praise for Jameson is genuine, although sometimes gently qualified with just the merest hint of claws:

> She became a very popular writer; and to the end of her life she proved that her power was genuine by the effect of appreciation upon the exercise of it. She did not deteriorate as a writer, but improved as far as the quality of her mind permitted. . . . Another great merit, shown from first to last, was that she never mistook her function; never overrated the kind of work she applied herself to; never undervalued the philosophy to which she could not pretend, nor supposed that she had written immortal works in pouring out her emotions and fancies for her personal solace and enjoyment. (p.431)

Her summing-up of Jameson's contributions to literature, to 'ameliorating the condition of women in England, by exposing the disabilities and injuries in the field of industry and the chance medley of education; and, again, in the diffusion of the knowledge of Art' (p.434) is again qualified, however: 'a great benefit to her time from her zeal for her sex and for Art; but likely to have been a greater if she could have carried less of herself and her experiences into her pictures and her interpretations of life' (p.435).

Martineau's apparent discomfort with unqualified praise, particularly when it applies to women, diminishes when she move outwards from the life to the social context. This is most noticeable in her sketch of Amelia Opie (†2 December 1853), 'Another of that curious class of English people—the provincial literary lion' (p.329), which provides the opportunity to discourse on the former importance of provincial towns like Norwich, 'the old glories of the provincial Athens' (p.335), which nourished Opie—and incidentally Martineau herself—and the life she represented. It is an amusing piece of social commentary which concludes that 'railways, free trade, and cheap publications have much to do with the extinction of the celebrity of ancient Norwich, in regard both to its material and intellectual productions. Its bombazine manufacture has gone to Yorkshire, and its literary fame to the four winds' (p.336).

Similarly the obituaries of politicians and members of the royal families of Europe proceed along standard lines of a life history of varying depth, then a disquisition upon important issues which the life has epitomised. Most of the first section in the collection on royalty gives her the opportunity to criticise European governments, to expound republican sentiments and, in the obituary of the Duchess of Gloucester (†30 April 1857), to inveigh against the 'demoralising Marriage Act':

> . . . there is, as we all know, a strong and growing popular distrust, in our own country and in others, of the close dynastic connexions which are multiplying by means of the perpetual intermarriages of a very few families. . . . Royalty will have quite difficulties enough to contend with, all through Europe, in coming

times, without the perils consequent on this law. Its operation will expose all the intermarried royal families in Europe to criticism and ultimate rejection by peoples who will not be governed by a coterie of persons diseased in body through narrow intermarriage, enfeebled in mind,—strong only in their prejudices, and large only in their self-esteem and in their requirements. (pp.27-28)

No comment.

Frequently the epitome is summed up in an appropriate image, such as the one she uses for Lord Brougham (†7 May 1868) who was staying in Cannes when the first 'daguerreotypes' were being produced there. He was asked to be part of a group photograph, and the 'artist explained the necessity of perfect immobility.' Lord Brougham, of course, moved too soon, and Martineau concludes, 'There is something mournfully typical in this. In the picture of our century, as taken from the life by History, this very man should have been a central figure; but now, owing to his want of stedfastness, there will be for ever—a blur where Brougham should have been' (p.104).

This sense of the life as epitome is nowhere clearer than in her troubled sketch of Robert Owen (†17 November 1858), which begins 'With Robert Owen dies out one of the clearest and most striking signs of our times' (p.305). The life is set in the context of the turbulent years of the turn of the century, and she describes in detail his schemes—New Lanark, the infant schools—and his legacy: 'The Christian Socialists are his disciples, politically, though not religiously; and the Secularists are his disciples, philosophically, though not as of course politically. He is, and will sooner or later be admitted to be, the father of the great social changes which are preparing, and already going forward, as the evidence of the Economy of Association becomes more clear' (p.312). It is with obvious reluctance, however, that Martineau faces up to Owen's 'imperfect view of the Human Being for whose benefit he lived, and would willingly have died' (p.312), which led to his utopian community ventures, and which illustrates most clearly the way in which his life stands as an epitome of the times: her view of the nineteenth century as a period of great hopes, endless possibilities, leading to the betterment of conditions for everyone, and a new order, which in the mid-century seems as far away as ever it did at the time of New Lanark.

In her damning portrait of King Frederick William IV of Prussia (†2 January 1861), another of her dangerous Stuart rulers, Martineau recognises with some clarity the special times in which she lives: 'the nineteenth century is one which demands and imposes action' (p.35), and 'evil was the destiny which made him a ruling Prince in our revolutionary nineteenth century' (p.41). Robert Owen and King Frederick William IV illustrate the Janus face of the early Victorian period: it is a time which can accommodate both the inept visionary and the autocratic ruler, but which will also in time sweep both of them away. In a sense this also encapsulates Martineau's task as a crusading obituarist for a Liberal newspaper. The medium of the daily press, particularly a paper such as the *Daily News* which prided itself on its modernity and radical difference from older established newspapers, allowed her the freedom to experiment with a new style of biography, to move away from the hagiographic form of obituary favoured by the *Times* and the *Athenaeum* and, in addition, to write not only about the Great Men of History, but also about those figures who were ignored by the *Times*, such as Charlotte Brontë (†31 March 1855) in whom she detects not only a morbid sensitivity, but also an admirable strength of intellect, 'a female writer who has discountenanced sentimentalism and feeble egotism' (p.362).

One is forced to wonder about her methods and resources here. The obituaries always appeared only a few days, a week or two at the most, after the subject's death, yet the information is frequently precise and detailed. A modern newspaper with obituaries on file, if not wholly written then certainly ready to be compiled at a moment's notice, reflects a modern interest in obituary comment and an obsession with the famous. Martineau would not have had such resources available to her, but her prodigious number of correspondents and acquaintances would doubtless have been able to supply her with anecdotes and details if necessary. It is clear, however, that the sense of immediacy which emerges clearly from these 'Sketches' and the personal engagement with the issues epitomised by a life suggest that her response is not only provoked by the death and the thoughts and, often, memories it evokes, but also by the way in which she sees her own place as revolutionary thinker within a revolutionary age.[8] The anonymity of the newspaper column allowed her a candour—and incidentally protected her against any charge of inaccuracy—which, when coupled with her own name in her *Autobiography* (written in 1855, but not published until 1877), was vigorously attacked in a major review by Margaret Oliphant as an offence against 'good taste, as well as against all family loyalty and the needful and graceful restraints of private life.'[9] Though ephemeral, the daily press as a medium demanded brevity and discrimination in the presentation of material, even while permitting an honesty which the signature might have inhibited. This freedom in turn called forth from her a personal and distinctive engagement with notable figures and issues of her time which represents a new approach to biography fitting the early years of an age of new journalism. For Martineau 'the true principle of Biographical delineation' (p.vii) not only demanded that personal engagement with both the faults and the virtues of her subjects. It also demanded a clear historical and political perspective which reflected both her own views and those of her readers.

Notes

[1] Harriet Martineau, *Biographical Sketches. 1852-1875*, new edn with autobiographical sketch (London: Macmillan, 1893), p.xi.

[2] Richard D. Altick, *Lives and Letters: A History of Literary Biography in England and America* (Westport, Conn.: Greenwood, 1965), p.78. Altick, for instance, has two brief references to Martineau, but does not include any mention of *Biographical Sketches* in his wide-ranging study.

[3] *Harriet Martineau: Selected Letters*, edited by Valerie Sanders (Oxford: Clarendon, 1990), pp.223, 226. Se also *Fifty Years of Fleet Street Being the Life and Recollections of Sir John R. Robinson*, compiled and edited by F.M. Thomas (London: Macmillan, 1904), pp.194-95.

[4] 'We have undertaken to discourse here for a little on Great Men, their manner of appearance in our world's business, how they have shaped themselves in the world's history, what ideas men formed of them, what work they did;—on Heroes, namely, and on their reception and performance; what I call Hero-worship and the heroic in human affairs.' This is the famous and influential opening sentence of Thomas Carlyle's *On Heroes, Hero-Worship, and the Heroic in History* (1841; London: George Routledge, 1897), p.5. The 'Great Man of History' view of biography—and incidentally of history—has been under sustained attack for a good deal of this century.

[5] Altick places the Victorian passion for the hero-worship style of biography within the context of Darwinism: 'Its popularity was, in effect, the Victorians' most defiant reply to the depersonalizing implications of contemporary thought. . . . Biography earned its way by being on the side of virtue against vice, by providing examples of honest, wise, generous, prudential, or profitably inventive conduct. Everyone who had anything to say about biography as a form of literature stressed its didactic duty' (p.86).

[6] First published in the *Monthly Repository*, 2 (December 1832), 301-14; republished in *Miscellanies*, vol.1 (Boston: Hilliard, Gray, 1836). 'Few have any idea of the all-powerful influence which the sense of personal infirmity exerts over the mind of a child . . . He not only gained power by vicissitude, . . . but pleasure fast following upon pain, the pain was robbed of its irritation . . . Scott's childhood was, in short, spent in *feeling*, the best possible preparation for after *thinking*' (pp. 5-6).

[7] Cf the comment in the *Times* at the time of Macaulay's death: 'The excitement which the first two volumes created, appearing as they did in all the hubbub of the French Revolution, presenting to us a picture in

remarkable contrast to that of the Parisian rabble, and calming down our own populace with the story of a nobler revolution, must be vividly in the recollection of our readers' (*Times*, 31 December 1859, p.7).

[8] Sir John Robinson (manager/editor of the *Daily News* from 1868) suggests that some at least of the sketches were written well before the death, and therefore were the result of considered thought, rather than immediate reaction (p.195).

[9] Quoted in Mary Jean Corbett, *Representing Femininity: Middle-Class Subjectivity in Victorian and Edwardian Women's Autobiographies* (New York/Oxford: Oxford UP, 1992), p.93.

5 Trollope, the *Times*, and *The Warden*

John Sutherland

It is tantalising that the three years of most significance in the evolution of Trollope's mature fiction should be among the least illuminated by the biographical record. Only seven personal letters are known to survive from 1853 to 1855 (some of them incomplete and dubiously dated), and none at all for the all-important year 1853.[1] It was during this period that Trollope had his first thoughts for *The Warden* and its successor, *Barchester Towers*, which were the novels which earned him his first critical and commercial success.[2] As pilots for the *Barchester Chronicles* they patented what posterity sees as the true Trollopian note in fiction. What inspired the author of *The Warden* to venture into what was new territory in the early 1850s—the comedy of ecclesiatical intrigue?

We are not helped by the account which Trollope gives in *An Autobiography*. The passage describing the genesis of the Barchester sequence is, as critics have noted (with a forgiving word) 'misleading'. As regards dates, the errors may spring from late-life forgetfulness, but other aspects of Trollope's account of the genesis of *The Warden* can only be ascribed to deliberate obfuscation. R.H. Super outlines the relevant issues clearly:

> When . . . Trollope published *The Warden*, he was 'often asked in what period of my early life I had lived so long in a cathedral city as to have become intimate with the ways of a Close. I never lived in any cathedral city,—except London, never knew anything of any Close, and at that time had enjoyed no peculiar intimacy with any clergyman' (*Autobiography*, pp.92-93). Yet both his grandfathers were clergymen, and as a schoolboy for

four years at Winchester he worshipped in the cathedral or college chapel three or four times a day. Moreover, he had known from infancy a Winchester prebendary, Dr. George Nott. And of course his frequent walks along the River Itchen had taken him again and again to St. Cross Hospital, the prototype of Hiram's Hospital in *The Warden*.

In telling how he hit upon the idea for *The Warden*, Trollope made a blunder as to dates that a modern editor has inadvertently restored from the manuscript. He conceived the idea, he wrote, at Salisbury, and twelve months later on 29 July 1852, he began the novel at Tenbury [in Worcester]. But his diaries show that he was in Salisbury in May 1852, and in Tenbury on 29 July 1853, each a year later than his recollection. [Trollope wrote *An Autobiography* in the 1870s]. Trollope himself was puzzled as he read over his manuscript, and remarked, 'On looking at the title-page, I find [*The Warden*] was not published till 1855' (*Autobiography*, p.97). When his son Henry published the *Autobiography* he spotted the error and corrected the former dates to 1852 and 1853, but the Oxford editor in 1950 reinstated the erroneous text of Trollope's handwriting and the blunder persists in current editions, including the Oxford World's Classics (*Autobiography,* pp.95-96).[3]

There are then two contradictory timetables for the composition and production of *The Warden*. According to the first, sanctioned by *An Autobiography*, conception occurred 'on the little bridge at Salisbury' in late May 1851, 'while wandering there on a mid-summer evening round the purlieus of the cathedral' (pp.93-94). He began writing the novel a year later in the summer of 1852 (29 July) at Tenbury (Trollope was, of course, criss-crossing England on post-office duties during this phase of his career). The manuscript of the resulting one-volume work (the shortest Trollope had hitherto submitted to a publisher) was delivered to Longmans around early October 1854. The work was read, approved, promptly accepted, contracted for, and published on 5 January 1855. In the same month, Trollope began writing *The Warden*'s sequel—*Barchester Towers* (initially also devised as a one-volume work). Due to the slow sales of *The Warden*, however (largely the result of the Crimean War, I would suggest), its successor was similarly interrupted and slow to appear. Begun in January 1855, *Barchester Towers* was not completed until November 1856 and was published (as a three-decker) in April 1857 after numerous delays in press.[4] If we follow the chronology given by Trollope in *An Autobiography*, these two novels—so vital in his career—occupied him for over six years. Never would he be so desultory again.

There are attractions in the 1851-52 genesis scheme. In a revealing essay 'Dickens and the Origin of "The Warden"', Lionel Stevenson points to a hitherto unregarded article in *Household Words*, 12 June 1852, which would explain both the venom of the 'Mr Popular Sentiment' satire in *The Warden* and, more importantly, the whole idea for the novel.[5] The article (which was probably not written by Dickens, but by his righthand man Henry Morley, a writer as popularly sentimental as his mentor) was on the subject of the Charterhouse asylum for indigent old men (the same institution which features so movingly in Thackeray's *The Newcomes*). It is, as Lionel Stevenson says, a 'long and detailed article' which gives 'full descriptions of the various buildings, the routines of administration, etc. More significant, however, was the persistent sarcasm with which the writer developed his thesis that the treatment of the old pensioners was harsh and humiliating, that the officials were scandalously enriching themselves, and that the original intent of the founder was flouted'. Quotation bears out Lionel Stevenson's contention. The author expatiates on the generous funds yielded by the foundation for the care of 'but eighty brothers', but while they scrape by with the barest of amenities (supplied on £1,000 a year), the 'Master' wallows in luxury:

> The Master, according to the words of the foundation, should be a learned, discreet, and meek man, unmarried, and aged, when appointed, above forty years. He should neither have nor accept of any place of preferment or benefit either in church or commonwealth, whereby he might be drawn from his residence, care, and charge of the Hospital; and if he do, in such case he shall leave this place, or be displaced if he refuse to leave it. His salary was fixed at fifty pounds, a very reasonable sum in those days [the early seventeenth century] . . . The Master's house, as it now stands, looks very much like a piece of the year 1611. Who is the *unbeneficed* divine residing here, devoting his whole care to the superintendence of the household of Poor Brethren? He is the venerable churchman, whose archdeaconry of London, whose post of canon residentiary of St Pauls, whose onerous duties as rector of St Giles, Cripplegate, whose chaplaincy to the Bishop of London, whose almonership of St Paul's (the whole yielding between two and three thousand pounds per annum) are not considered incompatible with the receipt of an additional eight hundred a year as Master of the Charterhouse, together with residence and partial board. The residence is humble in external pretensions, but inside luxuriously fitted, having thirty-three rooms, including all domestic offices; it is, in fact, one of the best ecclesiastical nests in London. (pp.84-85)

All this, of course, chimes nicely with the satirical description of Mr Popular Sentiment's new novel in monthly numbers, *The*

Almshouse, in Chapter 15 of *The Warden*. *The Almshouse* opens with a scene in a clergyman's house: 'Every luxury to be purchased by wealth was described as being there; all the appearances of household indulgence generally found amongst the most self-indulgent of the rich were crowded into this abode . . .' (pp. 206-07).⁶ Meanwhile the eight old men supported by the foundation starve on sixpence-farthing a day. And, in Trollope's novel, as the *Jupiter* indignantly records, the warden's stipend is 'eight hundred a year'; exactly the same sum as that of the Master of Charterhouse as described by Morley.

With all the enthusiasm of its first discoverer, Stevenson puts forward the Charterhouse article of 12 June 1852 as the prime source of Trollope's novel:

> Just six weeks after the publication of this outspoken assault upon a respected charitable institution, Anthony Trollope set seriously to work upon *The Warden*, his first novel of English life. Far from careful about details, he gives several inconsistent dates in *An Autobiography*, stating at one point that he began it on July 29, 1853; but [Michael] Sadleir and the Stebbinses are apparently correct in changing this to 1852. More than a year before, he had conceived the main idea of the story when taking his summer evening stroll in the close of Salisbury Cathedral; but, as he declares that he did not write one word during the subsequent year, one may doubt whether the whole plot had presented itself clearly to him on that first occasion. (p.86)

If, in fact, Trollope had begun to write *The Warden* shortly after the *Household Words* article, Lionel Stevenson's thesis would be very persuasive. But there is the contradictory evidence of the travel logs, which Henry Trollope and R.H. Super have taken note of, and which was not apparently available to Stevenson. If Trollope waited over a year to begin penning his riposte, the

Stevenson argument is considerably weakened. The *Household Words* article would have been old news by July 1853. But against the evidence of the travel logs, one can argue that the absence of any writing diary (such as Trollope habitually kept in later life) leaves the whole issue still open. There are so many gaps over these years, and such a huge expanse of unaccounted-for time in the putative period of *The Warden*'s composition, that it is quite likely that a seed was planted in July 1852 following the provocation of the *Household Words* article, some notes put down and stored away. There is, furthermore, something suspiciously symbolic-looking about the 'vista of Salisbury Cathedral from the little bridge' episode. In *The New Zealander* (the anatomy of England and the English which Trollope wrote in 1856, alongside *Barchester Towers*) he had taken as his theme the great historian Thomas Macaulay's symbolic tableau of a man of the far future, from a far distant place, standing on a broken arch of London Bridge (which has fallen down) contemplating the ruin of St Paul's. It seems likely that Trollope, in recalling the tableau in *An Autobiography*, was being imaginative rather than accurate. There is the further complication that Trollope gave a contrary account of the origin of *The Warden* and *Barchester Towers* to T.H.S. Escott:

> Both novels, in Trollope's own words to the present writer, grew out of *The Times* correspondence during a dull season of the fifties. The letters raised and argued, for several days or weeks together, the controversial issue whether a beneficed clergy man could be justified in systematic absenteeism from the congregation for whose spiritual welfare he was responsible. The ecclesiastic who had first supplied the subject for this newspaper was first vehemently attacked by open enemies or candid friends; he then received the best defence possible from zealous

partisans; and so, after an empty bout of argument, the matter ended.[7]

Taking this cue, and picking up references in the text (notably at the beginning of Chapter 2), Michael Sadleir assumed that Trollope was primarily concerned with the St Cross affair, which had been rumbling on since the late 1840s. The St Cross Hospital at Winchester supported fifteen old men. The 'Master' of St Cross since 1808 was the Reverend Francis North (1772-1861), after 1827 the sixth Earl of Guilford. The earl was what the *Times*, with heavy sarcasm, called 'a noble pluralist'. Since it was, following various ecclesiastical reforms, forbidden for a clergyman to hold more than two benefices, the mastership of St Cross had been redesignated a lay office, so that the richly endowed North might hold it with two other livings ('trickery', according to the Thunderer). It was estimated that by the early 1850s Guilford had received some £300,000 (Mr Harding, who has been Precentor for some ten years, will have received only £8,000). It is, however, important to note that in spite of Escott's comment ('and so, after an empty bout of argument, the matter ended'), the St Cross affair was not ended until 1855, some months after *The Warden* was published in January of that year. Guilford was obliged to retire and to make some reparation later in 1855.

Most modern biographers and the editor of the collected letters (N. John Hall) accept the 29 July 1853 *starting* date and Hall's 'Autumn? 1854' date for the termination of *The Warden*'s composition (the submission to Longman and their speedy response in October 1854 is reliably recorded). But recent biographers (and editors of *The Warden*, such as David Skilton) tend not to linger on two connected oddities: (1) Trollope must have known, if only by sight as a schoolboy, the Earl of Guilford from his three years at Winchester, 1827-30; (2) why did he deny so forthrightly knowing *anything* about Cathedral matters.

I suspect that Trollope was uncharacteristically 'misleading' on these issues because, as a serving civil servant in the early 1850s (at a period when reform was in the air), it would have been professionally inappropriate for him to have expressed an opinion on contentious political matters. What he offers in *An Autobiography* is the classic Whitehall sidestep. His private opinions were something else. Most commentators assume that *The Warden* was the result of the contemplative epiphany at Salisbury (whichever year it happened) and a longer-standing irritation about newspapers pontificating on the subject of church charitable trusts; something that had figured in the correspondence columns and the leader pages of the *Times* since 1849. It is assumed that Trollope was against corruption if and when it reached epic scale—as it reportedly did in the Guilford case. But, as it was traditionally controlled by gentlemanly English codes and hallowed tradition, Trollope was generally in favour of patronage and privilege. It was family interest, after all, which had got him his place at the Post Office in the first place. The egalitarian, meritocratic regime introduced by Northcote Trevelyan in 1853-54 would surely have excluded him, poor penman that he was in 1834. But 'measure in all things': Guilford's case represented, as David Skilton puts it, 'an extreme form of the evil which taints Barchester comparatively slightly' (p.xiv). Mr Harding's £8,000 plus perks over ten years may be tolerated; the Earl's £300,000 over 45 years is beyond the pale.

As it happens, I think Trollope had considerable sympathy for Guilford; almost as much as he had for that other vilified old man Septimus Harding. It seems likely that Trollope's sympathy for the Master of St Cross was increased during the course of writing the novel by the relentless persecution he endured from Printing House Square. It will be remembered that the satire on Tom Towers and the *Jupiter* comes very late in *The Warden*, in chapters 14-15 ('Mount Olympus', 'Mr Sentiment'). Tom Towers himself is introduced, in passing, some half way through the narrative, in Chapter 10. If one accepts the most persuasive timetable of composition, Trollope would have been writing Chapters 14 to 15 at some point in early 1854. He was, I think, particularly provoked by the third leader in the *Times* on 6

January 1854. It is a frankly gloating *ad hominem* attack on the Earl of Guilford (an 81-year-old man at the time). The newspaper's jubilation was excited by the news that the 'noble pluralist' had been induced to resign his two livings—but not, as yet, the mastership of St Cross:

> Lord Guilford has resigned his two livings of Alresford and St Mary's. The result is a great but not a complete victory. The calculation of the noble pluralist is, no doubt, that as he has but a limited number of years to live, all the benefit which he may hope to derive from the income of the two livings which he has just resigned must fall infinitely short of the aggregate sum of £90,000 which he is called upon to disgorge for the use of poor persons beneficially interested in the revenues of St Cross. Lord Guilford may be very sure that there are not twenty men who speak with English tongues out of the circle of his immediate dependents who will sympathize with him in what he may be pleased to consider his misfortune. From first to last the transaction has been a scandal to the name of North. It was begun in trickery, it has been supported by falsehood, and now Lord Guilford seeks to evade the consequences of discovery by shift and evasion. He will, however, find himself defeated by the law of the land, and public opinion is ready to confirm the sternest decision at which the law may arrive. The victory over a great pluralist is no ordinary one, and we may be proud when we think how large a share the press has had in producing the result. The era of the Norths and the Moores—of the men who dealt with the Church of England as stockjobbers deal with the funds—is well nigh at an end. Let us hear no more of 'dignified clergymen' when the 'dignity' is employed as a blind to conceal the real nature of

transactions which might be expected from a Jeremy Diddler or a Robert Macaire, not from a minister of religion, whose character, as well as his office, should give him a claim to our reverence and respect.

It is an obnoxiously complacent, self-serving, and callous editorial; designed to ruin, if nothing else, whatever lingering personal respect Guilford might enjoy among his circle of acquaintance. Trollope obviously thought it cruel. In Chapter 13 of *The Warden* it is a third leader in the *Jupiter* which brings Mr Harding to his determination to resign his wardenship. And in Chapter 14 Trollope expatiates on the irresponsibility of the *Times* when it embarks on one of its campaigns against corruption (sleaze, as we would say):

> Such is Mount Olympus, the mouthpiece of all the wisdom of this great country. It may probably be said that no place in this 19th century is more worthy of notice. No treasury mandate armed with the signatures of all the government has half the power of one of those broad sheets, which fly forth from hence so abundantly, armed with no signature at all.
> Some great man, some mighty peer—we'll say a noble duke—retires to rest feared and honoured by all his countrymen—fearless himself; if not a good man, at any rate a mighty man—too mighty to care much what men may say about his want of virtue. He rises in the morning degraded, mean, and miserable; an object of men's scorn, anxious only to retire as quickly as maybe to some German obscurity, some unseen Italian privacy, or, indeed, anywhere out of sight. What has made this awful change? An article has appeared in the *Jupiter*; some fifty lines of a narrow column have destroyed all his

grace's equanimity, and banished him forever from the world. No man knows who wrote the bitter words; the clubs talk confusedly of the matter, whispering to each other this and that name. (pp. 183-4)

My guess is that if Trollope had not felt constrained by his official position, he might have come out more strongly for Guilford in *The Warden* than he did. It was the same sense of constraint, even twenty years later, that led him, I suspect, to deny any personal knowledge of Guilford, of any clergyman, or any clergyman's workplace or working practices. This denial cannot, of course, have been absentmindedness (as the business of dates may well have been). It could further be argued that the hiatus in Trollope's novel-writing in the early 1850s can be linked to his promotion in the Post Office and new responsibilities. Between 1847 and 1850 Trollope published a novel a year. In 1851 he returned from Ireland and was assigned to the south-west of England on an especially responsible postal mission. Between 1850 and 1855 he published nothing. Thereafter he resumed his novel a year (or better) until the end.

Any reconstruction of how *The Warden* came about must necessarily be hypothetical, given the absence of record. But what seems plausible is that Trollope's first intention was to write a novel centred on some current 'scandal' being bruited in the newspapers. In this he may well have been influenced by Dickens's *Bleak House* and its attack on the Court of Chancery (something that had attracted the notice of the *Times*). Trollope chose the charitable trusts affair. He may conceivably have been drawn to it by his personal knowledge, or recollection, of one of the embattled principals. At the same time he was, as I surmise, warned by a superior, or felt himself inhibited now that things were going so well professionally, about compromising his career by writing fiction; particularly, that is, realistic Irish novels (in the aftermath of the Famine) or novels about revolutionary France (in the aftermath of the 1848 revolution). Hence the delays; and hence, perhaps, the turn from the subject matters of *The Kellys and the O'Kellys* and *La Vendée* to the less offensive tone of comedy represented by 'The Precentor' (later to become *The Warden*). Nonetheless, in choosing the charitable trusts business and making it the occasion of a counterattack on the *Times* (and, in passing, Charles Dickens), Trollope indicated his intention to intervene in the issues of the day—if less stridently than his trio of bêtes noires, Mr Pessimist Anticant, Mr Popular Sentiment, and the *Jupiter*. In one sense Trollope's judgment was sound. The St Cross affair did drag on—until mid-1855. As journalists now put it, the story 'had legs'. Other things being equal *The Warden* ought to have been topical when it was published, and the *Times*'s withers should have been painfully wrung by Trollope's topical satire.[8] But, unfortunately for Trollope's novel, the Crimean War intervened and with it came the Thunderer's finest hour (Dickens also achieved a new authority in public life with the formation of the Administrative Reform Association). *The Warden*'s satire looked like a popgun in the light of William Howard Russell's dispatches to Printing House Square. The attack on John Delane ('Tom Towers') now looked petty. The charitable trusts business, which had been on everyone's lips in 1853 and 1854, was entirely forgotten in 1855. It was small beer compared to Sebastopol or Balaclava. As Trollope records in *An Autobiography*, the sales of *The Warden* languished for the best part of a year and Longmans blew so cold on any proposed successor that *Barchester Towers*, with 86 manuscript pages written, was postponed for a year. Eventually, with peace, the Barchester Chronicles finally found their place in the reading public's heart.

It is, as I say, necessarily hypothetical. There are a number of dark pockets in Trollope's biography: his early years in London, his relationship with Rose (about whom we know little more than her name) and—most regrettably for my purposes here—what was happening in his mind and sensibility in the years between 1851 and 1853, the most formative period of his artistic life, as we may suppose. Let us hope that, even at this late date, some letters turn up to enlighten us.

Notes

[1] See N. John Hall, *The Letters of Anthony Trollope*, 2 vols (Stanford: Stanford UP, 1983).
[2] *An Autobiography*, edited by M. Sadleir and F. Page (1950; repr. Oxford: Oxford UP World's Classics, 1980, with introduction and notes by P.D. Edwards),. p.98.
[3] 'Truth and Fiction in Trollope's *Autobiography*', *Nineteenth-Century Literature*, 48.1 (June 1993), 76-77. All references to *An Autobiography* in the text, including Super's, are from the OUP World's Classics edition cited above.
[4] See 'Note on the Text', *Barchester Towers*, edited by John Sutherland (Oxford: OUP World's Classics, 1996), pp.xxix-xxxvi.
[5] 'Dickens and the Origin of "The Warden"', *The Trollopian*, 2 (September 1947), 83-89.
[6] References are to the World's Classics edition of *The Warden*, edited by David Skilton (Oxford: OUP, 1980, repr. 1994).
[7] T.H.S. Escott, *Anthony Trollope: His Work, Associates, and Literary Originals* (London: Lane, 1913), pp.103-04.
[8] The *Times* had an extraordinarily high conceit of itself in 1853-54. See, for instance, *The History of the Times: The Tradition Established, 1841-1884* (London: The Times, 1939), pp.158-65.

6 The Angry Young Gentlemen of *Tomahawk*

Christopher Kent

Social historians of Victorian Britain are currently in a state of turmoil over the problem of class. Long dedicated to bringing the neglected ordinary people of the past into history, they have done so mainly by aggregating and differentiating them into the collective identities of social class. The working class has been the master category of social history and its trajectory the master narrative. The recent retreat of intellectual Marxism and the reception of the linguistic turn are now forcing many social historians to recognize the extent to which their own ideology, art and desire have contributed to the making of the classes with which they work. Long accustomed to giving voice to the inarticulate in terms of class consciousness, they have been disconcerted to learn that contemporaries, who in some respects had better claims than they to speak for ordinary working people, did not use the language of a unified working class. The same applies to the middle class, except that, being more articulate, its putative members made it quite clear through their own contemporary writings—not least of them the novel—that they could not be confined to some pigeonhole labelled 'bourgeoisie'. Discovering that the middle class is a fluid discursive construct has been less of a shock to social historians, who being themselves largely middle class, like it or not, really knew that already.[1]

Ironically the social category that has long been regarded as least real in terms of traditional historical materialist thinking, was the most real—that is, the least reified—in terms of Victorian self- and-other classification and perception. That was the category of gentleman. Few would seriously claim that description today. For most its utter irrelevance is testified to by the fact that all men now pass without anxious self-scrutiny through the door that bears that word. But the question 'Is he a gentleman?' formed the keel of many a sturdy Victorian three-decker, and literary scholars have had much to say about the question of the gentleman in the novels of Thackeray, Dickens, and above all Trollope. Social historians should pay more attention to such valuable work; however, they should also pay more attention to the question itself. If 'Am I a gentleman?' evidently meant more to Victorians than the question 'Am I a member of the working class?', surely social historians should ask what this tells them. Here, as is so often the case, periodicals offer a good starting point.[2]

The 1860s was a time of particularly dense intersection for issues bearing on the interests and status of gentlemen, especially for those near its margins who patrolled the border, stemming the flow of incomers who wished to dwell in their blessed state. A journal of that decade was *Tomahawk*, an organ of embattled gentlemanliness that first appeared on 11 May 1867. It immediately caught public attention with its bold attacks on various public institutions, not least of them the Queen and the Prince of Wales. It soon claimed a circulation of fifty thousand, and its success caused unease in the camp of its chief rival, *Punch*.[3] It came to a mysterious and abrupt end, vigorous and slashing to the final number of 30 July 1870. Today it is chiefly remembered for its sensational colour-tinted centrefold cartoons by Matt Morgan.[4] But its text was as incisive as its pictures. The young gentlemen who wrote for it were a close-knit group with a distinct cast of mind, social and political.

Tomahawk's founder and editor was Arthur William à Beckett, who brought in his two older brothers, Gilbert and Albert. All three had clerkships in the civil service which gave them a secure base for budding careers in journalism and the theatre. Francis Albert Marshall was another young civil servant who would become a successful author of comedies and farces. Alfred Thompson, an ex-cavalry officer with a degree from Cambridge, where he was a founder of the Amateur Dramatic Club, was a Paris-trained artist. He would eventually go into costume design and theatre management. Frederick Clay was another civil servant, highly placed as private secretary to the Patronage Secretary at the Treasury. He had received musical training on the continent and was already embarked on a modestly successful career as a composer of light music for the stage and parlour. The fathers of both Clay and Marshall were wealthy beneficiaries of business fortunes and MPs of the liberal-radical stamp. Thomas Gibson Bowles was yet another *Tomahawk* staffer whose father was an MP. The illegitimate but acknowledged son of the liberal cabinet minister Thomas Milner Gibson, Bowles was a civil servant, dashing young man-about-town, enthusiastic amateur actor and part-time political journalist for the Tory *Morning Post*. T.H.S. Escott, fresh from Oxford, combined teaching classics at the University of London with writing 'middles' (social commentary editorials) for the *Saturday Review* and leaders for the Tory *Standard*. Shortly after *Tomahawk* was launched, Alfred Austin joined the staff. A briefless barrister and *Standard* leader writer, he was also a poet of Byronic pretensions who would eventually become, on the death of Tennyson, perhaps England's least distinguished poet laureate. Completing the *Tomahawk* team was its cartoonist Matt Morgan. The son of a minor actor and actress, he was the only member of the staff who lacked the birth, education, or occupation of a gentleman.[5]

The all-important claim of *Tomahawk*'s writers to the status of gentlemen was reasonably secure. Though none came from old or extensively landed families—their parents having backgrounds in the professions or the higher levels of business—they all had the public school and/or university educations which were deemed to confer gentility, except for Bowles and Clay, who made up for this lack by the excellence of their family and political connections. None had the classic qualification of the gentleman, leisure secured by adequate private means, but this had long since ceased to be a necessary prerequisite to gentility. A gentleman might have an occupation, but it should be a profession. The Church of England clergy and the bar were unquestionably gentlemanly, but the status of a civil servant was moot, that of a journalist dubious, and anything involving the theatre was generally regarded as well beyond the pale. While the first two conferred gentility, the latter two could jeopardise the status of any who brought their own gentility into them. The dilettante tradition to some extent buffered this conflict, since the gentleman dilettante was excused such occupational aberrations by being deemed 'not serious', meaning above all, 'not doing it for the money'—being essentially an amateur. But *Tomahawk's* young gentlemen did not quite fall within this tradition, mainly because they *were* doing it for the money. Clay, Bowles and Marshall might have the support of well-to-do parents, and Austen had income from a small legacy, but the others had only their clerkships, paying at best perhaps £200 a year at their level. They were serious about journalism and the theatre which offered valuable supplementary income and even the prospect of a full alternative career.

The financial attraction of founding a journal like *Tomahawk* was to challenge and defeat the hugely profitable *Punch*, the dream of every Victorian comic journal promoter. The à Becketts' father had been the first editor of *Figaro*, a successful comic journal of the 1830s widely acknowledged as *Punch's* chief predecessor, and he became a regular *Punch* contributor from its start until his death in 1856. *Punch's* main rival in the early 1860s was *Fun*, for which Matt Morgan had cartooned. The mid-1860s saw a spate of rivals such as *Mirth, The Mask, Moonshine, Quiz, Punch and Judy, Toby, Iris, Judy, Hornet* and *Will 'o the Wisp*, of which only the last three survived more than a year.[6] If a new journal seemed threatening, *Punch* might poach its staff, as it did from *The Man in the Moon* in the late 1840s.[7] The young Arthur à Beckett had earlier applied to join the *Punch* staff and been turned down, so he was anxious to make them regret their mistake.[8] Already at twenty-one he had become editor of the *Glow-Worm*, a light theatregoers' paper where he met several future *Tomahawk* writers.

Whereas the *Punch* staff were insecurely assertive about their gentlemanly status, drawing comfort still from the fact that

Thackeray had once been one of them, another of *Tomahawk*'s journalistic predecessors was much more secure in its gentlemanliness. This was the *Owl*, a smart, clever and expensive weekly *jeu d'esprit* founded in 1864, and carrying exclusive political and social gossip and wit from the highest echelons of the establishment. Self-consciously amateur (though not amateurish: it was well produced), it was pointedly intended neither to make money nor to circulate widely. It appeared only while parliament was in session, and even then not always regularly. Its editor was Evelyn Ashley, the dashing young private secretary and kinsman to the Prime Minister, Lord Palmerston. Its contributors included the brilliant eccentric Laurence Oliphant, whose neglected novel *Piccadilly* (1870; serialised 1865) provides perhaps the best picture of the social milieu which preoccupied *Tomahawk*'s writers. Both Bowles and Marshall belonged to the glamourous clique of *Owl* contributors. Such was that paper's mystique and reputation that its circulation and advertising revenue greatly exceeded its authors' intentions. Its considerable profits were spent on splashy parties for the contributors where expensive baubles were given to female guests.[9] Two other journals that flourished in the 1860s and did much to lessen the social stigma attached to journalism were the *Saturday Review*, known to be largely written by clever university men and exuding a distinct aura of intellectual snobbery, and the evening daily *Pall Mall Gazette*, a quality newspaper that was supposed to be, like its Thackerayan namesake, 'written by and for gentlemen'.[10] According to T.H.S. Escott, *Tomahawk* was intended to combine the best features of these three gentlemanly periodicals.[11]

Tomahawk's subtitle was 'A Saturday Journal of Satire'. E.P. Thompson once called satire a way of concealing political confusion, but it is perhaps more a way of responding to political and social confusion. There is an affinity between satire and toryism: both tend more to pessimism than optimism about human nature. Satire is a humour of anxiety that is sensitive to symptoms of danger, particularly in times of prosperity. The 1860s were propitious, being times of unparalleled economic growth, the effect of the great Victorian boom reaching down significantly into the labouring population. Related to this prosperity were the growth of organised labour and its increasing sense of entitlement to the franchise. Boom times revealed frictions within the banking system: when Overend, Gurney, Britain's largest brokerage house, failed in 1866, the aristocratic Bank of England refused to assist the upstart provincial bankers even at the price of a financial panic.[12] Outbreaks of cattle plague in 1865-66 revealed country gentlemen, usually placid about the misfortunes of others who fell victim to 'nature's laws', strenuously demanding government compensation when their infected herds were slaughtered (*Tomahawk*, 5 October 1867, p.321).[13] The ongoing controversy over the conduct of Governor Eyre in quelling disturbances in Jamaica raised the spectre of popular insurrection and the question of what degree of discretion and strength of nerve were necessary to those in authority (14 March 1868, p.110). Although the 1860s are now assigned to the age of equipoise, the political hypochondria of the satirist had plenty to dwell upon then.

A change of generation had just taken place in British politics: both parties had new leaders, both of whom were viewed with distrust by their parties. When it was said, by some, that neither Gladstone nor Disraeli was a gentleman, the judgment could invoke both traditional criteria of birth and fortune, which neither the son of a merchant nor the son of a Jewish man of letters met, and the newer moral criteria of trustworthiness and principled conduct. Having gained office by the defeat of a modest Liberal reform bill in 1866, Disraeli presided over the passage of the far more radical reform act of 1867. Having developed a reputation as an ardent defender of the established church, Gladstone as prime minister disestablished the Anglican church in Ireland.

The satirist prides himself on a strong sense of reality, but gnawed by the sense that the reality is seriously flawed, departing radically from how things should be, he prides himself much less on his splenetic resignation to that reality. Realism is also the price of being an insider, a status the satirist finds hard to resist.

Effective satire assumes a shared understanding between satirist and audience: the reader is 'one of us'. It can therefore resort to irony with some confidence, for irony can go seriously wrong when author and reader are not basically in tune. The insider status which *Tomahawk* conferred upon its readers was the journal's protection; it made those readers accomplices in its acts of aggression. They shared its anger, outrage and dismay, but they too were gentlemen, and like *Tomahawk* itself, could be trusted not to go 'too far'. In the view of many, however, *Tomahawk* did go too far. The most spectacular of the journal's acts of aggression was the one that gained it almost instant notoriety, its criticism of Queen Victoria. Contrary to the claims of its critics, *Tomahawk* was not criticising the institution of monarchy—no breath of republicanism tainted its pages—but rather the symbolic abdication emblematic of a wider social disorder (8 June 1867, p.51). It was the Queen who was the radical, failing to take her proper place at the head of London Society, even inflicting by her absence economic hardship on the many working people who depended on Society's patronage of the labour-intensive luxury trades (30 May 1868, p.213). But worse than all this was the usurpation of the empty throne by a complete nobody, John Brown, the Scottish servant to whom the Queen was attracted and whose rough familiarities with her shocked courtiers (and her own family). Here was an insider story that the press had suppressed, and which *Tomahawk* was the first to address openly. For this, of course, it was denounced as disloyal, even treasonous by chagrined and envious rival journals in a pattern familiar to this day. *Tomahawk* made no verbal reference to actual impropriety, but Matt Morgan's picture of Brown leaning on the empty throne, pipe in hand (Queen Victoria was well known to abhor tobacco) and staring defiantly at the lion of British public opinion, spoke volumes (10 August 1867).[14] Not content with chiding the Queen for absenteeism, *Tomahawk* also warned the rackety Prince of Wales not to follow the example of his unpopular predecessor George IV, who as Prince of Wales and Prince Regent was still a byword for immorality (29 June 1867, p.89). It even suggested

A BROWN STUDY!

(*Tomahawk*, 10 August 1867)

that the Prince be made Prince Regent to give his idle life some purpose in view of the Queen's evident distaste for the ceremonial role, and his talent for it (30 May 1868, p.213).

Underpinning *Tomahawk*'s exposé of royal shortcomings was the doctrine of snobbism. The journal's presiding genius was the spirit of Thackeray: its very title came from one of his fictional journals, and he was regularly invoked by its writers as their master.[15] This testifies to the impact of *The Book of Snobs*, that most controversial work which effected a transformation of the word from a relatively simple dismissive epithet for a social inferior to a richly ambiguous term that threatened to implicate the whole of English society, or at least its middle and upper classes, including even the author who admitted to being 'One of Themselves'. '*He who meanly admires mean things is a Snob*',[16] Thackeray's concise definition, was rendered less epigrammatically in *Tomahawk's* 'uncompromising detestation of all that is really low, of all that is beneath the English gentleman' (10 July 1869, p.20). The explicit reference here to the gentleman is significant. Though implicit in Thackeray, he was reluctant to attempt to pin down that equally fraught term, certainly in an explicit, mutually defining antithesis of gentleman and snob. Significant too is the fact that *Tomahawk*, in its own words, was 'not a snob'. Its anxious young gentlemen could not afford Thackerayan ironies on so vital a matter.

The doctrine of snobbism empowered *Tomahawk* to criticise the royal family. It was the snob whose superstitious worship of empty forms of monarchy, detached from its proper functions, weakened the very object of its worship by holding it above honest criticism. *Tomahawk*, then, was the truly loyal monarchist. Thackeray had signalled his semantic transformation of the snob when he revealed that even a king could be a snob, if that king were George IV. The snob said that a lord, and all the more a prince, was a gentleman by definition. Not so, argued *Tomahawk's* young gentlemen, who because of their more precarious position viewed themselves as the true guardians of gentlemanly standards, charged with maintaining its true ideal over its false, material definition. They found the example of the Prince of Wales being subpoenaed as a witness in a divorce action unedifying in the extreme, particularly when he had to deny under oath any act of adultery between himself and the plaintiff's wife—although, as *Tomahawk* pointed out, this sort of abdication of the responsibility to maintain high standards in high society was not confined to royalty (5 March 1870).[17] Readers' attention was drawn to numerous other examples. In 1867 the young Marquess of Hastings, already legendary for his fast life, completed his ruin at the Derby, losing £120,000 by betting against a horse owned by the man whose fiancée he had just run off with (25 May 1867, p.27; 21 November 1868, p.227).[18] The journal was studded with other allusions to depravity in high society. The son and heir of a recent lord chancellor was convicted for forgery. The scandal-racked family of the Duke of Newcastle continued its catastrophic plunge into bankruptcy and indecency. The society journalist Grenville Murray, illegitimate son of the spectacularly bankrupt Duke of Buckingham, was horsewhipped on the steps of a Pall Mall club by Lord Carrington, a boon companion of the Prince of Wales (10 July 1869, p.11). An army general was cashiered, not for seducing a governess—conduct the army apparently condoned—but for not paying his betting debts which was unforgivable (1 June 1867, p.47). Whether this was worse than the average bill of scandal for the English aristocracy is hard to say, but the degree of public attention it received was certainly rising. *Tomahawk*'s crowning example of the prevalence of 'brutal snobbism' is a small item from a London newspaper reporting an accident in which a cabman was taken to hospital with a broken leg after being struck by a carriage. The newspaper headlined the story 'Alarming Accident to Earl Grosvenor's Carriage' (1 May 1869, p.198).

Tomahawk was a forerunner of a new and influential type of journalism that proliferated from the 1870s onwards, the so-called society journalism that dealt heavily in gossip about the doings of the upper classes. *Vanity Fair* founded by Thomas Gibson Bowles was a direct offshoot; Henry Labouchère's *Truth* and Edmund

Yates's the *World* were two other notable examples of the genre. Not that such gossip was new but in earlier nineteenth-century scandal journalism it tended to have a radical provenance and conveyed hostility to the very institutions and existence of class, wealth and privilege.[19] The 'new' society journalism was more indulgent in tone, detached and somewhat amused by the misdeeds and foibles of the fortunate, tending more to the cynicism of tolerance, than the anger and bitterness of satire. *Tomahawk* was transitional in its style. It could be quite scathing in its invective—though it was Morgan's cartoons that carried the most potent charge of anger. Those who entered its contract of readership were presumed to share its moral superiority. *Tomahawk* lacked the somewhat cynical edge that often characterized later society journalism. There *were* standards, it proclaimed; they were in jeopardy, and it was the duty of proper gentlemen to assert and defend them. *Tomahawk*'s readers were not just social insiders; they were moral insiders. The tone of the British satirical journal *Private Eye* when it first appeared in the 1960s—in a social, political and economic climate strikingly similar to that of the 1860s—the clever, self-righteous, supercilious anger of the young ex-public schoolboys who launched it, bears an interesting resemblance to that of the young gentlemen who brandished the *Tomahawk*.

Though its criticism of the Queen and Prince of Wales gained it greatest attention, other issues are more indicative of gentlemanly anxieties. One of these was social mobility. *Tomahawk* stood for the maintenance of a stable class structure. It was not, however, hostile to the working man and supported the 1867 Reform Act which extended the franchise to the male artisan elite. It was, however, critical of liberal intellectuals who sentimentalised or idealised the working classes, particularly Professor E.S. Beesly, a leading English disciple of Auguste Comte (13 July 1867, p.113), and Mr. Edmond Beales, MA (their titles and degrees heavily emphasised), the old Etonian barrister who was chairman of the largely working-class Reform League (1 June 1867, p.39). Such renegade gentlemen were viewed as ingratiating themselves with the workers by exaggerating their political wisdom under the banner of *vox populi vox dei* (Latin and French phrases abound in *Tomahawk*). Its 'Dictionary of Reform Terms' offered some translations of Reform League jargon: for 'The Working Man'—'The Tavern Tippler'; for the 'Voice of the People'—'Window Smashing'; for the 'Deep-Toned Murmurs of a Mighty Nation'—'Beer, sometimes Gin' (17 July 1867, p.165). The British working people in its view were basically sound and did not wish to be elevated by the bourgeois patronage of working-men's clubs and other such agencies of moral improvement and social interference. It was, however, notably well disposed towards the Volunteer movement, the 1860s outburst of enthusiasm for amateur soldiering that brought deferential members of the working class under the officership of gentlemen like the editor of *Tomahawk*, himself commander of a volunteer unit. The journal's creed was faith in the readiness of the lower classes to accept the tactful leadership of proper gentlemen.

A more serious problem was the erosion of the gentleman ideal by those of the middle classes and below who claimed to be gentlemen and were encouraged in this illusion by journals such as the *Daily Telegraph* which 'thought it admirable to throw open its columns to the crude ideas and questionable grammar of correspondents evidently belonging to the lower ten million. Toms, Franks and Sams have been allowed to strut about in borrowed plumes.' The result? 'Caddism' of the worst kind with the *hoi polloi* airing their views on how much money one needed to marry or keep a servant (13 January1869, p.31; 29 August 1868, p.82). Cad was another of *Tomahawk's* favourite epithets. The Oxford counterpart to the Cambridge-based snob, it was to retain its original sense as a derogatory term for one's perceived inferiors, particularly when they were being assertive and less than deferential and when one had to share space with them. Work space being generally well demarcated, it was in leisure space that unregulated encounters were most likely to take place. One such space that particularly preoccupied *Tomahawk* was the music hall. Its writers were themselves much involved with the 'legitimate' theatre, though at its low end—the theatre of burlesque, pantomime and opera bouffe. But the music hall was non-legitimate, having no artistic authority structure of playwrights, directors, scene or costume designers, instead only an incoherent succession of variety turns, chiefly musical, claiming to exercise direct, egalitarian, even reciprocal communication between performer and audience. To worsen the confusion, that audience was more heterogeneous than that found in the West End theatres. It was becoming fashionable for upper-class men to frequent the halls, a fashion led by—who else?—the Prince of Wales. In the music hall audience cad met snob, low birth rubbing shoulders with low taste to their mutual satisfaction. *Tomahawk* reported in mock court-circular style the Prince's frequent visits to the Canterbury and the Oxford (25 May 1867, p.29) and foresaw an early knighthood for Arthur Lloyd, first of the *lions comiques* and a particular favourite of the Prince's, 'in recognition to his services to music' for writing such songs as 'Gish Bosh flipalong Gals and The Scrumptious Chambermaid' (8 June 1867, p.53).[20] The 'vulgarity' and 'stupidity' of music hall lyrics bellowed out by hideously dressed men and 'shrill' and 'saucy' women pained it deeply (14 September 1867, p.201). Such popular culture somehow seemed less coarse and indelicate when done by Mlle Theresa of the Alcazar in Paris, or at a *café chantant* (*Tomahawk* loved France). Anticipating a demand among snobs for songs suitable for singing 'in the style of the Great Vance' in Belgrave Square drawing rooms, *Tomahawk* offered such lyrics as:

> Aubrey de Lyle is my name
> A younger son! A younger son!
> Though Mammas don't consider me 'game'
> I'm up to fun! I'm up to fun! (6 July 1867, p.97)

The lot of the younger son in a primogeniture-based system has never rated very high as a social problem, however large it loomed as grievance for gentlemen born too late and with tastes beyond their prospects, an important segment of *Tomahawk*'s implied readership. Treated by society with the 'grossest ingratitude and the most unmitigated contempt', they were among those *Tomahawk* called the 'Unconsidered': 'Younger sons head the list, of course, and Government clerks, soldiers, professional men, and generally everybody who disgraces himself by working for his living and thereby, in effect, admits that Providence has not thought well enough of him to provide him with a living unaccompanied by the necessity for work'. These victims of snobbishness who performed the 'heavy work' of Society—'dancing with ill-looking girls destitute of money . . . chatting with chaperons . . . taking the governess down to dinner . . .'—might well form a union and bring Society to a standstill, *Tomahawk* warned (25 May 1867, p.34). If the grievances of the younger son may have contributed to the neglected phenomenon of gentry radicalism, a sort of hypersensitivity to social disequilibrium born of experience, the larger body of the 'Unconsidered' faced the more commonplace problem of combining employment with gentility. Since trade entailed a serious loss of caste, despite the ideology of downward mobility, the only occupations deemed gentlemanly were the public service professions, of which the civil service was the most marginal.[21] Elevating its social and intellectual status was an important project of mid-Victorian liberalism to which *Tomahawk* paid close attention. Its staff were of the last generation of patronage appointees before the advent of the competitive examination requirement and they were ambivalent towards them. Its pages were full of acid sketches of civil service clerks which dwelt on the numbers of snobs, swells, toadies, and flunkies among them, and drew attention to the inequalities of work load and social cachet between the posh Foreign Office, respectable Treasury and low Post Office (18 June 1870, p.238). The *Owl* itself, as *Tomahawk* remarked, was evidence of the idleness of the civil servants who found time to produce it (28 March 1868, p.131). Competitive examinations might increase the efficiency of the civil service, but a touch of unease about the examination mania as a portent of universal utilitarian egalitarianism marked *Tomahawk's* mock examinations for cabmen, MPs and poor law guardians, though perhaps not the one for haughtiness and insolence in government officials (14 December 1867, p.334).

Tomahawk's young gentlemen were *former* civil servants. What was their profession now? They were obviously journalists, but not ordinary ones. Certainly not inky-fingered denizens of Grub Street writing to order. The atmosphere of its pages was that of a club of high spirited, independent gentlemen: 'Tomahawk' the editorial persona (depicted occasionally in cartoons as the noblest of savages) was not an authority figure. One of its favourite targets was bohemia, the abode of pipe tobacco, gin and dirty linen, of hacks like G.A. Sala of the reviled *Daily Telegraph*, florid of nose and prose, and of cads like Edmund Yates, filling his columns with puffs, padding, and self-promotion (18 May 1867, p.17). *Tomahawk* had an early set-to with the ultra-bohemian Savage Club which enjoyed the patronage of the Prince of Wales, and whose secretary, Andrew Halliday, was anxious to make clear that it had no link with the journal (21 December 1867, p.347). The journal leapt at the opportunity to repudiate any hint of association with the Savage Club's snobs. Bohemia is the fascinating subculture where art, literature, theatre and journalism intermingle. Here the freemasonry of non-material callings, of culture and ideas is supposed to transcend the materialist concerns of the conventional social order; yet Victorian bohemia was very sensitive to social status, and its members were very insistent that they were gentlemen, in the 'best sense' of the term. However, bohemia had a high, as well as a low end, exemplified by Thackeray's beloved Garrick Club where more conventional gentlemen enjoyed the *frisson* of association with arty types (and vice versa).

A particular manifestation of high-end bohemianism that angered *Tomahawk's* staff was amateurism, 'the curse of the nineteenth century . . . the essence of all that is false and contemptible' (5 December 1868, p.249). This was not athletic but artistic amateurism, the convention which permitted gentlemen (and ladies) to perform in public and without loss of caste an art that was not their livelihood. It was triply offensive for demeaning the status of the profession and those who practised it as professionals, for debasing the critical standards, the amateur being treated with indulgence and receiving praise for substandard performance, and for fostering unjustified self-esteem in the amateur who preferred to think that he, or she, was in fact being judged by professional criteria. Amateur musicians and actors, the latter particularly numerous, inspired by Charles Dickens and his famous troupe, received frequent warnings in *Tomahawk*—among those warned, Thomas Gibson Bowles himself (3 August 1867, p.143). Amateurism exacerbated the notorious sensitivity of theatre professionals about their social position, as *Tomahawk's* young gentlemen were well aware by virtue of their own involvement with the stage, for they also felt the need to remind the professionals that they 'will not elevate themselves, or their profession by sneering at gentlemen or ladies (using the words in their conventional sense, i.e., persons of birth, position and education, who may choose to take to the stage)' (27 November 1869, p.249).

Amateur authorship was also the target of *Tomahawk's* scorn, although here the line between amateur and professional became hard to draw, anonymity drawing a veil over the vast majority of writers for the press, including themselves. Far from anonymous, but quintessentially amateur—and redolent of snobbism, of course—were Queen Victoria's own journals, excerpts from which were published in 1868 as *Leaves from the Journal of Our Life in the Highlands*. So successful was this volume that *More Leaves* followed. Forewarned, *Tomahawk* speculated about the imminence as well of '*Recollections of the Nursery*' by H.R.H. The Prince of Wales (Edited by his Nurse)' and '*My First Spelling Lesson*, by H.R.H. The Princess Beatrix' (3 August 1867, p.141).[22] Other victims of *Tomahawk's* antipathy to amateurism were 'Macaulay Fitzmuddle', the aspiring journalist who launches a paper 'The Hercules', recruiting his fashionable cronies and dismissing the professional as a 'low cad . . . Fellaw with brains—brains awfully bad form . . .' (12 December 1867, p.259). The civil service was of course a hotbed of amateur journalists, singers, and actors, as the *Tomahawk* staff well knew. So what then was *their* profession? What did that matter? Music, theatre, civil service, journalism—they were above all insiders, sharing with readers their intimate acquaintance with the arcana of the civil service (23 July 1871, p.26), their familiarity with how newspaper leaders are written (1 June 1867, p.41), their knowledge that most of the London theatre critics were also playwrights, anxious not to offend the managers who might take up their plays, and that most current British plays were little more than unacknowledged translations of French plays (20 October 1869, pp.149, 160).

Such knowledge was not conducive to complacency. There was an edge to *Tomahawk* absent in *Punch*. And a breadth of concern that has not been done justice to here. Its young gentlemen were also deeply concerned about young and not so young ladies, with the alarming knowledge that some of them resorted to makeup—the scandalous case of Mme Sarah Rachel Leverson, the criminal cosmetician was reverberating in the press[23]—and the alarming possibility of a women's franchise, first debated in parliament in 1867 thanks to John Stuart Mill. They were indignant about the inadequacies of the Poor Law, police harassment of the lower classes, tolerance of violence by the courts, anti-catholicism, and Irish Fenianism. They were also alert to the growing strength of Prussia, and the crumbling of Louis Napoleon's regime in France. *Tomahawk's* time was the time of Carlyle's *Shooting Niagara: And After?*, duly parodied in mock Carlylese as 'The Rocket and the Stick' (26 October 1867, p.250), and Matthew Arnold's *Culture and Anarchy,* knowingly alluded to in the title of one of *Tomahawk's* attacks on the music hall, 'Culture and Its Friends' (6 July 1867, p.97). Shortly after the journal's demise in 1870, Anthony Trollope began writing *The Way We Live Now*, a veritable compendium of its preoccupations. As it happened, Arnold was a civil servant; so was Trollope until his retirement in 1867. The angry young gentlemen of *Tomahawk* were certainly not alone.

Notes

[1] Patrick Joyce's *Democratic Subjects* (Cambridge: Cambridge UP, 1994) is the most recent contribution to a process that began with Gareth Stedman Jones's *Language of Class* (Cambridge: Cambridge UP, 1983). Dror Wahrman's *Imagining the Middle Class: Political Representation of Class in Britain c1780-1840* (Cambridge: Cambridge UP, 1995) specifically addresses the contingent construction of the middle class in early nineteenth-century political discourse.

[2] Martin Wiener's influential *English Culture and the Decline of the Industrial Spirit 1850-1980* (Cambridge: Cambridge UP, 1981) launched a debate over whether the economic 'failure' of modern Britain began with the surrender of the mid-Victorian middle class to the gentlemanly values and culture of the aristocracy; W.D. Rubinstein's *Capitalism, Culture and Decline in Britain 1750-1990* (London: Routledge, 1993) is the most spirited refutation of the 'Wiener thesis'. The historians' debate has not yet addressed the question of what needs were met by the idea of the gentleman, and they might benefit by paying more attention to the work of literary scholars such as Gordon N. Ray, *Thackeray: The Uses of Adversity 1811-1846* (New York: McGraw-Hill, 1955); P.N. Furbank, *Unholy Pleasure: The Idea of Social Class* (Oxford: Oxford UP, 1985); and Robin Gilmour, *The Idea of the Gentleman in the Victorian Novel* (London: Allen and Unwin, 1981).

[3] Henry Silver, Diaries, unpublished (*Punch* Office, London), 25 September 1867.

[4] Thomas M. Kemnitz, 'Matt Morgan of *Tomahawk* and English Cartooning 1867-1870', *Victorian Studies*, 19 (Autumn 1975), 5-34.

[5] The chief source on *Tomahawk*'s staff is Arthur W. à Beckett, *Green Room Recollections* (Bristol: Arrowsmith, 1896); *The à Becketts of Punch* (London: Constable, 1903); *Recollections of a Humourist, Grave and Gay* (London: Pitman, 1907). See also T.H.S. Escott, *Politics and Letters* (London: Chapman & Hall, 1886); *Platform, Press, Politics and Play* (Bristol: Arrowsmith, 1895). Additional information on Marshall, Thompson, Clay, Bowles, Escott, Austin and the à Beckett brothers comes from *Dictionary of National Biography* (Oxford: Oxford UP, 1922); Frederic Boase, *Modern English Biography* (London: Cass, 1965); Leonard E. Naylor, *The Irrepressible Victorian: The Story of Thomas*

Gibson Bowles (London: Macdonald, 1965); and Norton B. Crowell, *Alfred Austin: Victorian* (Albuquerque: U of New Mexico P, 1953). The last two authors do not mention their subjects' association with *Tomahawk*.
[6] Ted R. Ellis, 'Victorian Comic Journals', in *British Literary Magazines: The Victorian and Edwardian Age 1837-1913*, edited by Alvin Sullivan (Westport, CT: Greenwood, 1984), pp.501-13.
[7] M.H. Spielmann, *The History of 'Punch'* (London: Cassell, 1895), p.280.
[8] *à Becketts*, p.155. Both Arthur and Gilbert à Beckett (the younger) were invited to join the *Punch* staff a few years after *Tomahawk*'s death. Alfred Thompson also became a *Punch* artist, though not a staffer (Spielmann, pp.375, 383, 500).
[9] The *Owl* ran from 27 April 1864 to 28 July 1869. Starting at four pages, it rose to six, with two pages of advertisements. With so few pages, a high cover price of sixpence (*Punch* and *Tomahawk* were twopence for twelve pages), a circulation rising to six thousand, minimal editorial expenses, and advertising revenue, it must have been very profitable indeed. The fullest account of the *Owl* is in Reginald Lucas, *Lord Glenesk and the 'Morning Post'* (London: Alston, Riviere, 1910), pp.195-218.
[10] J.W. Robertson Scott, *The Story of the 'Pall Mall Gazette'* (Oxford: Oxford UP, 1950), p.24.
[11] T.H.S. Escott, *Masters of English Journalism.* (London: T. Fisher Unwin, 1911), p.262.
[12] Marcello De Cecco, *The International Gold Standard: Money and Empire* (London: Frances Pinter, 1984), pp.80-81.
[13] See also, W.L. Burn, *The Age of Equipoise* (New York: Norton, 1965), pp.212-16.
[14] The best study of the relationship between Brown and Queen Victoria, which concludes that they were intimate in every sense except the sexual, is Tom Cullen's *The Empress Brown: The True Story of a Victorian Scandal* (Boston: Houghton Mifflin, 1969). According to Lord Derby the Queen backed Brown in his insistence that he be treated 'like a gentleman' to the point of expelling the Duke of Edinburgh from Buckingham Palace for refusing to shake hands with him (*A Selection from the Diaries, 1869-1878*, edited by John Vincent, Camden Fifth Series, vol. 4 [London: Royal Historical Society, 1994], pp.200, 416). *Punch* alluded coyly to the ascendancy of Brown as early as July 1866 (Cullen, p.98) and its staff discussed publishing a more explicit cartoon on the subject in June 1867, but backed away (Frankie Morris, 'The Illustrated Press and the Republican Crisis of 1871-72', *Victorian Periodicals Review*, 25 [Spring 1992], p.115).

[15] Mr Bludyer, 'the famous editor of the *Tomahawk* . . . would "back himself for a slashing article against any man in England."' (Thackeray, *Ravenswing, Works,* vol.4 [London: Smith Elder, 1898], p.457).

[16] William M. Thackeray, *The Book of Snobs,* edited by John Sutherland (St Lucia, Qld: U of Queensland P, 1978), p.12. Sutherland's edition has a valuable introduction and etymology. Also of great value are the discussions in Ray, pp.373-83, and Leslie Stephen, 'The Writings of W.M. Thackeray', in William M. Thackeray, *Works,* vol.24 (1878-79), pp.15-78, reprinted in *Thackeray: The Critical Heritage,* edited by Geoffrey Tillotson and Donald Hawes (London: Routledge, 1968), pp.332-36.

[17] See also Cullen, p.121.

[18] Henry Blyth, *The Pocket Venus: A Victorian Scandal* (London: Weidenfeld & Nicolson, 1966), p.209.

[19] Donald J. Gray, 'Early Victorian Scandalous Journalism: Renton Nicholson's *The Town* 1837-42', in *Victorian Periodical Press: Samplings and Soundings,* edited by Joanne Shattock and Michael Wolff (Leicester: U of Leicester P, 1982), pp.317-48.

[20] As it happens, there were limits to the Prince of Wales's egalitarian bonhomie: 'Jolly John' Nash, one of the Prince's favourite *lions comiques,* made the mistake of slapping him on the back during one convivial occasion. He was dropped immediately and irrevocably (W. MacQueen-Pope, *The Melodies Linger On: The Story of Music Hall* [London: Allen, n.d.], p.313).

[21] F.M.L. Thompson, 'Aristocracy, Gentry, and the Middle Classes in Britain, 1750-1850', in Adolf Birke and Lothar Kettenacker, *Middle Classes, Aristocracy and Monarchy: Patterns of Change and Adaptation in the Age of Modern Nationalism* (Munich: Saur, 1989), p.31.

[22] Queen Victoria was encouraged by her advisors to publish as a public relations measure: to the first of many references to Brown in her journal she provided a twenty-two line footnote praising his merits and explaining his position in her household (*Leaves from the Journal of Our Life in the Highlands from 1848 to 1861,* edited by Arthur Helps [London: Smith, Elder, 1868], pp.128-29). The Queen set a fashion of royal literary amateurism that of course persists.

[23] Elizabeth Jenkins, *Six Criminal Women* (London: Pan, 1949), pp.9-33.

7   Margaret Oliphant: Journalist

Joanne Shattock

> [Mrs Lewes] thinks people who write regularly for the Press are almost sure to be spoiled by it. There is so much dishonesty, people's work being praised because they belong to the confederacy.[1]

This comment, recorded by George Eliot's friend Emily Davies in 1869, serves to reinforce one model of the professional woman writer in the nineteenth century, a model best represented by Eliot herself, in which journalism was an apprenticeship, abandoned when financial security was achieved and 'serious' writing could begin. Eliot's was a masculine success story, some would argue, both in the singlemindedness with which the writing was pursued and the critical acclaim and reputation which ensued.

For Margaret Oliphant George Eliot became the writer against whom she measured herself from the early days with Blackwoods, when it soon became clear that Eliot was the firm's most valued asset. Oliphant was touchingly honest about her mixed feelings for her celebrated contemporary. She resumed the writing of her fragmented autobiography in February 1885 after an interval of over twenty years, immediately after reviewing. J.W. Cross's *George Eliot's Life* for the *Edinburgh*. 'I have been tempted to begin writing by George Eliot's Life—with that curious kind of self-compassion which one cannot get clear of. I wonder if I am a little envious of her?', she recorded. Later she continued:

> I don't quite know why I should put all this down. I suppose because George Eliot's Life has . . . stirred me up to an involuntary confession. How I have been handicapped in life! Should I have done better if I had been kept, like her, in a mental greenhouse

and taken care of? . . . I was, after all, only following my instincts, it being in reality easier to me to keep on with a flowing sail, to keep my household and make a number of people comfortable, at the cost of incessant work, and an occasional great crisis of anxiety than to live the self-restrained life which the greater artist imposes on himself. . . . No one even will mention me in the same breath with George Eliot and that is just. . . . I am in very little danger of having my life written, and that is all the better in this point of view—for what could be said of me? George Eliot and George Sand make me half inclined to cry over my poor little unappreciated self. . . . These two bigger women did things which I have never felt the least temptation to do—but how much more enjoyment they seem to have got out of their life, how much more praise and homage and honour! . . . I do feel very small, very obscure, beside them, rather a failure all round.²

Oliphant's biographer, Elisabeth Jay, argues that a more appropriate analogy for Oliphant would be contemporary novelists like Fay Weldon, Anita Brookner, Penelope Fitzgerald, and Martin Amis, writers both male and female who successfully combine reviewing with creative writing, and who do not regard journalism, in Jay's words, as 'the financial penalty for being a minor artist'.³ She notes that Oliphant made her first submission to become a *Blackwood's* reviewer on the strength of her success as a novelist and short story writer—the reverse of the Eliot model. For Oliphant, Jay argues, reviewing fuelled her creativity rather than exhausted it. She was a voracious reader of the work of other writers due to the demands of her reviewing, and her own work was enriched as a result.

It could also be argued that to many nineteenth-century professional women writers Eliot was not necessarily the paradigm to which they subscribed. There were others among

Oliphant's contemporaries whose writing careers paralleled hers, women who worked in a variety of genres in which fiction and poetry were not necessarily privileged, energetic women whose work she knew. Harriet Martineau in many ways was much better placed to become the model for the Victorian woman journalist. Other possibilities include Anna Jameson, Geraldine Jewsbury, Mary Howitt and Eliza Lynn Linton. The list, as we know, could go on and on. In this essay I want to explore the issue of gender in the nineteenth-century periodical press by focusing on Margaret Oliphant as an example of a professional woman journalist.

Oliphant was undoubtedly a writer condemned by her industry. Virginia Woolf in *Three Guineas* invites her readers to 'deplore the fact that Mrs. Oliphant sold her brain, her very admirable brain, prostituted her culture and enslaved her intellectual liberty in order that she might earn her living and educate her children'.[4] The charge is that because she had to support her family, she wrote too much too quickly, that the biographies and literary histories, and, as Woolf describes them, the 'innumerable faded articles, reviews, sketches of one kind and another which she contributed to literary papers' (p.166) exhausted her creativity and prevented the writing of a few good novels. For her contemporaries it was her prolixity which was always commented upon. John Skelton, in an article in *Blackwood's* in January 1883, celebrating Oliphant's *The Literary History of England in the end of the Eighteenth and beginning of the Nineteenth Centuries* (1882) notes her 'unwearied and facile pen [which] has been constantly at work now for more than thirty years'. Skelton was writing primarily of her fiction, and he compares her not unfavourably with Scott, adding: 'I do not suppose that Mrs. Oliphant is one of the writers who consciously entertain or profess, what is called in the jargon of the day, "high views of the literary *calling*" but it may be said of her that she has never written a page which she would wish unwritten'.[5] Faint praise indeed.

Interestingly it was usually her non-fictional writing, in other words her journalism, which drew adverse comments. Edith

Simcox describes a conversation in 1878 with George Eliot, when the talk was 'of translations, ignorance in print, and the unprincipledness of even good people like Mrs. Oliphant who write of that whereof they know nothing' (*Letters* 9, 228). This was not a comment about a novelist who had produced some seventy-odd titles at this time. It was a comment on a too-prolific journalist. Henry James, writing sympathetically of Oliphant in an obituary, reflects that no one had practised criticism:

> ... more in the hit-or-miss fashion and on happy-go-lucky lines than Mrs. Oliphant. She practised it, as she practised everything, on such an inordinate scale that her biographer, if there is to be one, will have no small task in the mere drafting of lists of her contributions to magazines and journals in general and to 'Blackwood' in particular. She wrought in 'Blackwood' for years anonymously, and profusely, no writer of the day found a *porte-voix* [megaphone] nearer to hand, or used it with an easier personal latitude and comfort. I should almost suppose in fact that no woman had ever, for half a century, had her personal 'say' so publicly and irresponsibly.[6]

James's comment is interestingly double-edged. He notes the prolixity of her reviewing, but he also notes her influence. If we wanted further testimony to the latter we could recall Hardy's irritated description of her now infamous review of *Jude* ("The Anti-Marriage League", January 1896) as 'the screaming of a poor woman in *Blackwood's*'.[7] Jay argues that Oliphant's reputation suffered at the end of the century at the hands of a 'male clubland taking its revenge for the long years of George Eliot's supremacy' (p.245). It is too easy, I think, to see Eliot as the dominant force in women's writing from the mid-century onward. It was not necessarily so perceived by her contemporaries.

Oliphant's reviewing was phenomenal in its bulk and not inconsiderable in its impact. In her writing life of over forty years there were few of her contemporaries, male or female, not to mention writers of the past, whose work did not come under her scrutiny. In this she was the precursor not only of contemporary women writer/reviewers, but also of Virginia Woolf and Alice Meynell, two early modern women writers for whom journalism was a persistent strand throughout their writing lives.

Oliphant was in no doubt that she was entering a masculine world. She recognised that to make a living by writing for the periodical press it was the male-dominated press she needed to infiltrate. It was through her mother's intervention that she secured an introduction to George Moir ('Delta') of *Blackwood's*, a distant cousin. It never occurred to her or to her mother (as Jay points out) that she should attempt to get work from any of the women's or children's magazines or the more popular family-oriented periodicals which were coming into existence. Writing to John Blackwood in 1855 at the beginning of their long relationship, she expresses some doubt about her material: 'I am sometimes doubtful whether in your most manly and masculine of magazines a womanish story-teller like myself may not become wearisome' (*Autobiography and Letters*, p.160). In response to her self-doubt she evolved a neutral or ungendered voice for her reviewing which was on the whole more successful than George Eliot's comparable attempts to blend her voice with those of her male colleagues in the *Westminster Review*.

The opening paragraphs of her reviews are frequently self-consciously masculine or tended to expansive pronouncements, as if she were deliberately writing herself into an unfamiliar mode, after which the voice drops into a more relaxed tone:

> It is a dangerous thing to have your life written when you are dead and helpless, and can do nothing to protest against the judgment. . . . But if biography is thus dangerous, there is a still more fatal art, more radical in its operation, and infinitely more

murderous, against which nothing can defend the predestined victim. This terrible instrument of self-murder is called autobiography.[8]

This is the opening of her review of Harriet Martineau's *Autobiography*, uncharacteristically abrasive, and somewhat stilted, after which she assumes her normal tone. Other openings affect the magisterial or the near-platitudinous as in 'Greatness is always comparative: there are few things so hard to adjust as the sliding-scale of fame',[9] or 'Civilization, like every other condition of humanity, has its dark as well as its bright side',[10] the beginning of an article on the 1857 Matrimonial Causes Act. Occasionally she identifies herself as a woman, as in her 1866 article on Mill's proposals for female suffrage which begins: 'The present writer has the disadvantage of being a woman. It is a dreadful confession to put at the beginning of a page; and yet it is not an unmitigated misfortune'.[11] For most of her reviewing, though, Oliphant's voice is ungendered, carefully modulated, confident, not strident.

She began her reviewing career in 1855 when the controversy over anonymity versus signature was about to break. She remained wedded to the old system to the end, arguing in her 1882 *Literary History of England:* 'We believe that criticism is always most free, both for praise or blame, when it is anonymous, and that the verdict of an important publication, whether it be review as in those days, or newspaper as in our own, is more telling, as well as more dignified, than that of an individual, whose opinion, in nine cases out of ten, becomes of inferior importance to us the moment we are acquainted with his name'.[12] 'Anonymity is a great institution—I think I shall go in for that hence forward in everything but novels', she told Blackwood in 1870 (quoted by Jay, p.244), and she stuck to her decision. Her reviews in *Macmillan's* in the 1880s were initialled and the few in the *Contemporary Review* in the same period signed, but otherwise she remained anonymous throughout her forty years of reviewing. It was to prove a valuable key to negotiating the gender barrier in the world of journalism.

Most of her colleagues in the reviewing fraternity were men. A letter to Blackwood in 1873 reveals her sense of the university-dominated scene in which she found herself:

> I can only review books at all on the condition that I express my own feelings in respect to them. It is of course in your power to bid me refrain from reviewing any particular book or any books at all, but I can only say what I think and not what other people think, whatever the universities may say. I read every word of both books mentioned. . . . The tremendous applause which has greeted this performance is a good specimen of the sort of thing which I am anxious to struggle against—the fictitious reputation got up by men who happen to be 'remembered at the Universities,' and who have many connections among literary men. (*Autobiography and Letters,* pp.240-41)

Late in her career, perhaps with tongue in cheek, she wrote a series of articles in *Blackwood's* with the title 'The Old Saloon' (January 1887-December 1892), reminiscent of the 'Noctes Ambrosianae' of 'Maga's' early days and suggestive of a male clubland in which she took no part.

She wrote occasionally for the *Edinburgh* and the *Fortnightly,* and for the *Contemporary Review.* Two of her novels were serialised in *Longman's Magazine,* and others in *Macmillan's* and *Cornhill* to all of which she contributed occasional articles. In addition she wrote for the *Spectator* and for the *St. James's Gazette.* But *Blackwood's* gave her a central platform from which to speak throughout her career. John Blackwood was very much her mentor, performing a function similar to that played by W.J. Fox in Harriet Martineau's early reviewing days with the *Monthly Repository.* Unlike George Eliot, she had no G.H. Lewes to look after her business affairs, and she conducted all her negotiations, sometimes too diffidently, herself. But despite her enterprise and her independence, the ultimate journalistic prize eluded her. Her ambition was to equal her male colleagues, Trollope, Dickens, Thackeray and Leslie Stephen, as the editor of a serious journal, a position which would have brought with it financial security as well as status. Mrs Henry Wood's *Argosy*, Mary Elizabeth Braddon's *Belgravia, Howitt's Journal* or Mrs Gatty's *Aunt Judy's Magazine* would not have sufficed. But it was not to be. She edited a minor book series for Blackwood but the editorship of a periodical equivalent in status to the magazine did not come her way.

The spectrum of subjects she tackled could in no way be regarded as gendered. She wrote on fiction, poetry, religion, art, travel, history and biography. Politics she eschewed, and also science. She did not write much on philosophy, but it occasionally formed part of her articles on religion and other cognate subjects. She was sufficiently fluent in French to translate Montalembert, and she reviewed French literature competently. Not for nothing did she refer to herself as *Blackwood's* 'general utility woman'.

By Elisabeth Jay's reckoning she was even-handed in her reviews of male and female writers. Undoubtedly her reviews of her female contemporaries and predecessors stand out from her journalism in the way in which Virginia Woolf's do. Oliphant was perceptive about personal circumstances and the problems of writing for a living, and she was particularly attuned to the merits as well as the failings of women writers. She was generous and sympathetic to Mary Russell Mitford (*Blackwood's*, June 1854), for example. She showed a shrewd sense of the strengths as well as the conscious limitations of Jane Austen in a review of the Reverend Austen-Leigh's *Memoir* (March 1870), an article whose critical judgments stand up well today. She presented a convincing appreciation of the impact women made on the cultural scene even when they wrote comparatively little, in a review (April 1862) of recent biographies of Hester Piozzi and Mary Delany. She wrote intelligently of three female autobiographers, Alice Thornton, the Duchess of Newcastle and

Madame Roland, in a series of seven articles on autobiographies (January 1881-April 1883).

When it comes to her assessment of her female contemporaries, some of whom were her friends and others her rivals she is shrewd, generous, knowledgeable and devoid of spite. She leaps to the defence of Jane Carlyle (*Contemporary Review*, May 1883) the victim, as she saw it, of Froude's predatory biographical speculations, a subject which became for her almost an obsession. Her review of the *Memoirs* of Anna Jameson and of Fanny Kemble's *Records of a Girlhood* (*Blackwood's*, February 1879) salutes two working women who earned her respect for combining professional careers with the vicissitudes and demands of their domestic circumstances. Her review of Harriet Martineau's *Autobiography* (*Blackwood's*, April 1877) is sympathetic but measured in its praise. She disliked Martineau's air of self importance, the 'self applauses' of the work as she described them, her inflated sense of her influence on her times, her ill-tempered comments on her contemporaries, and her ungenerous treatment of her mother. Martineau's autobiography constructed a masculine success story, in Oliphant's view, the kind of autobiography she could never have contemplated.

Her review of J.W. Cross's *George Eliot's Life* in the *Edinburgh* is an intelligent assessment of Eliot as Cross presented her as well as an enthusiastic response to her early novels, the latter a position typical of most posthumous assessments of Eliot. She takes issue with Cross's chosen mode of presenting his material, that of letting Eliot tell her own story through her letters, comparing it with Froude's biography of Carlyle, and adding, 'Carlyle has been made out of his own mouth to prove himself a snarling Diogenes . . . and George Eliot by the same fine process has been made to prove herself a dull woman'. 'Is this the woman who wrote Adam Bede?' she asks disbelievingly after failing to find letters which demonstrated Eliot's humour.[13] Contemporary and posthumous assessments of the *Life* are in agreement with her.

She quotes at length the well-known passage from Eliot's Journal which Cross included, 'How I came to write Fiction' and comments, 'The reader will make the acquaintance of a remarkable character . . . the strongest of all female writers, he will find in her what is almost the conventional type of a woman—a creature all conjugal love and dependence, who is sure of nothing until her god has vouched for it, not even her own powers'.[14]

Two themes connect these reviews of works by women writers, their emphasis on women's work and on women's education. Both ideas were very much in vogue, and both, she contended, had existed long before the present movements for their improvement. Mary Russell Mitford and Jane Austen were excellent examples of how women had managed to become well educated long before ladies' colleges had ever been thought of, very much, she might have added, like herself:

> They were both well educated, according to the requirements of their day, though the chances are that neither could have passed her examination for entrance into any lady's college, or had the remotest chance with the University Inspectors; and it is not unconsolatory to find, by the illumination which a little lamp of genius here and there thus throws upon the face of the country, that women full of cultivation and refinement have existed for generations before ladies' colleges were thought of, notwithstanding the universal condemnation bestowed upon our old-fashioned canons of feminine instruction.[15]

Only occasionally in the Austen/Mitford article is there the slightest hint of envy that the section of society into which those women had been born was inestimably advantaged:

> They were well born and well connected, with a modest position which not even poverty could seriously affect, and the habit from their childhood of meeting people of some distinction and eminence, and of feeling themselves possessed of so much share in the bigger business of the world as is given by the fact of having friends and relations playing a real part in it. No educational process is more effectual than this simple fact, and Jane Austen and Mary Mitford were both within its influence. (p.290)

Jay argues that Oliphant had no chips on her shoulder as regards her own social background, and that she used her own career to celebrate the social mobility which the world of letters afforded. Occasionally in her reviewing there are hints to the contrary. On the question of work for women she sees significance in the current agitation for more opportunities:

> The present generation considers itself to have invented the idea that women have a right to the toils and rewards of labour, not withstanding the long array of facts . . . by which it is apparent that whenever it has been necessary, women *have* toiled, have earned money, have got their living and the living of those dependent upon them in total indifference to all theory.[16]

And she might have added, 'Like me'.

The writers she admired, writers of either sex, were those who worked for their living, who did not allow themselves the luxury of theorising about 'art' and its demands but for whom art and life and work were interwoven. In the introduction to her edition of the *Autobiography*, Elizabeth Jay writes of the 'intimate and complex relationship between the writing and the need that generated' which ran throughout Oliphant's writing life.[17] In the *Autobiography* Oliphant bristles with resentment against the images of a life dedicated to 'art', the literary 'success story' as projected by both Eliot's biography and Trollope's autobiography:

> I have never had any theory on the subject. I have written because it gave me pleasure, because it came natural to me, because it was talking or breathing, besides the big fact that it was necessary for me to work for my children. . . .They are my work, which I like in the doing, which is my natural way of occupying myself, though they are never so good as I meant them to be. And when I have said that, I have said all that is in me to say'. (*Autobiography and Letters*, pp. 4-5)

Oliphant's conservative views on the woman question are well known, her attacks on Mill's *The Subjection of Women*, her opposition to the vote, to divorce, views all the more disappointing to contemporary readers who regard her as a truly professional woman.

For her, journalism, work which could be undertaken in the home in a way that plain sewing could also be undertaken by women with talents in that direction, provided the ultimate solution for women who needed or sought financial independence but who at the same time refused to compromise their domestic responsibilities and roles. Nor did she regard journalism as an inferior form of work. Jay is right I think in arguing that for Oliphant journalism was not an apprenticeship which was to be shed as soon as success in a higher sphere looked distinctly possible. Neither was it the routine but not unpleasurable chore which paid for the bills, as it was, one suspects, for Woolf. For Oliphant writing biographies, literary histories, and 'the innumerable . . . articles, reviews, sketches of one kind and another' was inseparable from her total writing life, a life which itself was inseparable from the domestic circumstances which demanded it. She did not place her various kinds of writing in a hierarchy. 'Margaret Oliphant: Journalist' was a title of which she would have been proud.

Notes

[1] *The George Eliot Letters*, edited by Gordon S. Haight, 9 vols (New Haven and London: Yale UP, 1954-78), 8, 466. Further references to this work are given after quotations in the text.
[2] *Autobiography and Letters of Mrs Oliphant*, edited by Mrs Harry Coghill, introd. by Q.D. Leavis (Leicester: Leicester UP, 1974), pp.5-8. Further references to this work are given after quotations in the text.
[3] *Mrs Oliphant: 'A Fiction to Herself': A Literary Life* (Oxford: Clarendon, 1995), p.4.
[4] *Three Guineas* (London: Hogarth, 1938), p.166.
[5] *Blackwood's*, 133 (January 1883), 73.
[6] 'London Notes, August 1897', in *Notes on Novelists* (London: Dent, 1914), p.358.
[7] Thomas Hardy, April 1912 Postscript to the Preface to *Jude the Obscure* (Harmondsworth: Penguin, 1978), p.42.
[8] *Blackwood's*, 121 (April 1877), 472.
[9] 'Modern Novelists', *Blackwood's*, 77 (May 1855), 554.
[10] *Blackwood's*, 83 (February 1858), 139.
[11] 'The Great Unrepresented', *Blackwood's,* 100 (September 1866), 367.
[12] Quoted by John Skelton, 'A Little Chat about Mrs Oliphant', *Blackwood's,* 133 (January 1883), 90.
[13] *Edinburgh Review*, 161 (April 1885), 517-19.
[14] *Edinburgh Review*, 161 (April 1885), 515.
[15] 'Miss Austen and Miss Mitford', *Blackwood's* (March 1870), 290.
[16] 'Two Ladies', *Blackwood's*, 125 (February 1879), 206.
[17] *The Autobiography of Margaret Oliphant: The Complete Text* (Oxford: Oxford UP, 1990), p.vii.

8   Benjamin Kidd:
     Social Prophet as Journalist

Paul Crook

Benjamin Kidd was a social prophet. True to that tradition, he burned like a Roman candle, then fell to earth, and is now largely forgotten. He was, if you like, the Alvin Toffler of the 1890s, extrapolating to the future, celebrating human potential, but dramatically warning also of the perils of mammon, egoistic individualism, the misuse of science, failure of nerve and values, prophesying a militaristic and totalitarian future—a dark eugenic world—if humans could not discover for themselves a new consciousness, an alternative mode of life to that of secular materialism. He would have liked the title of Theodore Roszak's counter-culturist book *Unfinished Animal* (1976). Feeding off Darwinism and the new genetic ideas of the 1890s and 1900s, Kidd detected a fatal bi-polarity within the process of social evolution, a dialectic clash between the titanic forces of primal recidivism and civilised morality. The human animal was indeed unfinished. This metaphor was to be taken up with a vengeance during the Great War of 1914-18, when commentators spoke freely of 'man the fighting animal', and of the frailty of culture, when instinctivist theories promoted a reductionist image of a belligerent and territorial humankind reminiscent of present day sociobiology. Later, in *The Ghost in the Machine* (1967), Arthur Koestler would famously attribute human 'schizophysiology' to our ancient 'animalistic' brain. Kidd, in his more hopeful moments, trusted in the evolutionary payoff of human social sympathy and mutualist endeavour. He anticipated Teilhard de Chardin's concept of the 'noosphere' of the future, by which human self-consciousness, powers of communication, cooperation, cognition and higher ethics would enable the species to transcend the limits of physical evolution, opening up vistas of a cosmic movement towards wider community and, ultimately, oneness with the divine.

The book in which Kidd most imaginatively projected his ideas was his *Social Evolution* (1894), which became an amazing bestseller. It went through numerous printings in Britain and America (including, to his chagrin, many pirated editions in the United States). It was translated into at least ten languages, Arabic and Chinese among them. Who would have expected such a success from an obscure civil servant of impecunious Irish Protestant origins?

Benjamin Kidd (1858-1916) was born in Bandon, son of a policeman in the Royal Irish Constabulary, and of the daughter of a Farranhavane landowner. The young Kidd was educated at a small country school in Ennis, County Clare, where he quickly evidenced a passion for knowledge, and a classic Victorian determination to succeed through industry and abstinence. Psychologically Kidd came to combine shyness and anal-retentive parsimony with an at-times almost occult self-belief, spikiness and semi-mystical idealism. He read voraciously, acquiring an idiosyncratic mix of *fin-de-siècle* ideas, part traditional, part new, which he expressed in a dramatic, often overblown, style. Not surprisingly he gravitated to occasional journalism, serving a useful apprenticeship in that trade well before the appearance of his 'big book'.

His first journalistic writings were naturalist essays, a popular genre with the Victorians, who relished the essayists' descriptive power and joy in nature—too luxuriant and anthropomorphic for today's tastes. As a child and youth Kidd roved the River Fergus estuary and acquired an enduring love of wild-life and field studies. This was sharpened by an almost obsessional interest in Darwinian biology. *The Origin of Species*, he later wrote, caused an 'intellectual Saturnalia' in almost every department of thought.[1] Kidd—despite his pan-religious tendencies—was vastly influenced by the giant figures of Charles Darwin, Herbert Spencer and T.H. Huxley. He closely followed the scientific debates that arose during the revolutionary advances that took place in genetics in the last decades of the nineteenth century. Kidd undertook experiments on animal behaviour: his son later insisted that 'he seemed to understand by some instinct the inflexions of the unspoken language of beasts'.² He kept in his menagerie at various times cats, toads, frogs, wild rabbits, blackbirds, jays and cuckoos. During his early London days he kept colonies of ants, bees and wasps in his study. His first publication was an article on the weather for *Chambers's Journal* in November 1884. During the 1880s and 1890s Kidd wrote a spate of papers on natural history for journals such as *Chambers's*, *Longman's Magazine*, the *English Illustrated Magazine*, *Cornhill Magazine*, and *Littell's Living Age*. He continued sporadically to write on the subject to the end of his life.³

Kidd wanted to popularise biology, but he also had a serious scientific purpose in testing hypotheses. For instance, his 'Habits and Intelligence of Bees', published in *Longman's* in June 1885, debunked exaggerated claims for bee intelligence. Kidd explained apparently complex and purposive behaviour, such as construction of hexagonal-celled hives, by reference to natural selection and a few simple instincts. This was a very topical discourse, and Kidd took care to obtain advice from Sir John Lubbock, whose classic study *Ants, Bees and Wasps* (1872) had conditioned the rise of fashionable instinct theory (widely applied to humankind at the end of the century)—and was also to exert influence upon Peter Kropotkin's anarchist mutual aid theory (there were to be fascinating parallels between Kidd's and Kropotkin's ideas). Kidd's nature essays brought him attention and also welcome extra earnings. *Longman's* paid around £1 per page, excellent money.

In 1877, at the age of eighteen, Kidd passed the lower-division civil service examination and moved to London as clerk to the Board of Inland Revenue. There he began a spartan regimen of study, self-improvement, and involvement in civil service reform. He gained publishing and editorial experience by preparing civil service examination textbooks, guides and journals. He collaborated with H.J. Maywood to produce a 128-page shilling booklet, *Guide to Female Employment in Government Offices* (published by Cassell in 1884). Cassell drove a hard bargain. The authors were to share a royalty of 10 per cent on sales over and above 3000 copies. Unfortunately it sold only 2628 copies by 1891. Cassell refused to re-issue it and, after an irritable correspondence, sold the plates to the authors for three guineas and released them from copyright. From such events Kidd learnt caution about publishers and about subjects like copyright, royalty agreements and protection of author's rights. He even acquired editorial experience. Somehow or other, despite being a Liberal sympathiser, he was given a role in editing and distributing the first volume of the Conservative party handbook, *The Constitutional Yearbook* (1885), the brainchild of Richard Middleton, the chief party agent. By 1890 Kidd was earning £4 per month in preparing for press the weekly *Civil Service Competitor*. He also assisted with the *Civil Service Review* and the *Civil Service Manual*.

The administrative reorganisation of the civil service in the 1870s had broken down both patronage system and rigid departmentalism and resulted in the unionisation of lower-division clerks. In 1883 Kidd became secretary of the lower clerks association, which by 1888 had welded together 3000 members. Its impact was so marked as to merit attention, even censure, during the hearings of the Ridley Commission on Civil Establishments.[4] Kidd lobbied the leading Tory politician Randolph Churchill, later Lord Salisbury's Chancellor of the Exchequer after the fall of Gladstone in 1886.[5] Then, in October 1886, an article of Kidd's on civil service reform appeared in James Knowles's leading journal, the *Nineteenth Century*. This represented something of a coup for an unknown writer. Some of his criticisms of the open competitive system were vindicated following the Ridley Report. Uniform hours, comparable pay for comparable work, promotion by merit within top grades of the division, and greater mobility between lower and higher divisions were instituted. Kidd continued to write on the subject for the *Pall Mall Gazette*.

In the 1880s and 1890s Kidd was to be profoundly influenced by August Weismann's germ plasm theory, which raised key biological issues of heredity, cell structure and sexual reproduction. Kidd wrote on cell fusion and the advantages of sexual over asexual reproduction in a paper for *Longman's* in September 1890 entitled 'The Battle of the Eggs'.[6] Kidd tried to expound Weismann's view that sex was indispensable for biological progress and wrote an article on 'The Evolution of Sex', but editors of family journals were frightened off by the title.

In June 1890 Grant Allen, the Canadian-born science journalist (also novelist and feminist), stirred much interest with a review of hereditarian theory for W.T. Stead's new *Review of Reviews*, which featured a monthly science summary.[7] Allen—although himself a Lamarckian—showcased Weismannism as the latest fashion: 'it has become almost a test of orthodoxy with the Oxford and London biologists'. Kidd, who became a close friend of Allen, made a pilgrimage to see Weismann at Freiburg University in the summer of 1890, and the interview was to be a major stimulus to the writing of *Social Evolution*. Kidd's account of the visit for *Review of Reviews* depicted Weismann as Darwin's heir apparent,[8] and Kidd was to absorb from Weismann some of the traditions of German Idealism and Transcendentalism. Science was seen at the highest level as a revelation of the absolute. Reason alone could never make knowable the ultimate reality that embodied the world as spirit. Kidd was to use this vision in the fight against purely materialist and positivist philosophies.

Now married with a young family, Kidd hawked his writings to the periodicals, and angled for a journalistic job, with disappointing results. He wrote to the editor of the *English Illustrated Magazine*: 'Thy servant knoweth that authors are an irritable race who never cease from troubling'.[9] Kidd boldly offered himself to C.F. Moberly Bell, the business editor of the *Times*, as a weekly column writer on parliamentary affairs, but

Bell fended him off. The two men became acquainted and Kidd even became a house guest of the editor during the 1900s, but he was never able to talk his way on to the staff of the *Times*.

Kidd became an overnight celebrity when his *Social Evolution* was published by Macmillan in 1894. The publication owed not a little to journalistic contacts, Kidd winning backing from his chief at Inland Revenue, Alfred (later Lord) Milner, who commended the manuscript to publishers. Milner was one of Benjamin Jowett's brilliant young Oxford imperialists and 'race patriots', later High Commissioner to South Africa (1897) and a prime mover in triggering the Boer War. Also influenced at Oxford by Arnold Toynbee, Milner developed a consuming passion for empire and social reform, a type of social imperialism that Kidd was to champion. Milner was politically close to Joseph Chamberlain's Liberal Unionists, and Kidd was to gravitate to that circle. Milner had tried journalism—he was assistant editor of W.T. Stead's *Pall Mall Gazette* in 1883—before he became private secretary to the Whig nabob Lord Goschen, and subsequently under-secretary for finance under the famous pro-consul Lord Cromer in Egypt. Kidd's book would probably not have seen the light of day without the support of such a Whitehall mandarin. C.J. Longman, in fact, rejected it, the reader reporting 'there is nothing very new or startling in it'.[10] But Macmillan's reader John Stuart MacKenzie, Scots philosopher and fellow of Trinity College Cambridge, favoured publication. MacKenzie and Kidd became friends, and it was MacKenzie who initiated Kidd's life-long association with Trinity College. At a Trinity Feast Commemoration in December 1894 Kidd met such illustrious men as Henry Sidgwick, Leonard and Francis Darwin (Charles's sons), Alfred North Whitehead, and Frederick Maitland. This was only the beginning of a spectacular widening of horizons.

Macmillan contracted for one printing of 1500 copies of *Social Evolution* on a half-profit basis, but refused to arrange a separate American edition or secure American copyright. Extensive pirating cost Kidd heavily in lost royalties. He proved a difficult customer for Macmillan (and his other publishers): he made heavy corrections to proofs, sent detailed advice to editors on production and publicity, pestered the office for data on sales, tracked down reviews, sponsored translations, insisted on star billing in lists, and negotiated more money for future printings (two-thirds profit for second and following printings, 15 per cent royalty for the second and later American printings, half-profit for Gustave Fischer's German edition). The earnings from *Social Evolution* made Kidd financially independent and he eventually retired from the civil service (1897) to become a full-time writer, with entry into English intellectual and club life.

He was to find life on the fame machine both fascinating and alarming. He was sustained by friendships, most notably from within the world of journalism, particularly with John Saxon Mills, Grant Allen, W.T. Stead and William Clarke. And from the young Saxon Mills, a Liberal-Imperialist, came almost discipleship. The two worked together in the cause of tariff reform in the 1900s. Kidd helped Allen to get published his controversial treatise on *The Evolution of the Idea of God* (1897), although disagreeing '*toto coelo*' with its thesis that ancestor-worship was the basis of religion.[11] Kidd and Allen shared a fatal attraction to synthetic philosophies propounding universal laws. The influence of Allen's feminism was to bear fruit in Kidd's last work, *The Science of Power*.

Kidd was drawn into Liberal political circles by William Clarke, radical journalist and acrid anti-imperialist. Clarke had broad interests and learning, was on the staff of the *Spectator* and the *Daily Chronicle*, and wrote for a number of political and literary reviews in Britain and America. For a time he dabbled in socialism. His Fabian essay 'The Industrial Basis of Socialism' (1888) attacked American trusts, and may have influenced Kidd in his perpetual suspicion of monopoly capitalism. Clarke loved America, despite feeling that it was diseased by the malevolent spirit of jingoism and 'manifest destiny'. Clarke sided with the Americans, Kidd with the British, during the war panic of 1895 over Venezuela. Clarke thought that Kidd was too much under the influence of the expansionist Stead: 'Do not use the cant phrases of that charlatan W.T. Stead: you are too much of a thinker to wear his cast-off rags. . . . Unlike you I do not desire to see the English race everywhere. I do not like the creature well enough'.[12]

Kidd harboured hopes of obtaining a journalistic job through his American connections. In September 1894 he met William Price Collier, the visiting and energetic representative of the New York *Forum*, controlled and edited by the southerner and reformer Walter H. Page. Kidd and Collier dined and clubbed together and came up with the idea of launching a European *Forum*, an international review with Kidd as editor. When Page vetoed the project, as competition was already too stiff in this field, Kidd was deeply disappointed. In something of a huff, but also to escape the limelight, he withdrew from his clubs and public life until 1902 and began to write another big book on evolution and civilisation. However, the outbreak of war between Spain and the United States in 1898 caused him to publish a short book *Control of the Tropics* (1898), comprised of articles originally written for the *Times*. The ideas expressed were to influence a generation of administrators and politicians, including Milner, Lord Lugard, Joseph Chamberlain and President McKinley. Kidd emphasised the critical importance of tropical resources for the world's industrial nations. He linked a bio-political defence of empire with a social reform programme at home, together with a colonial policy of trusteeship abroad. This would deliver 'a higher type of social order', and eventually independence, to indigenous peoples. Kidd traced racial differences to cultural rather than genetic factors. He attributed the hegemony of the white races to a superior, but perhaps only temporary, 'social efficiency'.

The book seemed supremely opportune to expansionists in the United States, and Kidd was lionised when in 1898, shortly after the end of the war, he made a two-month trip to North America. He was taken in hand, with splendid American hospitality, by Walter H. Page, now editing the *Atlantic Monthly* in Boston, and by William B. Howland, treasurer of the New York *Outlook* which apparently paid his expenses. They took him into East Coast society and intellectual circles. The press pestered him for interviews (he gave a 'scoop' to the *Outlook* on 10 September, and was interviewed by the *Times-Herald* and *Chicago Chronicle*). He received a stream of visitors at his New York hotel: readers, businessmen, doctors, attorneys, clergy, teachers, secretaries of debating clubs and women's groups wanting him as a speaker. He evaded most of these, but was obliged to give a keynote address on the Philippines problem to the Twentieth Century Club, arranged by Edwin D. Mead, editor of the *New England Magazine*. For this he received a fee of one hundred dollars. The lecture appeared in the *Atlantic Monthly* in December, and was much quoted. He met William H. Rideing, editor of the *North American Review* and E.W. Burlingame, editor of *Scribner's Magazine*, while within a week of his arrival George P. Brett, president of New York Macmillan (since 1896 a separate American corporation), had secured Kidd's signature to a contract for publication of his next *magnum opus*. Clearly American publishers were much more proactive than their British counterparts.

Kidd travelled to California, Canada briefly, then to 'futurist' Chicago, where he saw at first hand a clutch of flourishing universities and colleges willing to offer adventurous courses. He toured Chicago University's celebrated school of sociology, organised by Albion W. Small and George E. Vincent, an experience that led him to campaign vigorously for the introduction of sociology into British universities. Kidd met, and strongly influenced, 'Social Gospel' circles, Protestant reformers who wanted to apply the 'social law of service' to empire and world politics—most notably Richard T. Ely of Madison State University; Lyman Abbott, editor of the *Outlook*; Washington Gladden, Josiah Strong and W.D.P. Bliss (who had already recruited Kidd to write for his *Encyclopedia of Social Reform*). On his return to England Kidd granted an interview to the *Echo* (9 November 1898). He suggested 'the transportation of our theorists to America for a term of study, and the subsequent locking up of them for a six months' period of silent reflection'.

Kidd's *Principles of Western Civilisation* appeared in 1902. However, he was to suffer the classic fate of first-book successes. Kidd's later works were not without influence, but none achieved the extraordinary impact of *Social Evolution*. People found *Western Civilisation* overblown and obscure. In it Kidd put forward an unDarwinian type of evolutionary teleology, suggesting that 'projected efficiency'—stressing the collective future needs of the human species—was more important than present efficiency or short-term individual interest in human evolution. It would be the basis of a futurist world order. Oddly enough the book's most significant impact was probably in China. It inspired Mao's early mentor Liang Ch'i-ch'ao and was to have a considerable influence on Chinese Marxism.

Kidd kept up his journalism, now less for money than to propagate his reformist ideas for a world susceptible to degeneration. Page, having founded the new publishing house of Doubleday, Page and Company (1899), established the landmark *World's Work*, an American magazine devoted to politics and practical affairs. Kidd found himself pressed into service for the persuasive Page. He also did occasional pieces for the *Daily News*, a morning Liberal paper edited by E.T. Cook, a supporter of Lord Rosebery, the leading Liberal Imperialist. Cook and Kidd shared a desire to emancipate Liberalism from antiquated notions of laissez faire and 'Little Englandism'. In 1900 Cook asked: 'Could you not from time to time write a leader suggested by crucial events?'[13] Kidd duly produced appropriate pieces, getting the 'best rate' of three guineas per column—not up to the £6 per column paid him by the *Spectator* for 'specials'. He wrote for the *Daily News* until it was bought out in 1901 by a rival anti-empire group associated with Lloyd George. The death that same year of his valued friend William Clarke left a vacancy on the *Spectator*'s staff that Kidd offered to fill. The editor St Loe Strachey countered: 'I am afraid we could not run in double harness'.[14] Such rebuffs, together with the poor reception given to *Western Civilisation*, reminded Kidd that he was still an 'outsider' in the English intellectual and political establishment. His writings recurrently exhibited elements of alienation, which may also explain his periodic flights into a protective private world.

After a trip to South Africa in 1902, Kidd immersed himself in a political and journalistic campaign for tariff reform. He joined a group of 'Milnerites' and Liberal Imperialists, adopting (or having thrust upon him) the role of theorist for the 'Limp' minority within the Liberal party, while enthusiastically supporting Joseph Chamberlain on the Unionist side of the political fence. Kidd joined the Liberal League when it was founded in February 1902 by Lord Rosebery, Edward Grey, R.D. Haldane and their circle, which soon included the firebrand Saxon Mills (editor of the *Cape Times* during the Boer War). Press backing came from the Harmsworths' *Daily Mail* (and their journal the *New Liberal Review*), Harold Harmsworth's *Leeds Mercury* and *Glasgow Herald*, and Robertson Nicholl's nonconformist *British Weekly*. Chamberlain's charisma won Kidd over at about this time. Perhaps he was flattered that Chamberlain had openly praised *Control of the Tropics* in 1898 for the American *Scribner's Magazine*. Chamberlain, once the epitome of middle-class radicalism, had defected to the Conservative camp over Home Rule, becoming an apostle for big nations, big empires, big corporations. His plan for a massive British trading empire based upon an imperial *Zollverein* impressed Kidd.

During the tariff reform years of 1902-06, Kidd was closely involved with press circles sympathetic to the Chamberlain-Milner school of empire. When the *Daily News* began refusing to print his 'heresies', Kidd turned to the *Daily Mail* and the *Manchester Daily Despatch*, as well as writing for friendly journals such as the liberal *Westminster Gazette* and the conservative *Spectator*. He became a close associate of leading press Milnerites, such as G.E. Buckle, editor of the *Times*, Leo Amery, a talented *Times* leader-writer, J.L. Garvin, leader-writer for the *Daily Telegraph*, and Leo Maxse of the *National Review*. Kidd fulfilled a promise he had made to Milner that he would proselytise for him in the quality press. Kidd helped Milner build up a powerful press following, a political factor of considerable importance at the time.

Kidd and Saxon Mills pursued a dream of starting their own newspaper or periodical, all to no avail. 'I have pondered your schemes of journalistic venture' Mills wrote to Kidd in December 1902. 'I am inclined to think that we should see E.T. Cook to stand in with us in a Liberal Weekly . . . I could get the money I think. I fear there is little opening for a monthly whereas there is an 'aching void' for a weekly.' A fortnight later he wrote: 'I hope you are thinking of a third person for our journalistic trinity. [H.G.] Wells would suit excellently.' In February he summoned Kidd urgently to a four-pm meeting at the National Liberal Club: 'I have another idea about another paper which I think I can get very reasonably'.[15] Kidd pestered Moberly Bell to launch a new journal, but Bell curtly dismissed the idea as economically risky.

In May 1903 Chamberlain launched a personal crusade for selective customs controls and imperial preference, a move that Campbell-Bannerman described as 'playing Old Harry with all party relations'.[16] Chamberlain gathered around himself a 'brains trust' that included Amery, Maxse, Halford Mackinder, Saxon Mills, and, of course, Kidd. Chamberlain's keynote Birmingham speech of 15 May owed not a little to Kidd's Colonial Institute lecture of 7 April on 'The State in relation to Trade'. Kidd became the school master of tariff reform, dashing off newspaper comments galore,[17] reworking his ideas for a range of journals, labouring long over major new articles such as one on tariffs for Knowles's *Nineteenth Century* (July 1903). This was to be the political phase of Kidd's life. He disseminated his ideas throughout a number of intellectual clubs, including the Co-efficients, the Compatriots, the Round Table and the X Club. He joined the Tariff Reform League, and even harboured parliamentary ambitions. All this was ended by Campbell-Bannerman's Liberal electoral victory of 1906.

Kidd buried himself in work at his rural retreat in Tonbridge (where he had moved in 1904). He agitated in the cause of British sociology, something for which he has never been given much credit. He infiltrated his ideas into the 1902 edition of the *Encyclopaedia Britannica*, writing the first separate article on sociology. In 1903 he was a founding father of the British Sociological Society; in 1906 he addressed the Royal Institution on the subject (focusing on group selection); then wrote a long pamphlet *Two Principal Laws of Sociology* (1907-08). Soon after came his *Individualism and After*, the Herbert Spencer lecture for 1908, which (a trifle ungraciously) attacked Spencerian Social Darwinism for being too closely linked with 'red-toothed' laws of conflict.

During this time, Kidd kept in touch with affairs through his journalist friend J.L. Garvin, associate of the press baron Lord Northcliffe. Between 1905 and 1908, Kidd wrote over ninety pieces for Garvin's Chamberlainite review, the London *Outlook*. Garvin had clawed his way up from Irish immigrant stock in Birkenhead to become what Alfred Harmsworth regarded as the greatest journalist in England. As leader-writer for the *Daily Telegraph* from 1899, Garvin acted as Chamberlain's first lieutenant, in the thick of the fiscal reform fray. He was offered the editorship of the *Outlook* in January 1905 by its owner C. Sydney Goldman, and made it into a sixpenny review without peer in London. During his stormy two-year editorship, Garvin attracted a corps of talented writers, Kidd amongst them. The two men became close friends. Many of Kidd's pieces were political, but he wrote prolifically on the natural and social sciences. At last, in a modest way, Kidd found his niche, his platform, in journalism, using to the full his broad reading and interests. As Garvin once flattered him: 'You give us "atmosphere"'.[18] The *Outlook* paid him £2 or £3 for reviews and 'middle' articles, and in good weeks he would make £5 or £6. He wrote some of his best work here, being a writer who benefited from deadlines and editors who curbed his verbosity. It was when he tried to be more ambitious, in his books, that he elevated himself onto a more rarefied and abstract plane. Promising world-shattering new syntheses, he often disappointed readers with general and imprecise formulations.

Kidd's new career nosedived after Garvin's departure to edit the *Observer*, although he continued to write occasionally for the *Fortnightly* and Percy L. Parker's *Public Opinion*, to give oracular comments to the press, and to write for encyclopaedias (for instance, he furnished the entries on 'Civilisation' and 'Darwinism' for *Hastings's Encyclopaedia of Religion and Ethics*). Apart from an involvement in the suffragette movement in 1912, Kidd spent his last six years in cloistered study at Ditchling, Sussex, working on his last book *The Science of Power* (1916). It was an apocalyptic tome. Well before 1914, Kidd was gloomily prophesying a global conflict for resources and renouncing both Darwinism and imperialism as doctrines of pagan force. He finished his first draft only days before the outbreak of war which forced him into renewed study of Prussian militarism and prolonged re-writing, even though he was grievously ill. He died from a heart attack on 2 October 1916, a month after finishing his book. Kidd had started his literary career by celebrating biological progress and western superiority. He ended it with a searing indictment of western civilisation. But, rather like H.G. Wells at the end of his life, he managed to dredge up some hope for the future. Perhaps peace and altruism were attainable in a collectivist society, with women playing a key role. Violet Tweedale fictionalised the themes of *Science of Power* in her novel *The Veiled Woman* (1918).

The press, for which Kidd had laboured long—labours almost completely unremarked by historians—gave him a respectful farewell. But even here there were signs that the times had passed him by. The left was decidedly unkind, forgetting his social reformism and anti-capitalism, portraying him as a rugged Social Darwinist. Harold Laski's debunking of him in the *New Republic*[19] epitomised the type of misinterpretation and neglect of his ideas which helped to eclipse Kidd's reputation for many years to come.

Notes

[1] B. Kidd, 'Darwinism', in *Encyclopaedia of Religion and Ethics*, edited by James Hastings, (Edinburgh, New York: Clark, 1911), 4, pp.402-05.
[2] Franklin Kidd, 'Benjamin Kidd: Author of Social Evolution, Principles of Western Civilisation and The Science of Power (Biographical)', typescript (10 fos), 1918, in Benjamin Kidd Papers (hereafter BK), Cambridge University Library, UK, Add.MS.8069 (BK32, p.3).
[3] For a checklist of Kidd's writings see D.P. Crook, *Benjamin Kidd: Portrait of a Social Darwinist* (Cambridge: Cambridge UP, 1984), pp.439-49. Franklin Kidd later assembled a collection of his father's naturalist pieces, entitled *A Philosopher with Nature* (London: Methuen, 1921).
[4] *2nd Report of Royal Commission on Civil Establishments, Minutes of Evidence, Parliamentary Papers* (1884), 47, 435ff.
[5] Randolph Churchill to Kidd, 6 April 1883, 1 May 1883 (BK, SB1).
[6] Kidd was paid £15 for the article. C.J. Longman rejected the first draft, but Kidd replied: 'you nasty crumpy old editor, your fruitful contributor . . . has, just this once, an opinion that there is something in the paper' (Kidd to C.J. Longman, 24 September 1889 [BK10]).
[7] Grant Allen, 'The New Theory of Heredity: Our Scientific Causerie', *Review of Reviews*, 1 (June 1890), 537-38.
[8] Benjamin Kidd, 'Darwin's Successor at Home: Our Scientific Causerie', *Review of Reviews*, 2 (December 1890), 647-50.
[9] Kidd to editor *English Illustrated Magazine*, 24 February 1891 (BK). He added that 'having fortunately provided himself with another occupation in addition to that of writer he hath, so far, managed not to die fasting'.
[10] C.J. Longman to Kidd, 15 November 1893 (BK).
[11] Kidd to Grant Allen, 31 March 1896 (BK): Kidd disagreed with the book '*toto coelo*, its conception, argument, conclusion—all. I am utterly amazed that a Darwinian could have written it'. Allen died in 1899.
[12] William Clarke to Kidd, 10 December 1895 (BK, C112).
[13] E.T. Cook to Kidd, 5 February 1900 (BK).
[14] J. St Loe Strachey to Kidd, 15 May 1901 (BK, S238).
[15] J. Saxon Mills to Kidd, 27 December 1902 (BK, M316); 14 January 1903, 22 February 1903 (BK, M320).
[16] Quoted by Julian Amery, *Life of Joseph Chamberlain* (London: Macmillan,1969), 5, 193-94.
[17] For example, Hammond Hall, the editor of the *Daily Graphic*, commissioned him to do a series of articles and graphs showing the merits

of tariff reform. Kidd held out for £10 per thousand words, with a maximum of £200 for the series, an impressive sum.

[18] J.L. Garvin to Kidd, 28 April 1906 (BK, O18).
[19] H.J. Laski, 'A Sociological Romance', *New Republic*, 9 (30 December 1916), 235-37.

9 Paper Heroes: Special Correspondents and their Narratives of Empire

Judy McKenzie

Early in 1875 George Augustus Sala wrote a gossipy letter to his friend Edmund Yates. Sala, acting in his capacity as a special correspondent for the London *Daily Telegraph*, was in Spain to cover the royal progress of the newly crowned Alphonso XII from Madrid to Murriedro. After mentioning a number of his travelling companions, mutual acquaintances from diplomatic and press ranks, he exclaimed: 'Forbes was here, bragging his head off. Clever men are, I take it, mainly unbearable; but he is the most intolerable celebrity (except Stanley) I ever met'.[1]

Yates often found in Sala's letters appropriately pithy observations to publish verbatim in 'What the World Says', a weekly gossip column in his journal the *World*, but he resisted the temptation this time. No doubt he recognised the irony in Sala's comments since Sala, of course, could be classed as an 'intolerable celebrity' himself. Just like Archibald Forbes and Henry Morton Stanley, Sala had risen from obscurity to fame by publicly 'bragging his head off'. All three were celebrated journalists who had made their names as special correspondents for popular daily newspapers; all three were experts in sounding their own trumpets in print, on the lecture circuit, and in that Victorian institution, the post-prandial speech.

The success of the *Daily Telegraph* and the *Daily News*, two of London's largest-selling newspapers, was facilitated to a large degree by the popularity of these three journalists: canny and pragmatic 'braggers' who not only reported 'news' in a personalised and colourful fashion, but who, because they stimulated public interest in themselves, also became objects of 'news' in their own right. As well as possessing all the qualities of efficient reporters, they were superlative salesmen who learnt to further their own careers, and those of their papers, by creating, both in their writing and in their public life, a particular persona designed to sell themselves and their work to the reading public. They wrote and spoke themselves into fame in the pages of the press and on the lecture circuit throughout England, America and the British Empire.

Public fascination with all three depended on their ability not just to record events in an interesting and colourful fashion but to project themselves into those events—to be there. As historians of the press have pointed out, they pioneered a narrative style of reportage based on themselves as hero/authors. F. L Bullard refers to Forbes's 'thrilling narratives';[2] Philip Knightley demonstrates how through his 'thrilling accounts' the intrepid war correspondent 'rapidly became the hero of his own story';[3] Lucy Brown describes the writings of the special correspondents, with 'their expeditions to forbidden cities in Turkestan or to the deserts of Khartoum', as providing late-Victorian England 'with the equivalent of *Mandeville's Travels*', a twelfth-century travel guide of fabulous adventures.[4]

The blurring of the boundaries between report and personal narrative, between 'truth' and interpretation, which made the work of these special correspondents so attractive to readers, was enhanced by the fact that they usually transferred their 'fabulous adventures' from the pages of newspapers to books. Reports that had been published separately over a period of time took on a more cohesive narrative quality when bound together in book form; rescued from the ephemeral pages of the newspaper, the tale of adventure could be read and re-read. As the authors of books rather than journalism, special correspondents were freed from the jurisdiction of newspaper editors and had more control over the presentation of their 'stories'. This enabled them to identify themselves even more directly with the events of their narratives, usually by means of a preface or other commentary added to the text. In the preface to *My Diary in America in the Midst of War*, a collection of his *Daily Telegraph* reports on the Civil War, Sala rounded on American critics who had the temerity to suggest that he had intruded himself and his opinions too much into the action: 'Should a strong man be ashamed to avow that his Book is Himself, and that in whatsoever he writes that treats of individual thought or individual opinion, he must be, to a great extent, his own hero?'[5]

The later Victorian era has been recognised as a period in which British life was being reinvigorated by a sense of imperial mission associated with 'a renewed militarism, a devotion to royalty, an identification and worship of national heroes, together with a contemporary cult of personality, and racial ideas associated with Social Darwinism'.[6] It is no coincidence that the careers of Forbes, Sala and Stanley flourished at this time, since by then the popular press, with its ever-increasing capacity to influence public opinion and propagate ideas, was exercising considerable power over the public mind. In fact, these three, arguably the leading journalists of the day, can be seen as both instigators and products of the *Zeitgeist*, for it was the pursuit of these very themes in their writing that brought them success and defined their identities as special correspondents.

Moreover, since the main aim of the emerging capitalist press was to generate income, its entrepreneurial proprietors, anxious to attract readers in an increasingly competitive market, tended to pander to popular tastes by favouring the coverage of the kinds of events that had already been shown to stimulate sales. Initial success led to more of the same as the Specials, in accordance with the policy of their journals, skewed their reporting towards saleable narrative. In this way, special correspondents created their public and were, in turn, its creations. The pragmatic nexus between demand and supply is implicit in T.H.S. Escott's perceptive remark about Sala: 'Never was there a journalist who had so thoroughly mastered the tastes and requirements of the colossal circle of readers to which he appeals. Seldom has there been one of whom it may be said that he has created the appetite which his writings satisfy'.[7]

The same dynamics are apparent in the relationship between Forbes and his audience. The outstanding success of Forbes's coverage of the Franco-Prussian War, which increased the circulation of the *Daily News* from 50,000 to 150,000 copies (Brown, p.33), resulted in his being sent thereafter to make the most out of even the smallest skirmish. It was in the interests of both Forbes and the *News* that the public's desire for militarism be both encouraged and assuaged. The Zulu War in 1879 is a good example—and it had a bonus in the death of the Prince Imperial (the young Eugène Louis, son of Napoleon III) whose body, according to news reports, was dramatically transfixed by seventeen Zulu spears. In this case, interest in heroic public figures *and* in things military was satisfied; an interest that was both generated and harnessed by Forbes and his newspaper.

Forbes even managed to incorporate into the battle the technology associated with his role as a reporter to create some heroic action for himself. His ride from the field of British victory at Ulundi to lodge his news at the telegraph office, 110 miles away through enemy territory, was widely lauded and publicised. A mounted Forbes, with the burning township in the background, was depicted on the front cover of the *Illustrated London News*. It was even suggested that he should receive the Victoria Cross (9 August 1879). Two years earlier during the Russo-Turkish War, Forbes had brilliantly capitalised on a similar ride by arriving unannounced to inform the Czar of the unexpected Russian victory at Shipka. In both cases, he drew attention to himself by turning his trip to the telegraph office into a newsworthy event in its own right. He transformed himself, a non-combatant, into the 'hero of the hour'.[8] Readers became just as enthralled by the special correspondent as they were by his news.

Stanley rose to fame in a similar fashion. The search for Livingstone, which had provided such a journalistic coup for the *New York Herald*, was recreated by the London *Daily Telegraph* when they sent Stanley out to Africa again a few years later. The *Herald*, not wishing to be left out, agreed to help finance the venture in return for publishing rights. Even though Livingstone had died, both papers capitalised on his name by advertising that Stanley would 'follow in Livingstone's footsteps'. But it was now

(*Illustrated London News*, 9 August 1879)

Stanley not Livingstone who was the focus of attention. Throughout his career Stanley clearly recognised that his popularity with the public stemmed from that initial meeting, and he made sure that his name thereafter remained coupled with that of Livingstone.

There can be no doubt that, as exciting public figures, Forbes, Stanley and Sala captured the Victorian imagination, and that, as influential journalists, they had a hand in creating the imperialistic ethos that characterised their times. Although it is unlikely that any one of them would have considered himself to have been overtly 'pushing' an imperialistic ideology, as John MacKenzie points out in *Propaganda and Empire*, it was the 'constant repetition of the central ideas and concerns of the age' (p.3), the continual reinforcement of themes and images, that set up a self-generating ethos which verged on propaganda. An investigation into the journalism of these men shows it to be exactly this: a constant harping on imperialistic themes, Forbes with war, heroism and militarism; Sala with famous figures and pageantry; Stanley with African exploration, Christian mission and paternalism.

It is difficult to assess the influence of popular culture on the opinions and attitudes of people who absorbed its influences. Any such assessment of the impact of Forbes, Sala and Stanley on their public must therefore be to a large extent speculative. However, by examining a unique situation that occurred during the last quarter of the nineteenth century, a persuasive case can be made to show that these special correspondents did indeed have a significant impact on one particular section of the British public. The unique situation takes the form of a series of individual lecture tours to Australia that were undertaken by the Specials between 1882 and 1891. The extent to which their writings and the public images they engendered during their tours influenced the attitudes, and the actions, of the colonials demonstrates clearly that they had indeed become heroes of their own 'narratives' of empire: travelling propagandists who peddled dreams of imperialistic adventure.

The Australian context is a useful one because it permits each visitor to be examined within a brief timeframe of concentrated activity that was very well documented in the colonial press. The collected contemporary documentation gives insight into the relationship between the visitors and their audience, between what they presented and how they were received. At the same time the sequential nature of the tours (Forbes, 1882-1883; Sala, 1885-1886; Stanley, 1891-1892) facilitates a comparative assessment of their impact. The evidence to be used has been gleaned from performance advertisements, reviews, interviews and detailed reports of public receptions.

The colonial context is significant because it is one where the concepts of patriotism and empire were heightened by distance and nostalgia, and where, divorced from colonial experience, the events and personalities that made up the visitors' subject matter had taken on the qualities of myth. The reality of such great deeds and larger-than-life figures was one from which the colonists were excluded, but one to which they began to aspire, as shown by the excitement that surrounded the decision of New South Wales to send a contingent of colonial troops to fight in the Soudan in 1885—the year Sala visited the colonies and three years after Forbes's visit. The colonial enthusiasm for engaging in imperialistic activity for the first time at *this* time seems significant enough to make Australia a particularly good place to study the influence of these men.

By the time the Specials had reached the colonies their writings and their images had become set—ossified in the colonial mind. All three had passed the peak of their careers, and the interest of both visitors and colonial hosts alike tended to be focused on their past: on what they had done, on what they had seen. The lectures were characterised by an emphasis on past glories. In other words during their colonial tours the Specials were identifying, and were identified by, the themes that they had been writing about for so long. The reiteration of all the old 'chestnuts' is reflected in the titles they gave their lectures, and reviews of the lectures reveal that their subject matter was indeed a condensed version of the themes that had become their trademarks. For all of them, it represented the concentrated matter of their careers as journalists.

The reception received by the Specials showed that their writings, and the public personae that had grown up around them, were very familiar to their hosts. Their influence on the colonial mind was clearly acknowledged. As the chairman Robert Garran told Forbes in a welcoming speech at the Athenaeum Club in Sydney: 'You knew nothing of us until tonight but we all knew you long ago'.[9] Another speaker, Colonial-Secretary Bede Dalley, reminded the assembly that they were entertaining a man 'who has helped by his writings in the public Press the English-speaking people throughout the world to comprehend the course of modern history'. In words which blurred the distinction between soldier and journalist, Dalley presented an image of Forbes, pen in one hand and sword in the other, 'engaged in writing contemporary history at the watch-fires of contending armies . . . who by his participation in danger, and the vigour of his compositions in his own person signally illustrates the valour of one profession and the power of the other'.[10] Forbes couldn't have said it better himself.

This introduction set the tone for Forbes's colonial visit. He was clearly an expert on things military and should be listened to. Throughout his tour he was continually asked for his advice on how the colonies should defend themselves, and he gave it freely. Comments made in an interview with the *Argus* in June 1882 were republished a number of times, and a lively correspondence ensued.[11] Forbes toned down the militaristic approach he applied to European affairs when he offered advice to the Australians. He advised against forming a large army because there was practically no military danger for Australia: 'When I look at the enormous distance which separated you from the nations of the old world, I am forced to the conclusion that you are better situated than any other people or country of which I have cognizance as regards your prospects of escape from war'.[12]

At the same time that his very sensible advice was being read in the colonial papers, Forbes was lecturing to packed audiences at the Melbourne Opera House. His repertoire of lectures comprised: 'The Inner Life of a War Correspondent'; 'Kings and Princes I Have Met'; 'The Armies of Europe'; 'Warriors I Have Known'; and 'Lecturing Experience in Both Hemispheres'. They were clearly designed to stir the blood, and the lecturer's demeanour and appearance on stage were theatrical and very much in character with his subject matter. A review of 'The Inner Life of a War Correspondent' describes how Forbes *plunged* into his subject' and details at great length the medals which covered his chest: 'The Orders of Knighthood of the Star of Roumania, St. John of Jerusalem, Charles III of Spain, Remembrance Cross of Saxony, and St. Stanislaus of Russia, the Iron Cross of Prussia, the Takova Cross of Servia [sic], the Roumanian Cross of Danube, and the Russian, German, Servian and Roumanian war medals'.[13] It is no wonder that *Melbourne Punch* saw fit to dispel the rumour 'that he requires a poker down his back to support the weight'.[14]

Forbes presented his lectures with verve, 'interspersing the discourse with graphic descriptions of the many stirring scenes he has witnessed in war, together with numerous perils of his own personal experiences, and relieving the narrative with anecdotes which have always a strong spice of humour'.[15] War, when Forbes described it, was clearly glamorous, dangerous and, yes, fun. Yet, according to his advice, the colonists were destined by geographic accident to miss out on it. To them the rallying cry to jingoism, which was the underlying theme of his lectures, was one that thrilled yet thwarted.

An article Forbes published in the *Nineteenth Century* soon after he arrived home from his Australian trip recognises the frustration in the hearts of the colonists, but disparages the jingoism he found there as being a luxury that they *could* afford:

> The Australian glowed over Ulundi, and thrilled and swelled at the Tel-el-Kebir tiding. Military successes

get into all our heads, and the man who has personally helped them has a glow of self-satisfaction. But his feeling is nothing so intense as is the elation of good people who have won a battle vicariously . . . in all his community there is not one weeping woman, and it has not cost him a rap. Oh! British Jingo, don't you wish you were an Australian?[16]

In the light of Australia's experience in the first World War, Forbes's comment is agonisingly ironic, almost as ironic as the fact that Forbes didn't seem to recognise that it was his influence which undoubtedly gave rise to the jingoism he perceived in the colonials: their yearning to share in the exciting adventure of war that he so vividly described. This influence is implicit in the praise accorded him by Dalley, the man who, two years later, was responsible for sending the New South Wales contingent to the Soudan; the first time, apart from the Maori Wars, that colonial troops had fought under the British flag:

> We are honouring a brave soldier and a brilliant journalist—a man who has moved about in the most hotly contested scenes and places of bloody conflict. . . . It is something for us individually to meet such men, and to look upon those whose great mission it is to give mankind, in Wordsworth's lines, the 'Expressive records of a glorious strife; / And competent to shed a spark divine / Into the torpid heart of daily life'.[17]

Of Forbes's competency to arouse the colonists with his narratives of war, there can be no question. As the jingoism surrounding the departure of the Soudan contingent attests, the Australians were spoiling for a fight. Public interest in the whole affair, with flags and streamers flying, shows that it did indeed inject some excitement into ordinary lives.

To Sala, following in Forbes's footsteps in 1885, the jingoistic nature of the Australians was made even more apparent. His visit coincided with the patriotic fervour associated with the departure of the Soudan contingent, which had sailed out of Sydney harbour just ten days before he arrived. At Sala's official reception Dalley, now Acting Premier, was in full cry. He took the opportunity to remind the visitor of the 'portentous step' that had just been taken and to announce with fervour the 'thorough and absolute identification of ourselves as colonists with the fortunes of the Empire'.[18] Dalley was anxious to make an impression on his visitor, since Sala, as well as lecturing on his own account, had been commissioned by the London *Daily Telegraph* to write a series of articles on the colonies. As the Sydney *Daily Telegraph* remarked, such an account 'circulated in the columns of the most largely circulated of the London morning dailies will be worth shiploads of handbooks and pamphlets'. Sala assured his hosts that he deplored 'the ignorance that exists in the mother country of the state and condition and legitimate wants of her dependencies' (16 March, p.4).

Dalley welcomed Sala, as he had welcomed Forbes, like an old friend: 'He is for the first time a visitor to this distant colony, and yet he is as well-known to us as if he had lived here for a quarter of a century'. Sala, however, was perceived as a much more urbane figure: more bon viveur, than man of action: 'One of the most accomplished and liberal hosts in the dispensation of a graceful and unrivalled intellectual hospitality' who 'has enlarged our information by his descriptions, amused us by his charming inventions, and assisted us to understand the bearings of great international questions by his comments and his observation'.[19]

Dalley's summing up of Sala's appeal was reflected in the titles of the lectures that Sala had prepared for colonial tastes: 'Wars, Revolutions and Tumults'; 'Shows and Pageants'; 'Costume, Culture and Cookery'; 'Two Princes of the Pen: Dickens and Thackeray'; 'Famous People: including General Gordon, Lord Wolseley, the Duke of Wellington, Victor Emmanuel, Abraham Lincoln, Lord Palmerston, Sir Edwin

Landseer'; and 'The Englishman in America'. His first lecture, 'Wars, Revolutions and Tumults', was 'a summary of all the wars, revolutions and tumults that have occurred in Europe since the fateful and memorable year 1848 down to the equally fateful and memorable year 1870, with the narrator as a principal figure in the story'.[20] It was reported that he delivered his personal account of European history to a 'bumper house', that his audience 'hung upon his lips', that it gave 'rounds of applause in the proper places', and that it 'greeted his peroration with a tempest of cheers'.[21] Sala's takings that night were a record-breaking three hundred pounds.

By his third lecture, 'The Englishman in America', Sala's audience had fallen from an initial fifteen hundred to one hundred people, and his takings to twenty pounds. Why, with a reputation and name such as his, was his tour failing almost before it had begun? Unfortunately for Sala his celebrated urbanity led to his downfall. His style and delivery were too low-key and his intelligent concentration on historical cause and effect dampened down his more bellicose subject matter. Sala, who had embarked on his trip at Forbes's suggestion, with the specific aim of making a 'nest egg' for his old age, had failed to anticipate the mood of the colonies. He had become a victim of the legacy of jingoism that Forbes had left behind: compared to Forbes, Sala was a disappointment. It was not until he added another title to his list, 'Russia: What She Is and What She Means', that Sala could command a decent audience again. 'Russia' played on colonial fears of Russian attack and quickly became the preferred lecture. In fact, according to the *Brisbane Courier*, in Queensland it was the only lecture that could rally audiences:

> The great journalist made his debut at the Protestant Hall on Tuesday night, his subject being 'Russia'. On Wednesday he lectured on 'Dickens and Thackeray', and on Thursday on 'Wars and Revolutions'. At the first lecture there was a large crowd. The hall was packed and many were unable

to gain admission. On Wednesday and Thursday however the audience were scanty. There was not only room for all who came there, but there would have been room for more. The lecture on Russia is to be repeated tonight at the Opera House and here our visitor will have another good gathering.[22]

Although Sala was not intrinsically a jingoist, for pragmatic, pecuniary reasons he turned himself into one. He couldn't quite bring himself actually to endorse the fairytale of an imminent Russian invasion, but he did continue to give his successful 'Russia' lecture long after Gladstone had announced that Britain and Russia intended to negotiate their differences. Like Forbes, Sala expressed amazement at the extravagance of Australian militarism, expressing concern that a 'Federated Australia—as a Nation on a National footing—might involve Great Britain in a war that would cost millions of treasure and rivers of blood'.[23] Sala disparaged colonial jingoism, but, like Forbes, he clearly had a hand in it. The focus of both correspondents on the glory of war and the honour to be won there contributed to the wave of militaristic and patriotic propaganda that primed Australia for that apotheosis of jingoism, the 'Great' War, which thirty years later would set the 'rivers of blood' flowing at Gallipoli and on the fields of Flanders, a war for which the 'mother country', not her young colonial offshoot, would be to blame.

By the time Stanley arrived in Australia he had become a true icon of Empire. Newspaper advertisements publicising his Australian lectures give some idea of the way his audiences would have revered him. They were the work of R.S. Smythe, a very able promoter who knew exactly what would appeal to colonial audiences. Smythe's epithets were designed to honour an empire builder. They included: 'Explorer, Missionary, Hero; The Man Who Found Livingstone; The Hero of the Dark Continent; The Most Remarkable Man Who Ever Stood on a Lecture Platform; The Pioneer of the Congo; The Columbus of Central Africa; The Tacitus of the Cannibals and Pygmies; The Apostle of

Christianity in Uganda; The Arch-Enemy of Slavery'. Audiences came to see the man whose adventures they had been reading about for nearly two decades. Even though his stories may have grown a little too familiar, Stanley's celebrity status was enough to draw them in. After his first appearance the *Argus* reviewer gushed: 'Everyone knows how Stanley found Livingstone, and from any other lips but Stanley's would not care to listen to the narrative again, but to view with their own eyes the man who did it they would give a great deal' (12 November 1891, p.6).

To the postcolonial sensibility, Stanley is the epitome of the imperialist. Reviews of his lectures show him to be judgmental, paternalistic and aggressive; he believed in white mastery and annexation to secure valuable resources. To him, the native Africans were anthropological specimens rather than human beings. In his lecture on 'Pygmies and Cannibals' he described 'some beautiful human animals' he had seen 'among the women', regaling the audience with 'several amusing stories of their characteristics'. Most of his nineteenth-century colonial audiences seem to have thought Stanley incapable of wrong and rarely questioned his attitudes. He was praised as 'a masterful man, a man who will do his duty at all hazards, and who during his expeditions has been accustomed to exercise the power of an autocrat, and to send a criminal to his grave as readily as to give the order for marching'.[24] The Queensland Branch of the Royal Geographic Society deemed his explorations to be 'noble self-sacrifices' by which 'British trade and the influence of civilisation have been extended to the remotest parts of the earth, adding to the happiness and prosperity of millions of the race'. In response Stanley pontificated that 'geographic explorations were the beginning of all commercial enterprise'.[25]

The whole thrust of Stanley's Australian tour was to give the aura of moral respectability to empire building. Even though he was still an American citizen, the National Anthem was played at his performances to acknowledge the part that Stanley had played in opening up Central Africa to Great Britain and other European powers 'whereby 150 millions of Africans have a prospect of becoming civilised and Christianised'.[26] (As a prerequisite for knighthood the Welsh-born Stanley was readmitted as a British national on 20 May 1892 soon after his return from Australia.) Stanley's identification with the 'saintly' Livingstone and his missionary activities heightened the sense of Christian morality that he had built up around himself. The greeting, 'Dr Livingstone, I presume', which had started off his largely media-manipulated career as an explorer, became one of the most celebrated phrases of the nineteenth century. Although Stanley claimed that he had made the absurdly stiff salutation because he couldn't think of anything else to say,[27] the incongruity of such formality in the 'wilds' of Africa made the words a stroke of promotional genius. They were perfect both for the music hall and for the lecture platform. As the *Argus* reported, Australian audiences eagerly anticipated their delivery at Stanley's first lecture in Melbourne: 'The audience waited expectantly for the famous "Dr. Livingstone, I presume", and applauded heartily when it came' (12 November 1891, p.6).

Stanley had left England for Australia when the controversy over his handling of the Emin Pasha expedition was threatening to damage his carefully contrived reputation. His Australian tour, largely a public relations exercise and an opportunity to salve his ego, provided a respite from his critics and gave him a chance to bathe in the adulation of the unsophisticated colonials. His lectures were designed to reinforce the idea of empire, particularly the British Empire, as a moral duty, and empire building as a noble vocation.

Although now relegated to the murky screens of microfilm readers, the visits to Australia of Forbes, Sala and Stanley left behind them a legacy which persists today. As well-known public figures, and as journalists whose work had been syndicated throughout the colonies for many years, the advocacy of the special correspondents for the 'mother country' both fulfilled and engendered British patriotism and pride of Empire in colonial hearts. Blinkered by their own cultural mindsets and their egoistic and pragmatic drive for self promotion, these men failed to comprehend the impact that their words would have on the young land they could only see as a 'little England', an offshoot of the 'old country', a milch cow for their pockets.

On the eve of Federation and about to come of age, the colonists, more or less ignored by the English, were frustrated by their distance, both geographically and culturally, from the 'mother country' and its fabled glories. The combined feelings of slight, frustration and patriotism manifested themselves in the jingoism that Forbes and Sala decried. Sala failed to recognise the significance of the Soudan War for the Australians: that it was their first assertive move to attract some positive attention. Forbes failed to recognise that what he defined as the 'vicarious' luxury of Australian jingoism was actually its spur: the colonials didn't want a vicarious experience, they wanted the real thing. And they were determined to get it.

Of course, it would be simplistic to suggest that the special correspondents can be held responsible for the eagerness of the Australians to participate in England's wars, but their influence is clear. It was only by shedding blood on the battlefields of the Boer War and the first World War that the colonists could truly claim to have a part in the 'glorious' traditions the special correspondents had so skilfully depicted, and in doing so create for the Australians of the future their own myths, their own 'glories'. Paper heroes aside, history is, after all, a vicarious business.

Notes

[1] Sala to Yates, 3 Feb 1875, Letter 463, Edmund Yates Papers in the University of Queensland Library.
[2] *Famous War Correspondents* (New York: Beckman, 1974), p.vii.
[3] *The First Casualty* (London: Deutsch, 1975), p.42
[4] 'The Treatment of the News in Mid-Victorian Newspapers', *Transactions of the Royal Historical Society*, 5th Series, 27 (1977), 29.
[5] G. A. Sala, *My Diary in America in the Midst of War,* 2 vols (Tinsley: London, 1864), 1, p.14.

[6] J.M. MacKenzie, *Propaganda and Empire* (Manchester: Manchester UP, 1984), p. 2.
[7] T.H.S. Escott, 'A Journalist of the Day', *Time* 1 (1879), 120.
[8] Quoted in R.T. Stearn, 'Archibald Forbes, Special Correspondent', *Journal of Newspaper and Periodical History*, 8. 2 (1992), 7.
[9] Sydney *Daily Telegraph*, 8 May 1882, p.3.
[10] Sydney *Daily Telegraph*, 8 May 1882, p.3.
[11] For instance: *Argus*, 6 June 1882, p.6; *Sydney Morning Herald*, 6 June 1882, p.6; 8 June 1882, p.3; *Sydney Mail*, 10 June 1882, p.928.
[12] *Argus*, 6 June 1882, p.6.
[13] *Argus*, 23 May 1882, p.6.
[14] *Melbourne Punch*, 18 May 1882, p.197.
[15] *Argus*, 23 May 1882, p.6.
[16] *Nineteenth Century*, 14 (October 1883), 724-25.
[17] Sydney *Daily Telegraph*, 8 May 1882, p.3.
[18] *Sydney Morning Herald*, 16 March 1885, p.5.
[19] *Sydney Morning Herald*, 16 March 1885 p.5.
[20] Melbourne *World*, 24 March 1885, p.4.
[21] Melbourne *World*, 24 March 1885, p.4.
[22] *Brisbane Courier*, 28 April 1885, p.3.
[23] Brisbane *Figaro*, 30 May 1885, p.673.
[24] *Sydney Morning Herald*, 1 December 1891, p.5.
[25] *Brisbane Courier*, 15 December 1891, p.5.
[26] *Argus*, 26 November 1891, p.8.
[27] F. McLynn, *Stanley: The Making of an African Explorer* (Oxford: Oxford UP, 1989), p.148.

10 Literature and Politics in the Queensland Colonial Press

Chris Tiffin

> The Englishman all over the world appreciates his daily paper. Queensland Englishmen are no exception to the rule; hence it follows that the literature of the colony as represented by the Press is large and varied. Every town possesses its newspaper; some, three or four—daily, weekly, and bi-weekly. Many of these journals are of a very high class and nearly all are of moderate tone, which causes them to present a very vivid contrast to the highly-spiced sensational journals of our cousins over the Pacific.[1]

In the nineteenth century cheaper paper and mechanised presses made the newspaper a medium of communication that could be produced rapidly, disseminated widely and discarded easily (or recycled as cabin-trunk liners). With the invention of the telegraph and steam transportation, the newspaper took on the notes of immediacy and universality. In the colonial situation, of course, this 'immediacy' was rather tempered by distance and the sparseness of settlement, and newspapers had a longer shelf life through being recirculated much more extensively than they were in Great Britain. For isolated people with little access to reading material, a month-old newspaper or issue of a journal could afford information and interest long after it would have appeared stale and useless in other environments. In 'Remailed' Henry Lawson celebrates the practice of bush mates in different districts or colonies who never actually wrote letters, but who carried on an elaborate staccato correspondence by sending old newspapers backwards and forwards with items marked that referred to mutual acquaintances or supported their case in past arguments. He rather sentimentally suggests that this is the ultimate form of publication:

> It is supposed to be something to have your work published in an English magazine, to have it published in book form, to be flattered by critics and reprinted throughout the country press, or even to be cut up well and severely. But, after all, now we come to think of it, we would almost as soon see a piece of ours marked with big inky crosses in the soiled and crumbled rag that Bill or Jim gets sent him by an old mate of his—the paper that goes thousands of miles scrawled all over with smudgy addresses and tied with a piece of string.[2]

Colonial papers did not just seek to inform or entertain, however; like English papers they were often started to promote political agendas. In Queensland James Swan the founding editor of the earliest paper, the *Moreton Bay Courier* (1846), was a protégé of John Dunmore Lang,[3] so the paper advocated free emigration. Four years later the squatter interests countered with the *North Australian Free Press* to argue for the reintroduction of transportation of convicts to the district (Knight, pp.297-98). This opposition between the squatter interests and those of the urban liberals remained the major journalistic paradigm for the rest of the century. Political allegiance was often partisan and fierce. Journalist and editor R. Spencer Browne recorded the difficulty he experienced as editor of the *Observer* trying to maintain objectivity on the one hand and answer the demands of a committed proprietorship on the other: 'It was very hard to keep on the lines of policy which the directors, or a majority of them, desired, and to secure a measure of public confidence. . . . The "Observer" was bought for the purposes of strong party onslaughts.'[4] In such circumstances, editorial independence was fragile at best and often nonexistent. As Browne comments dryly about two of the proprietors, 'Both Morehead and Perkins seemed to regard an editor, or a newspaper man of any sort, as a kind of retainer or hanger-on'(p.67).

Distance and remoteness dictated various aspects of colonial publishing practice including 'the introduction of weekly papers . . . to provide a weekly summary of news for the outback dwellers. This was essentially a mail subscription service for frontiersmen who did not make a daily trip to town.'[5] A second impact of remoteness was the heightened importance of foreign news. In the early days before telegraph lines to the colony were completed, the *Moreton Bay Courier* would expand by four pages when English mail ships had just arrived (Knight, p.278).[6] Later the selection and rewriting of telegraph news became one of the most important jobs on the paper.

The primitiveness of the local book-publishing industry and the repeated failure of attempts at magazine publishing meant that newspapers had to take on a broader publishing role. This was especially true of the weeklies which, as Elizabeth Webby argues, were far more than a weekly digest of news:

> They were particularly directed at country readers to whom a daily newspaper, received days late, was an unnecessary luxury. Their magazine features, however, also made them attractive to city readers. Though individual titles offered different emphases, and the mix also changed from decade to decade, by the end of the century these weeklies normally included a summary of the week's news, an illustrated section (greatly extended when reproduction of photographs became possible), rural news and affairs, sections on sport, drama, mining, and commercial matters, women's and also often children's pages, serialised and other fiction and

poetry. Because of their wide circulation and the financial backing of their parent papers, they were a far more important source of income for local writers than monthlies like the *Cosmos*.[7]

Nora Murray-Prior, a comfortably-off pastoralist's wife, describes a Sunday morning in 1880 in a way that suggests the place the weekly paper held in the household routine:

> Having dismissed Mr Cramp in peace, nursed the baby, read up the serial story in the Queenslander, put a few late roses & honeysuckle loosely together in the centre vase & some cottage beauties & white jessamine in the specimen vases, (not on the mantel piece where the heat is too much for them), I may as well finish my solitary morning by writing to you.[8]

The newspapers were often the sole outlet for local fiction or poetry, as book publication until the 1890s almost inevitably required a subscription list or authorial payment for the production costs. Literature was useful to the journal, however. In situations where the supply of news was by no means guaranteed, literary contributions acted as fillers and could be manipulated to perfect columns or pages. The easiest way of doing this was to adjust the leading with which a story was set.[9] More drastic methods of page adjustment were to excise a sentence or paragraph of the story, or even abandon the episode.[10] Fiction seems to have been regarded by most colonial journals as more expendable than the editorial material or market reports. Publishing local literature was, however, a marketing tool which encouraged readers' participatory identification with the paper. In a technique later perfected by the Sydney *Bulletin*, the newspapers would solicit contributions in order to procure this sense of identification. Although most often associated with the literary pages, this encouragement of community authorship sometimes inflected other sections of the paper:

> Nothing can tend more [to the advancement of agriculture] than the full interchange of information of all those engaged in farming pursuits in the different districts. . . . It is hoped that the farmers will freely use [the] open column for giving to, or eliciting from, one another, much valuable information of a character which nothing but experience can supply.[11]

By far the most important of the Queensland weeklies was the *Queenslander*, which first appeared on 3 February 1866 and was published from the offices of the *Brisbane Courier*. At the time the *Queenslander* was founded, the sole proprietor of the *Courier* was the wool-merchant Thomas Blackett Stephens, but only two years later financial difficulties forced Stephens to amalgamate the *Courier* with another struggling daily newspaper the *Observer* and form, with some of its directors, the Brisbane Newspaper Company.[12] The original shareholders of the company comprised three squatters, one woolbroker, one planter-merchant, one solicitor, one butcher, and the Brisbane Collector of Customs (Cryle, p.89), a mix which resulted in such differences of political opinions that in 1873 the business was sold by auction. It was quickly resold to a partnership which included Gresley Lukin, and he steered the papers successfully for the remainder of the decade. In 1880 he was bankrupted through unsuccessful land speculations,[13] and was succeeded as editor by Charles Hardie Buzacott.[14]

It is important to reiterate that the *Queenslander* was not just a cut-and-paste compilation from the weekday issues of the *Courier*, which by 1866 was publishing its own twelve-page digest of the month's news for rural, intercolonial, and 'Home' readers. Not only did the *Queenslander* produce its own editorial matter, but it included much material, especially of a leisure nature, which did not appear in the *Courier*. The *Queenslander* aimed at a wide readership, and therefore struck a generally progressive but moderate tone, eschewing party politics on the one hand and anything inappropriate for family reading on the other. It was, in the words of E.B. Kennedy, 'a most useful and reliable weekly paper'.[15]

Although the *Courier* was the 'serious' flagship of the company, both Lukin and Buzacott devoted attention to the *Queenslander* as well. Lukin radically redesigned the paper in 1875 when the old twelve-page, seven-column broadsheet was transformed to a 32-page, four-column tabloid with an illustrated masthead and cable news on the front page instead of advertisements. He also introduced a Christmas supplement of fiction and poetry. In 1882 Buzacott expanded the 32 pages to 40 and improved the layout and use of headings.

As a publisher of literature, the *Queenslander* provided an outlet for local writing, and reprinted fiction, poetry and literary news from Britain, the United States, and to a lesser extent, the Continent. The dominant form of local writing was lyric verse, but there was a good sprinkling of topical satire, bush sketches and stories, including a significant number of pieces with a Pacific setting. Two of Marcus Clarke's novels were serialised in the 1870s, while serial fiction by George Essex Evans, Catherine Helen Spence, James Brunton Stephens, Francis Adams, Mrs Campbell Praed, Mary Hannay Foott, Price Warung, and Ernest Favenc appeared in the 1880s. Theatre reviewing was detailed but sporadic; a succession of long reviews of performances might be followed by some months of neglect.

Apart from the actual publication of fiction, poetry and essays, the paper also monitored local and overseas literary culture. Lectures on Australian poetry, meetings of the Moggill Penny Reading Group, and a talk by Mary Hannay Foott to the East Moreton Teachers Association were all reported, as well as any new books added to the collection at the Brisbane School of Arts Reading Room. Topics discussed included journalism in the bush, place names in Australia, and a proposal for a Brisbane university. The paper regularly printed obituaries of leading English and American writers such as Tennyson, Stevenson, and Browning, but also ventured on discussions of such diverse topics as the socialism of William Morris, the use of violets in poetry and drama, the new poet laureate (Alfred Austin), and morality in literature.

Local writing was supplemented by overseas material. Wilkie Collins, William Black, Mary Elizabeth Braddon, Hall Caine, Joseph Hatton, Edna Lyall, George Macdonald, Henry Seton Merriman, Margaret Oliphant, James Payn, and Mrs Henry Wood all published novels in the *Queenslander*, while verse or shorter fiction came from Tennyson, Mark Twain, Bret Harte, Rudyard Kipling, Robert Louis Stevenson, and Arthur Conan Doyle. Just how the overseas material was secured is not clear, and it may be that in the early days scant notice was paid to concerns of copyright. By the late 1870s, however, the paper was regularly proclaiming of its imported serials that 'the right of publication in Queensland . . . has been purchased by the Brisbane Newspaper Company.' This was probably intended to forestall piracy by opposition papers, but it does suggest that, at least for serials, some formal licensing system was in place. Paragraphs, shorter prose and poetry were regularly republished from English and American papers with attribution given, but there is nothing to suggest that any reprint fee was paid. If the rights to a serial were purchased, one would expect that copy of the whole work would have been provided to the paper by the author or agent. There is some evidence that at least in the early days the *Queenslander* simply took its serials from other journals and reset them episode by episode as they were received from England. On 29 September 1866 the paper announced that it was rationing the episodes of Mrs Notley's *Norman and Grind* on the curious grounds that the story was too saccharine for weekly inclusion (p.5). A few months later, however, the paper was forced to come clean and admit that the problem had been one of supply:

> A correspondent requests us very earnestly to continue the publication of "Norman and Grind" weekly until it is finished. We should be happy to comply with this request, but it is beyond our power

to do so—the story is reprinted from the *Englishwoman's Magazine*, and we publish it as quickly as received. (29 December 1866, p.5)

A typical early issue of the paper contained an episode of a serial consisting of a full page of seven columns, a short story or sketch, three or four short poems, and some literary notices or reviews. There were also poetry and stories for, and sometimes by, juveniles on the Children's Page, and semi-literary material under the heads of 'The Essayist' and 'The Sketcher'. After Gresley Lukin took over, the selection on the literary page was more discriminating, and a smaller group of more talented local writers tended to appear in the 'Original Poetry' and 'The Storyteller' columns. Less finished sketches, and topical and sentimental verse continued to appear in other sections of the paper, however, such as 'The Sketcher', 'Flotsam and Jetsam', and 'Facts and Fancies'.

Looking at the overall pattern of publication, it is clear that local verse and short fiction were appealing to the editors, but for serial fiction, which remained the lynchpin of the literary pages, British novels were preferred. There are approximately three times as many episodes of serial fiction as there are individual stories, and of these as many are British as Australian and American put together. Such a British dominance is not true for either verse or short fiction, however, as the following table shows. (Except for translations of verse, only tiny amounts of material from other countries were published.) The table gives the percentages of types of item which can be assigned to Australia, Great Britain, the United States or other countries on the basis of either known authorship, setting or subject matter, or source from which the item was reprinted. An item which was written by an American author but set in Australia is counted as both Australian and United States. Despite the lack of exactitude in definition, the table gives an indication of the focus of the literary contents of the paper.

Assignment of *Queenslander* items to country of origin

	Aust.	Brit.	US	Other
All Items	61%	24%	14%	>1%
Verse	68%	16%	13%	>3%
Short Fiction	44%	25%	30%	>1%
Serial Fiction	39%	51%	10%	>1%

Like other colonial institutions, the colonial newspaper had an ambivalent attitude to Europe and Britain. While it could be prickly and defensive when local aspirations seemed disregarded or thwarted, there were frequent outbreaks of europhilia in its columns. The visit of Prince Alfred, the Duke of Edinburgh, called forth not only fulsome coverage of official events, but also a stream of loyalty odes in the literary pages. These identified themselves as issuing from ethnic groups. The Scottish welcome to the Prince (8 February 1868, p.3) was quickly followed by a 'British' one and a 'Highland' one (22 February 1868, p.3), and not to be patriotically outdone, German settlers of Drayton and Toowoomba pledged their welcome and loyalty in German verse (7 March 1868, p.4). The latter poem had been written to be read to the Prince when he arrived in Toowoomba. Unfortunately the Prince was whisked straight through to the great sheep station at Jondaryan along with the official party, occasioning much popular criticism and the burning of an effigy of Arthur Palmer, the Colonial Secretary.

The respect and hospitality accorded to visiting dignitaries would not survive much criticism of the colony, however, and the fate of Anthony Trollope in the pages of the *Queenslander* is instructive. Trollope came to Australia in September 1871 as part of a ten-month tour of Australia and New Zealand, commencing his travels in Queensland in order to avoid that colony during the hot summer months. He spent a fortnight there and on his departure was accorded a banquet hosted by the Parliamentary Librarian and attended by the leaders of both Houses of

Parliament, most of the Cabinet, the Leader of the Opposition, and the Chief Justice. It was an all-male affair, allegedly because there was not enough space for the ladies, and the fully reported speeches were full of expressions of imperial loyalty and hopes that the colony would one day have a literature to rival that of the mother country. Trollope got a laugh for his self-deprecating remarks about being a new chum doing colonial experience and knowing very little about Queensland, and although his speech reads as a little tired and perfunctory, the evening passed off pleasantly in a fug of genial sentiment (30 September 1871, p.3).

Trollope left for Sydney in the 'Blackbird' a couple of days later, but was still in the southern colonies when his dispatches started to appear in the London *Daily Telegraph* and to be reprinted in colonial papers. Trollope's remarks on Queensland occasioned a storm, not just because of the usual colonial defensiveness, but because he involuntarily bought into two of the major running disputes in the colony—the use of land and the sources of labour. Farmers' groups met to deplore Trollope's assertion that Queensland farming land was marginal and that it should be given over to grazing, and the East Moreton Farmers' Association voted to publish a refutation of his pronouncements. The tone in which Trollope's remarks were reported was initially injured and respectful rather than angry. In announcing the Moreton refutation the *Queenslander* continued:

> That Mr. Trollope wilfully maligned or misinterpreted Queensland in his letters 'home', we do not believe. Men of his stamp—literary men of experience—are about the last men on earth to do a thing of the kind; and in his case if there was any motive whatever it would tend to give a cheerful description of a country where he was kindly and courteously received. But he has said hard and very incorrect things of this country, and we are very glad that an opportunity to rectify these assertions is still open to him, and that he will be aided in his

corrections by the parties maligned. (9 March 1872, p.4)

This measured tone soon changed to one of hostility, however. A fortnight later 'Bob Bandicoot' took Trollope to task for his implicit support of the use of Pacific Island labour, dismissing Trollope's opinions collected on his 'lionising tour through the colonies' as 'garbled, superficial and as unreal as the life he portrays in his novels'. 'His indirect defence of kidnapping is simply amusing to anyone acquainted with the facts connected with that vile and, to Englishmen, disgraceful traffic' (23 March 1872, p.3).

Trollope got into further trouble for a dismissive remark about the worth of the Queensland gold discoveries, and an assertion that the goldfields were now exhausted. This provoked a denunciation of 'the charlatan who is so free with his opinions on farming, mining and other technical matters, as if he had watched us a dozen years in place of as many days' (23 March 1872, p.3). Again this outburst was not just provincial over-sensitivity to a negative comment. Both the squatters and the liberals agreed on the need to increase the white labour force of the colony, and an assisted passage scheme for migrants to Moreton Bay had been established long before the colony achieved separation from New South Wales. (Indeed, the perception that the Sydney area was monopolising immigrant labour added impetus to the Separation movement.) The lure of gold had been a major inducement for new settlers, so the colony was horrified that this inducement was being disparaged by Trollope. Moreover the colonies were keenly aware of the potential of newspapers to create favourable impressions in the minds of prospective colonists. When the New Zealand parliament debated rates of postage on newspapers sent to England via the new Panama route, it was argued that the government should absorb the additional charges because the circulation of colonial papers in Britain acted as 'a most powerful colonizing agent' (*Queenslander*, 29 September 1872, p.11). In the event Trollope was terribly wrong about the future of gold production. Charters Towers was discovered in 1872, the Palmer River field in 1873 and Mount Morgan in 1882, between them producing more than £40,000,000 worth of gold in the next thirty years.[16]

The *Queenslander* was somewhat mollified when Trollope seemed to revise his earlier opinions in later despatches. 'He would no doubt have done more justice to Queensland in his letters to the *Daily Telegraph* had this colony been the last, instead of almost the first, which he visited' (18 May 1872, p.3). All was not forgiven, however, and a month later, on 15 June 1872, the paper gleefully reprinted a sardonic paragraph from the Melbourne *Leader*:

> Mr. Anthony Trollope is pursuing his investigations very conscientiously. The last time I saw him he was at the bottom of a ditch apparently analysing the nature of the soil in the neighbourhood of Brighton. I thought at first that he was studying agricultural chemistry, but it turned out that he had been following the hounds and had come to grief in a very awkward watercourse. (p.2)

For the last third of the century, the *Queenslander* provided a steady budget of fiction and poetry for its readers as well as encouraging and publishing both junior and adult local writers. If appearance in the literary pages of the *Queenslander* was ephemeral, it still offered publication with the production costs borne by a publisher, a significant readership, and a springboard to subsequent republication in more permanent form. With its publishing of rough verse satires of local politics; its 'Literary Letters' from London and Melbourne; its theatre reviews; its reporting on new acquisitions at the School of Arts Reading Room, and on meetings of the Johnsonian Club and Reading Societies; its theatre and book reviews; and its constant culling of literary paragraphs and longer essays from English and American periodicals, it maintained a sense of a literary culture which the colony found difficult to support in other ways. Although it is clear that colonial newspapers did not rank fiction and poetry among the higher priorities, they still made an enormous contribution to the maintenance and development of colonial literary culture.

Notes

[1] A.J. Boyd, 'Queensland: An Introductory Essay', in *Queensland: Its Resources and Institutions*, edited by Price Fletcher (Brisbane: Government Printer, 1886), p.15.
[2] *While the Billy Boils* (Sydney: Angus & Robertson, 1896), p.126.
[3] See J.J. Knight, *In the Early Days: History and Incident of Pioneer Queensland* (Brisbane: Sapsford, 1895), pp.152-53.
[4] R. Spencer Browne, *A Journalist's Memories* (Brisbane: Read, 1927), pp.68-69.
[5] J. Manion, *Paper Power in North Queensland: A History of Journalism in Townsville and Charters Towers* (Townsville: North Queensland Newspaper, 1982), pp.1-2.
[6] The Sydney-Brisbane telegraph line was completed in 1861 and Australia was connected to Great Britain and Europe in 1871.
[7] 'Journals in the Nineteenth Century', in *The Book in Australia: Essays Towards a Cultural and Social History*, edited by D.H. Borchardt and W. Kirsop, (Melbourne: Australian Reference Publications in Association with the Centre for Bibliographical and Textual Studies, Monash University, 1988), p.61.
[8] N. Murray-Prior, Letter, 2 May 1880, MS OM71-81, John Oxley Library, Brisbane.
[9] Examples of manipulation of leading can be seen in the *Queenslander* at 10 March 1867, p.2; 18 May 1867, p.2; and 13 November 1869, p.6.
[10] Unpublished research by Toni Johnson-Woods shows that the *Brisbane Courier* on several occasions commenced publication of a serial only to abandon it after a few episodes. Since on occasion the serial was running simultaneously in its sister publication, the *Queenslander*, supply of copy could not have been the cause.
[11] *Brisbane Courier*, 25 January 1866, p.1.
[12] D. Cryle, *The Press in Colonial Queensland: A Social and Political History 1845-1875* (St Lucia: U of Queensland P, 1989), p.88.
[13] *Australian Dictionary of Biography*, 5, 108.
[14] *Queenslander*, 20 August 1887, p.293.

[15] *Four Years in Queensland* (London: Stanford, 1870), p.63.
[16] *Our First Half-Century: A Review of Queensland Progress* (Brisbane: Government Printer, 1909), p.146.

11 Learning Journalism in Australia: Francis W.L. Adams, an Englishman Abroad

Meg Tasker

> The talent for journalism is, if not a high one, a distinct one, and is unfortunate enough to have too much justice done it by the popular taste for which it caters and too little by the cultured taste which it criticises and adapts.[1]

Thus Francis William Lauderdale Adams (1862-1893), commenting on his own new profession to the Queensland poet and journalist James Brunton Stephens in 1887. In their correspondence, which traces his increasing involvement with journalism, Adams claimed to have had no experience in journalism until he started his literary career in Australia. He quickly found, however, that writing for newspapers as well as literary periodicals was the only way for a young writer to survive in Australia. His comments on the state of Australian society in his later articles and books are clearly informed by the work he did during his stay in Australia, including editorial leaders on social and political issues as well as the more literary work (book reviews, fiction, poetry and essays) which he contributed to a number of Australian journals. Adams's very successful sortie into Australian journalism is interesting not only because it allowed him to make a more informed appraisal of Australian society, but because it demonstrates quite emphatically the importance of journalism in the cultural and literary life of Australia towards the end of the nineteenth century.

Adams's brief stints of employment as an attaché at the British Embassy in Paris, then as an Assistant Master at a private school on the Isle of Wight, ended when, at the age of 22, he became too ill to continue his duties and turned his attention instead to writing full time. He had started to establish himself as a writer of poetry and fiction when he set off for Australia in 1884 on the advice of his doctor. He was followed soon after by his first wife, Helen. Still writing poetry and fiction, he worked for several months as a tutor on a station at Jerilderie, NSW, but eventually moved to Queensland, where he lived between 1886 and 1890. During that time Helen died, followed a few months later by their infant son. Adams married an Australian, Edith Goldstone, travelled in Asia, and settled again in Brisbane before returning to England in 1890 to attempt a more purely literary writing career.

Francis Adams would later write about journalism in *The Australians* (1893),[2] claiming that the state of journalism in Australia was superior to that in Britain for two reasons: the press was more independent, and it was more open to left-wing ideas. He also stated what was to become a commonplace about Australian literary culture: that it was almost entirely tied to daily and weekly newspaper publication. During the nineteenth century Australian monthly and quarterly magazines were few and often had relatively short runs. When W.T. Stead announced the Australasian edition of the *Review of Reviews* in 1892, it was in terms that acknowledged both the lack of literary journals in Australia and the difficulty such publications would have in competing with the cheaper English journals:

> The monthly magazine or review has become more and more the arena for the serious discussion of the problems of life. The monthly magazine or review represents the higher thought of our time, and, hence, a good monthly magazine is as indispensable for the culture of a democracy as a well-endowed University, or a good common school. Australia at the present moment has no monthly magazine of the first class. The *Centennial*, of Melbourne, died; the *Quarterly*, of Sydney, as its name implies, only appears once in three months. The very success of

the *Review of Reviews* in Australia stands in the way of the publication of monthly magazine. The field is occupied by a cheap competitor from London: what room is there for a monthly which would be Australian indeed, but which, by the nature of things, could neither be so cheap, so profusely illustrated, or so varied in its contents as its English or American rivals?[3]

Stead wrote this in 1892. When Francis Adams arrived in Melbourne at the end of 1884, he had with him a sheaf of essays on English literature—Matthew Arnold, Tennyson, Dante Rossetti, *Othello*—which quickly found their way into the monthly *Victorian Review*.[4] According to Frances Gill's obituary/appreciation of Adams, he had written the essays during the voyage to Australia,[5] but it was not long before he started to write material of more local interest, with an essay on Adam Lindsay Gordon appearing in the quarterly *Melbourne Review*,[6] and several short stories and poems appearing in the Melbourne *Australasian* between May 1885 and April 1886.[7]

One of these, 'Leonard', responded directly to the *Australasian*'s preference for Australian material. Adams wrote to James Brunton Stephens that he wished he hadn't written it, for 'I threw over "writing to order" years ago in London, and am as surprised I repeated the thing as a man is who wakes from a for[t]night's return to some drug or other'.[8] Despite the *Australasian*'s preference for Australian material, Adams's next contribution, a serialised story titled 'Nellie: A Tale of the Mutiny', was not only about the Indian Mutiny of 1857, but turned out to have been published five years earlier in the British *Family Herald* under the title of 'Jack's Heroine'.[9] The editor of the *Australasian* was so cross about what he regarded as a deception on Adams's part that he published an angry apology to his readers with the second instalment of 'Nellie'. These incidents do not necessarily suggest that Adams wasn't interested in writing about Australia—rather, that he had to make a living publishing whatever he could in the short interval before he felt qualified or had the material to do so.

It is typical of Adams that within a year he did feel qualified to write on several Australian topics, including 'Melbourne and Her Civilization', 'Sydney and Her Civilization', and 'Dawnwards: An Australian Dialogue', collected together in *Australian Essays* and published in Melbourne and London in 1886. When, some years later, Adams sent a copy of *Australian Essays* to the Queensland politician and statesman Sir Thomas McIlwraith, he commented that the essays 'were written when I had been in Australia not much over a year, and there are naturally things propounded in them which I should modify, and in some cases even suppress or change, now. But, such as it was, the little book made me two dear friends—Carl Feilberg [editor of the *Brisbane Courier*] and Brunton Stephens'.[10] In fact he had already made Brunton Stephens's acquaintance by correspondence in 1885, through his campaign to rescue paintings by the artist Adelaide Ironside, which were rotting away in a shed behind the temporary Sydney 'Picture Gallery'.[11] In this early correspondence Adams addresses Brunton Stephens formally as 'My dear Sir', but also makes an appeal to their shared status as writers: 'two old literary wolves like us'. Adams was at this stage more interested in Stephens's poetry than his contributions to various newspapers and journals. In 1885, writing from the station at Jerilderie, Adams is still thinking in terms of the contacts he had made in Melbourne, on the *Melbourne Review* and *Victorian Review*. By 1887, however, both these journals had closed down, and Adams had moved on, both physically and in his publishing outlets, to Sydney and Brisbane.

By June 1885 Adams had begun to believe that 'No literary life is here possible except that of the journalist—*Laboremus*!', but in writing to Brunton Stephens he declares his own lack of journalistic experience in a way that emphasises the primacy of literature:

> For me (since you speak of me) I know nothing of the pressmen, and am inclined to be more afraid of them than even in England. There are no men of literature here, & so one is spared the counterbalancing fear of that factitious whirlpool of 'great men' whose insincerity drove Keats into himself, Tennyson into his 'Island of Cowslips and Primroses', and furnished Carlyle's world-disgust with those poignant portraits we know of. Browning alone of contemporary men of letters, as it seems to me, has kept his sincerity unflawed without running away—much praise to him for it![12]

The rest of the letter deals with things literary and artistic, as though Adams wants to maintain his status as a 'real writer' rather than seek advice on establishing a journalistic career. He may not have realised how much he would need to engage with this journalistic literary life himself, let alone that he would be fêted as one of the best 'leader' writers in the country before too long. It is worth noting, however, that in September 1885, only three months later, Adams declares himself to be 'a member, a very humble member' of the Australian press.[13] He does so, however, in order to attack the cultural standards of the press, in particular the kind of journalism represented by the popular English journalist George Augustus Sala, who wrote for several Australian newspapers during his tour of Australia in 1885 but was best known for his colourful, personal work in the English press (for Dickens's *Household Words*, albeit anonymously, and the London *Daily Telegraph*). All through his own career as a journalist Adams would be careful to distinguish between various types of journalism and to keep even the most serious newspaper writing in perspective as being, in his view, less enduring and important than other kinds of intellectual and literary work.

By December 1886 Adams had moved to Brisbane and was writing to Brunton Stephens affectionately as 'mon cher'. The following letter shows not only how far their acquaintance had developed, but also that Adams has ceased to stand back from the life of the 'pressmen' he had referred to so mock-nervously in the earlier letter:

> Just a line to say I haven't been around because I have been so busy with (1) *Courier* work (2) changing abode (3) proof correction. I am bringing out a complete edition of my poetical work, and now you'll be able to say your say about it. Herewith is Heney's letter, so *candidus*, ingenuous and nice. Send it me back: I like it. And you too will, I guess: hence my despatch of it. How are you? Drop me a line to say. I will try to get around again presently, [illeg] yours, FWL Adams.[14]

The letter from Thomas Heney was a response to Adams's review of Heney's book of poetry, *Fortunate Days*, in the *Brisbane Courier* (29 November 1886, p.5). If *Australian Essays*, which was published in June 1886, really did provide an introduction to his mentors at the *Courier* (Brunton Stephens and Carl Feilberg), as he claimed in his letter to McIlwraith, he must have started to write for that newspaper very soon afterwards. His earlier, rather diffident, claim to be a humble member of the Australian press had a slim foundation, so far as the existing evidence suggests, in his contributions of stories and poems to the *Australasian*.

It appears that James Brunton Stephens helped Adams to acquire the skills and opportunities to make a living by writing for daily and weekly newspapers as well as the more literary monthlies and quarterlies he had started with in his Australian writing career. In September 1888, for instance, Adams writes to Brunton Stephens to thank him for the opportunity to take over the 'Stenogram' column for the *Courier*: 'Whether I should ever have taken to journalism at all without your guiding hand is a question, or how else I should have stumbled along through these last 3 years of wretched health I can't tell'.[15] By 1887 Adams had achieved some status as a journalist in Brisbane, writing to

Brunton Stephens in a ruefully sarcastic vein about his own vanity in thinking he had been a poet:

> But you must not make me so proud with your praises of my 'fascinating prose-style'! Poor old Browning told me he found great interest and pleasure in my verse, Tennyson too said some thing in that way, and so did Oscar Wilde and Mary Robinson and a fair number of other English imbeciles, some of whom took the pain to write to me with absurd expressions of their belief; but these sort of people are different. When I think of the extraordinary consensus of opinion in this matter between Carolus [Carl Feilberg], Spencer Browne, the *Courier* reviewer and you, I am, I confess, really staggered. I think of what these other people said and quail for their insincerity. How unkind, how really and truly unkind, to bolster up a poor fellow in such a 'crank' and get him to waste so much valuable time—time, wh. might have otherwise been spent, perhaps, on writings like my *Courier* leaders, which are in a style (Forgive my vanity in quoting; but it is Carolus who speaks, and he, Spencer Brown, the reviewer and you, are my new lights now that the old ones are all extinguished)—in a style that 'might please all the English-speaking peoples'. That phrase has got into my heart.[16]

But what was it that Adams was writing for the *Courier*? Given that the editorial leader columns, for which he was so highly praised, were unsigned, it is difficult now to identify his contributions. R. Spencer Browne, in his *A Journalist's Memories*, recalls that in the late 1880s 'there were some general and special writers, and a good many leaders came from "outside"'.[17] Adams was just one of several freelance leader contributors, including the radical William Lane who became editor of the *Queensland Worker* in 1890 and later led the 'New Australia' expedition to Paraguay. Adams is supposed to have written book reviews as well, but since these were also unsigned they can only be identified on external evidence, such as the letters about his review of Thomas Heney's book. It is somewhat easier to trace his leaders for the *Darling Downs Gazette* in the lead-up to the 1888 Queensland elections, because the editor, John Zillman, discussed Adams's contributions in his memoirs, crediting him with helping to return Sir Thomas McIlwraith to power.[18] Nonetheless Adam's reputation as a journalist extended beyond the pages of the *Brisbane Courier* and beyond Queensland. When Adams left for England in 1890, the Sydney *Bulletin* recorded the fact in the following terms: 'That accomplished literary man, Mr. Francis Adams, leaves for England this week on a health voyage, taking with him the sincere regards of many friends and admirers in all the Australias. Mr. Adams will, during his absence, continue to contribute to the Australian press' (3 March 1890, p.7).

Adams was probably never on the staff of the *Bulletin*, although his younger brother Harry Beardoe Adams worked there as a sub-editor for a time before moving to Queensland (also suffering from tuberculosis).[19] His contributions were many, however, and he enjoyed advance publicity in its pages for his book of socialist verse, *Songs of the Army of the Night* (1887). In *The Australians* Adams was to praise the *Bulletin* as the only truly national journal, read at all levels of society and in town and country alike. His praise is qualified: 'The *Bulletin* is the one really talented and original outcome of the Australian press, but its literary criticism is that of clever, sixth-form schoolboys and imperfectly-educated pressmen, and all it knows about culture is to perpetually spell it "culchaw"' (p.47). Adams was reasonably happy with the politics of Australian journalism, but not so with its cultural development, as we see in his further description of the *Bulletin*: 'Republicanism seasoned by Socialism, Fiscal Protection as a means to the first, and ruthless and unscrupulous satire of all authority as a means to the second—this is its "policy". It has, however, its limitations, as we have seen, and they are grave in so powerful a general influence' (*Australians*, p.56).

Politically, however, not only the *Bulletin* but even the mainstream press has more independence and integrity than its British counterparts, he argues, because 'its legitimate profits have so far been large enough to keep it pure' (p.48), and the influence of 'Society' and 'wealth' is not yet strong enough to dominate it (p.48). On the whole, he found Australian journalism less conservative and more secular:

> There are no Conservative newspapers in Australia in the English sense: the choice is between Liberalism and Radicalism. The Melbourne *Argus* paid for its erstwhile effort after undisguised Toryism by the transformation of a feeble rival [the *Age*] into one of the most powerful and richest newspapers in Australia and by the loss of all political influence. Its Sydney fellow, the *Morning Herald*, the richest of all . . . has been too wise to take any decided position whatever. (pp.48-49)

His account of Australian newspapers is succinct and decisive, summing up the character, policy and fortunes of the major papers in a matter of pages, but with a particular eye to the political stance of each. Given his earlier account of the various colonies, he says: 'One would have thought that the restless political energy of Queensland would have produced something journalistically fresh and characteristic, but this has not been the case, and Brisbane still astonishes the new arrival by the leisurely issue of a single twopenny morning paper'(p.52). Writing in *The Australians* for a general, rather than a specifically working-class, English audience, he does not mention the smaller socialist newspapers he himself had worked for while in Brisbane. His opinion of the *Brisbane Courier*, however, is quite favourable. As *The Australians* was written from the distance of England, it is not necessary to suspect Adams of currying favour with his former employers when he says, 'the *Courier* has never wanted the saving faculty of progressiveness, and each new phase of the desires and aspirations of the community has found in it more or less satisfactory expression' (pp.52-53).

Moreover despite the *Courier*'s unfriendly reviews of his own work (particularly *Songs of the Army of the Night*), Adams clearly found it not unduly restricting as a source of bread-and-butter journalistic work. In 1889 he wrote to William Michael Rossetti: 'I wrote the leaders here in the *Courier*, the local "stupid paper", from the start of the strike. Why, they were *straight socialism*. I doubt the *Pall Mall* would give me the same hand I got in an Australian "capitalist organ"!. Think what that means!'[20] The *Pall Mall Gazette*, acknowledged by Adams as one of the more liberal English journals, was edited by W.T. Stead, whose journalistic innovations provoked the following comments from Matthew Arnold:

> We have had opportunities of observing a new journalism which a clever and energetic man [W.T. Stead] has lately invented. It has much to recommend it; it is full of ability, novelty, variety, sensation, sympathy, generous instincts; its one great fault is that it is *feather-brained*. It throws out assertions at venture because it wishes them true; does not correct either them or itself, if they are false; and to get at the state of things as they truly are seems to feel no concern whatever.[21]

Adams was on good terms with W.T. Stead after his return to England, but his admiration for the spirit of modernity, which he may or may not have seen reflected in the best of the 'new journalism', was not as strong as his admiration for the high cultural ideals espoused by Arnold. Certainly he viewed with 'a jaundiced eye' the 'triumphal progress' of George Augustus Sala during his lecture tour of Australia in 1885, and reflects pessimistically in his preface to *Australian Essays* (1886) on the adequacy of the press to create the 'current of true and fresh ideas' which, according to Matthew Arnold, 'the first of living critics', should be the role of criticism in contemporary culture. He wishes that journalism could be supplemented by 'the ideas of such personages as Goethe, Emerson, Renan, Arnold, and so on: writers, of course, familiar to us all, and whom I, at any rate must still continue to consider as not wholly exhausted'.[22] This element of compromise in Adams's own performance as a journalist is evident not only in this Preface and in the correspondence with Brunton Stephens already quoted, but also in the work he did after returning to England.

Adams arrived in England in June 1890; within three and a half years he was dead. He suffered from tuberculosis and throat cancer, and his suicide in September 1893 did little more than cut short his final massive haemorrhage. At the time of his death, he was working on *The New Egypt*, based largely on his own visit to Egypt in the winter of 1892.

In England Adams used the now-familiar medium of periodical and newspaper publication to promote and develop material for his last books, *The Australians* and *The New Egypt*. His contacts with Stead, Massingham and the irrepressible Frank Harris (*Fortnightly Review*) provided him with good outlets for articles and publicity for his books, to the extent that one reviewer complained not only of his style ('rank journalese') but of the 'boom' in Francis Adams's work that succeeded his death.[23] One of the many obituaries that followed his sensational death in September 1893 summarises:

> In Australia Mr. Adams was best known as a journalist, and on his return to this country he wrote several magazine articles on Australia and Australians [in the *Fortnightly Review*]. These had some obvious defects, but they showed abundant gifts for vivid description, artistic presentment, and shrewd judgment. Mr. Adams was also the author of some critical essays and of several stories. Last

> winter he went to Egypt, and the book which he wrote on his return is now in the hands of the publishers. Mr. Adams, we may state, was the author of the remarkable series of interviews with his Highness the Khedive, Lord Cromer, and the Egyptian Ministers which excited so much attention at the time of their publication in *The Westminster Gazette* a few months ago.[24]

While it is understandable that an obituary in the *Westminster Gazette* would mention the interviews it had published, it is worth noting that earlier they attracted attention from other quarters, not least Stead himself, who wrote to Adams:

> My dear Mr Adams, And so you are the Famous Interviewer of the *Westminster Gazette*! That explains some things. Your interview with the Khedive is the only smart thing that the *Westminster Gazette* has done since it came into existence. I wrote the moment it appeared heartily congratulating Cook upon having obtained it. He did not tell me that it was you who did it. Had he done so, it would have added to the interest with which I read it.[25]

Stead's use of interviews in the *Pall Mall Gazette* in the 1880s had been an innovation; by 1893 it was a familiar genre.[26] Francis Adams took advantage of its scope for personal comment and impression in the series of interviews which challenged the mainstream conservative portrayal of the main players in the Egyptian crisis: the British consul, Lord Cromer, and the Egyptian leaders, Abbas II, Khedive of Egypt, Riaz Pasha and Tigrane Pasha.[27]

Adams's book *The New Egypt* attempts to fill out the record, to express, more fully than the medium of the newspaper interview would allow, Adams's impressions not only of the young Khedive, but of the political situation in Egypt and his views on British foreign policy. It was unfinished at the time of Adams's death, but his own words express the strong sense of the difference in genre that made him seek a more lasting and more independent voice through other forms of publication than those of the professional journalist: 'Abbas Hilmi was, and is to me, just what he seemed standing up in those boots of his, which figure so appositely in an interview recorded for a public devoted to personal trivialities' (p.163).

Francis Adams may have learnt journalism during his time in Australia, but he never forgot its limitations; it was a part of his repertoire as a writer, rather than the main thrust of his career. As he indicated to Brunton Stephens, writing for newspapers provided him with the means to stay alive; at the same time, however, it demanded time and energy that he would have preferred to spend on more enduring work. Added to this pressure to earn money was the relative difficulty of having books published in Australia.

Adams's attitude to the Australian press, as to Australian culture more generally, was one of condescending approval. He praised its qualities of independence and freshness, feared that it might be corrupted by conservative Anglo-Australian forces, and argued that it had the potential for fostering a new and unique offshoot of English culture along democratic lines.

Yet it seems Francis Adams found that a literary culture which depended so heavily on weekly and daily publications was too narrow to satisfy his own ambitions as a writer. His return to England was not a health voyage in any literal sense: he arrived a physical wreck, and spent his remaining three years searching for warmer climates and avoiding the bad air of London. It was the desire to make his mark in a broader literary culture, rather than the climate or the politics or the economics of Australian life, which sent him back to England, despite his own prophecies of a 'new Athens' in the Antipodes. His time was too short to wait for it to mature.

Notes

[1] Francis Adams, 'The Prose Work of Marcus Clarke', *Sydney Quarterly Magazine*, 4.2 (June 1887), 115-35.
[2] *The Australians* (London: Fisher Unwin, 1893). Further references to this work are given after quotations in the text.
[3] [W.T. Stead], 'To the English-Speaking Folk Under the Southern Cross. Why the "Review of Reviews" Takes Root in Australia', *Review of Reviews* (Australasian edn) (July 1892), 11.
[4] Articles by FA published in *Victorian Review*: 'Tennyson' (1 January 1885), 241-61; (2 February 1885), 408-16; 'Arnold' (2 March 1885), 522-41; (1 April 1885), 682-90; 'Dante Rossetti' (1 June 1885), 198-209; (1 July 1885), 281-86; 'Introduction to Othello' (1 January 1886), 229-37.
[5] Frances Gill, *Table Talk*, 22 September 1893, p.4.
[6] 'The Poetry of Adam Lindsay Gordon', *Melbourne Review*, 10 (April 1885), 196-210. The *Melbourne Review* ran from 1876 to 1885.
[7] The *Australasian* was the weekend magazine published by the *Argus* which 'gave more scope to literary matters . . . and catered for a more sophisticated audience' than its rival, the *Leader*, which was published by the *Age*: *A Colonial City: High and Low Life: Selected Journalism of Marcus Clarke*, edited and introd. by L.T. Hergenhan (St Lucia: U of Queensland P, 1972), p.xxiv.
[8] NLA MS 3271/1, FA to JBS 24 June 1885.
[9] 'Jack's Heroine', *Family Herald* (4 June 1881), [n.p.]. Republished with minor revisions as 'Nellie: A Tale of the Mutiny', *Australasian*, serialised in 3 parts: 27 March 1886, p.618; 3 April 1886, p.666; 10 April 1886, p.714.
[10] FA to McIlwraith 27 November 1888, Oxley Library, Queensland, OM1 64 McIlwraith/Palmer papers 19/111 2483.
[11] *Australian Essays* (Melbourne: Inglis, 1886), p.58. Unfortunately Adams was unsuccessful in persuading the Gallery to hang Ironside's three major paintings, which were subsequently reclaimed by the Redman family and sold at the turn of the century: Jill Poulton, *Adelaide Ironside: The Pilgrim of Art* (Sydney: Hale, 1987), p. 113.
[12] NLA MS 3271/1, FA to JBS from Jerilderie, 24 June 1885.
[13] Preface, *Australian Essays*, p.x.
[14] NLA MS 3271/1, FA to JBS from Red Hill, Brisbane; Heney's letter (enclosed) dated 8 December 1886.
[15] NLA MS 3271/1, FA to JBS from 'Eryx', Kennedy Terrace, Red Hill, Brisbane, 25 September [1888].

[16] NLA MS 3271/1, FA to JBS from Toowoomba, [18 or 20] February 1887.
[17] Reginald Spencer Browne, *A Journalist's Memories* (Brisbane: Read, 1927), ch. 7.
[18] J.H.L. Zillmann, *Career of a Cornstalk* (Sydney: Duncan & Macindoe, 1914), p.49.
[19] Fred J. Broomfield, a friend of Adams's who wrote for the *Bulletin* and later corresponded with Morris Miller on bibliographical and literary subjects, took issue with Mackenzie Bell's statement in *Half-hours with Representative Novelists* ([London: Routledge, 1927], 1, pp.78, 95-97) that Adams was on the staff of the *Bulletin* while in Australia: 'Adams was never on the staff of the Bulletin. The 'B' took his work, as did also the S.M.H., the Brisbane Courier, the Melb. Argus. Adams would never tie himself down to any journal, and always claimed to write from his own standpoint. His contributions to the Australian press were invariably signed by his proper name, save a few pieces of verse, or peculiarly personal sketches, when he generally used the pen-name of "Frank Hawkesbury"'. (NLA MS 87/2/65, 7 February 1934 [709]). While Broomfield is not always accurate in his recollections of Adams (who probably never contributed to the *Argus*, although he did write for its weekend magazine, the *Australasian*), I have found no evidence that Adams was on the *Bulletin*'s staff, except in English sources (the Shrewsbury School Register, and a brief biographical note by Adams's posthumous editor, H.S. Salt).
[20] Angeli-Dennis Papers, UBC, FA to WMR 7 November 1889.
[21] 'Up to Easter', *Nineteenth Century* (May 1887), 638; quoted in Henry Mayer, *The Press in Australia* (Melbourne: Lansdowne, 1964), p.23n.
[22] Preface, *Australian Essays*, p.x.
[23] Anon, 'The Poetry and Prose of Francis Adams', *Saturday Review*, 78 (21 July 1894), 75-76.
[24] 'Suicide of Mr. Francis Adams', *Westminster Gazette*, 5 September 1893, p.5.
[25] The letter continues: 'I will see what I can do about your Book. I have not yet had the pleasure of reading it, but I shall see what I can do this month. Hoping to see you when you come to London, I am, Yours sincerely, W.T. Stead'. The book referred to is almost certainly *The Australians*, which was reviewed in the *Review of Reviews* (London edition) in May 1893.
[26] [W.T. Stead], 'The *Pall Mall Gazette*', London *Review of Reviews* (January 1893), 139-56. The article was prompted by the establishment of

the *Westminster Gazette* by E.T. Cook, a former colleague of Stead's on the *Pall Mall Gazette*, who took over as its editor in 1889. Stead quotes Cook's opinion that interviews had, since the 1880s, become a 'stale matter of course', and his facetious speculation that the next innovation might be interviews with spirits.

[27] Interviews with Lord Cromer, *Westminster Gazette*, 21 February 1893, pp.1-2; Abbas II, Khedive of Egypt, 3 March 1893, pp.1-2; Riaz Pasha and Tigrane Pasha, 29 March 1893, pp.1-2. All reprinted in *The New Egypt: A Social Sketch*, edited by J.W. Longsdon (London: Unwin, 1893) pp.131-88. The editorial introduction to the second interview comments: 'Whatever else may be thought of the exposition of the Khedive's views which it is our privilege to publish this morning, the interview will, at any rate, make one thing clear; and that is that the estimate of his Highness hitherto current in this country requires considerable revision. Mr. Chamberlain's insults were, it is clear, wanting not only in tact, but in truth. So far from being an empty-headed fanatic, the Khedive is a lad of courage and of character. It is very desirable that this revised version of his Highness's personality—to which our interview will, we hope, do something to give currency—should be recognised in this country'.

12 Jean Rhys and Dominican Autoethnography

Sue Thomas

In the theoretical preamble to 'Three Women's Texts and a Critique of Imperialism' Gayatri Chakravorty Spivak takes as her object of investigation an 'abject' 'imperialist narrativization of history', strategically eschewing a reading which would 'touch' the 'bio-graphy' of the author. She does, however, cursorily implicate Jean Rhys's biography in her 'reinscription' of *Jane Eyre*: she suggests that *Wide Sargasso Sea* is the 'scene of writing' of Rhys's origins, birth 'on the Caribbean island of Dominica', and of 'the interest of the white Creole'. Spivak assumes the transparency of these signifiers of a 'named life'.[1] As Laura Chrisman argues, in Spivak's essay 'one colony, India, inadvertently begins to occupy a privileged site of representativeness, of conceptual supremacy for imperial "worlding", at the expense of other colonies such as those in Africa and the Caribbean'.[2] My project is to begin comprehending Rhys's 'worlding' as a Dominican. Born Ella Gwendolen Rees Williams in 1890, she left the island in 1907 to finish her schooling in England. She would remain an expatriate in England and Europe, returning once to Dominica for a holiday in 1936. I situate Rhys's representations of white Creole culture and people and Dominica in relation to late nineteenth- and early twentieth-century Dominican autoethnographic inscriptions of nature, and tropes of place. 'Autoethnography' is a concept developed by Mary Louise Pratt in *Imperial Eyes: Travel Writing and Transculturation*: 'If ethnographic texts are a means by which Europeans represent to themselves their (usually subjugated) others, autoethnographic texts are those the others construct in relation to or in dialogue with those metropolitan representations'. Autoethnography is integral to 'transculturation'—'how subordinated or marginal groups select and invent from materials transmitted to them by a dominant or metropolitan culture'—and the questions it raises: 'How are metropolitan modes of representation received and appropriated on the periphery? . . . with respect to representation, how does one speak of transculturation from the colonies to the metropolis? . . . How have Europe's constructions of subordinated others been shaped by those others, by the constructions of themselves and their habitats that they presented to the Europeans?'[3]

James Anthony Froude reworked Dominican discourses of nature and place in *The English in the West Indies or, The Bow of Ulysses* (1888), a provocative travel book which has an important place in Rhys's family history. The anxieties evoked for Froude by his 1887 visit to Dominica are apparent in two insistently repeated motifs—drift and indifference—both related to the spectre of England's mere 'titular dominion'.[4] In *Voyage in the Dark* (1934) and *Wide Sargasso Sea* (1966) Rhys transculturated for a metropolitan audience the historical master narrative Froude developed through these motifs, in the process also engaging with and 'rewriting' or 'writing back' to Dominican autoethnographic discourses familiar from her childhood and adolescence.[5] Indifference, too, is part of Rhys's autobiographical figuration of oceanic desire for maternal solace and favour and attachment to place.

Dominican journalism published between 1880 and 1907 is my main source of autoethnographic expression. The principal language spoken in Dominica was a Normandy-based French patois. English was the language of government, education, the press, and a significant portion of trade and commerce. The editor-proprietors of the Dominican papers, four-page weeklies for most of the period, were 'coloured' Creoles, members of a class termed the 'Mulatto Ascendency' in Dominican history. Their proprietorships follow colonial American patterns of creole editor-proprietorship, the printer-journalist,[6] the politician-journalist,[7] and the journalist-editor models. The *Dominican* (1839-1907) was edited by Alexander Rumsey Lockhart from 1872 until 1880, and by Augustus Theodore Righton, known popularly as Papa Dom, from 1880 until 1907. Rhys has a journalist-editor character Papa Dom in 'Again the Antilles' (1927), and in two late stories, 'Fishy Waters' and 'Pioneers, O Pioneers' (1976). Lockhart and Righton were Government Printers. Lockhart was probably a descendant of Rhys's slave-owning greatgrandfather James Potter Lockhart.[8] The *Dominica Dial* (1882-1893) was edited by William Davies, influential leader of the Ascendency in the 1880s and 1890s, and the *Dominica Guardian* (1893-1924) was owned initially by William Davies, Sholto Pemberton, A.R. Lockhart and Henry Hamilton, the elective members of the Dominican Assembly until the imposition of Crown Colony rule in 1898, with Joseph Hilton Steber as sub-editor and manager. The Assembly consisted of elected members (called electives) and members nominated by the governor (and usually drawn from the small class of white public officials). Davies took over the editorship to campaign against Crown Colony rule. Steber, a professional journalist, became editor in his own right. Righton and Steber had received early training under A.R. Lockhart.

In 1880 Lockhart published in the *Dominican* an article he thought 'highly interesting and graphic', designed 'to bring the resources of the country to the notice of persons abroad as a means of inviting settlement and capital'.[9] The article called 'Dominica & Its Boiling Lake', by two locals Dr H.A. Alford Nicholls and Edmund Watt, conflates three standard late nineteenth-century Dominican discourses about 'nature': scientific systematisation; the picturesque sublime; and capitalist invigoration. The explicit purpose of the writers is to make 'the loveliest, the most interesting, but one of the least known islands of the New World' and its 'advantages' more 'generally known'. Nicholls and Watt associate the presence of English authority in Dominica after 1770 with 'fresh survey'. They implicitly situate themselves in a line of knowledge-production and discovery: chart making; uncovering of 'submerged' geological history; interior survey of geological formation, vegetation, animals, climate (p.[3]). The local scientific authority cited is the highly esteemed Dr John Imray, who practised in Dominica from 1832 until his death in 1880. The obituary in the *Dominican* memorialised his political integrity and his botanical work: bringing to 'scientific notice' through his correspondence and collaboration with Sir John Hooker of Kew Gardens 'our rare and curious plants and flowers', and the introduction of 'new and valuable plants', including limes and Liberian coffee for commercial cultivation on his plantations.[10] He is constructed as a 'benign, decidedly literate . . . "herborizer"'; Pratt associates such figures with the expansion of 'Europe's "planetary consciousness" . . . marked by an orientation toward inner exploration and the construction of global-scale meaning through the descriptive apparatuses of natural history' (p.15). Imray's protégé Nicholls continued his botanical work, concentrating on scientific agriculture, his labours culminating in the prize-winning *A Text-book of Tropical Agriculture* (1892), reprinted eight times by 1926; scholarly recognition in Great Britain, the United States, and the Caribbean; and knighthood.[11] In their 1880 sketch Nicholls and Watt draw attention to 'many plants of economic value' in the 'primeval forest', the 'large tracts of virgin soil, as rich as can be found any where in the tropics', waiting to be 'mapped out in thriving plantations', and the commercial possibilities of 'systematic' sulphur and silver mining. Primeval forest and virgin soil are the canonical local images of Dominica.

Nicholls and Watt's transformative vision of economic modernisation entails a reinvigoration of the planter class by 'a portion of the tide of wealth in men and money now turned to the East'; they seek to entice what Pratt calls the 'extractive vision' of a European 'capitalist vanguard' (Nicholls and Watt, p.[3]; Pratt, p.150). Editorials and letters to the editor in all local papers, and evidence to the 1893 British Royal Commission on the condition and affairs of Dominica published in the *Dominica Guardian* show that the coloured middle class and small landholders generally shared this desire for recapitalisation. Tradesmen and labourers were keen for the work supplied by plantation owners; irregular employment in that sector meant by 1893 that they had difficulty paying the road tax.[12] As planters, William Davies and A.R. Lockhart gave evidence to the 1897 West India Royal Commission which enquired into depression in the sugar industry: Davies urged more popular representation in government, Lockhart immigration and capital. Both proposed credit schemes. In Nicholls's elaboration of his vision of modernisation before the 1897 Commission he lauded 'scientific principles of agriculture' as opposed to the 'primitive', 'wasteful' and 'unwise' farming practices of predominantly black small landholders.[13]

Pratt observes that the 'concrete relations of labor and property' seldom figure in the writing of the capitalist vanguard or in (white) Creole civic consciousness: 'In the esthetic (as in the political) realm, the unquiet American multitudes [of subjugated peoples] could not be dealt with' (p.180). Nineteenth-century travellers to Dominica often presented it as a twin spectacle: naturally picturesque from a distance, but with the human transformation of the landscape in a state of decay. For Anthony Trollope the decay was graphically emblematised in the 'thick, rank grass' growing through the cobblestone roads of Roseau, the capital. Froude was also disturbed by this spectacle. Trollope, like others, essentialised and pathologised the decay as a failure of civic character, an entropic reversion of all racial groups to the stereotypical 'nature' of black people: 'chattering, idle, and listless'.[14] Nicholls and Watt, however, present subjugated peoples in both negative and positive aesthetic registers. Epitomised and delegitimated as the 'Crown Land squatter', the small landholder is represented as a rapacious and unsystematic despoiler of the 'riches' of the forests. Pacification is presented approvingly: once 'warlike' Carib Indians 'now gentle in demeanour and timid in nature' are contained in duly allotted 'Indian Country', yet still 'skilled' in hunting and seafaring; and bucolic fishermen ply 'the gentle art' with 'intense satisfaction and great good humour', turning to (white) spectators with a '"Look you, Master, what I have done!"'(p.[3]).[15] The dialect speech, a sharp contrast to the language and stylistic registers of the authors, essentialises in linguistic caricature 'the difference that separated white from black'.[16] Nicholls and Watt do not refer to the coloured and black middle class, with whom the Crown and white officials were engaged in a fierce contest over political authority and financial responsibility. Unequal relations of labour and property, particularly as they concerned ability to pay land, horse and road taxes, were forcefully articulated by small landholders William Gabriel Marie, Henry Le Blanc and Fagan Pinard at the 1893 Royal Commission.[17]

The ambitions and sense of propriety of the middle class produced some alternative visions of political, social and economic modernisation. To the coloured journalists the stock historical image of the coloured or black person in a state of 'nature' was the 'beast of burden' under slavery;[18] the contemporary image was of the rowdy '"pests"' who 'infected' the streets of Roseau, and confirmed the racially traducing prejudices of 'morbid' white minds.[19] In his 1896 obituary of Joseph Fadelle, Righton lauded the free middle class of the 1820s and 1830s who contributed to the 'regeneration of their race' by acquiring the 'essentials' of *knowledge, morals*, and wealth' in order to enter political and legal contest with white authorities. (After the passing of the Brown Privilege Bill in 1831, the qualifications for enfranchisement were maleness and a specified measure of property.) The activities of the Young Men's Mutual Improvement Society (for non-white men) in March and April 1888 indicate the kinds of knowledge valued: reading of essays in English, grammatical exercises, dictation, and classes on 'Arithmetic, Synonyms and Geography'.[20] Obeah (a metonym for African religion) was represented as 'barbaric';[21] and the clergy and the press were extolled as the 'two most powerful agents fighting towards the advancement of civilization'('Moralizing', p.[3]). Civic space is mapped in such a way that filth, 'unhallowed mire', metaphorically comes to stand for people outside 'a thrifty, industrious, and moralized class' fit for orderly and 'healthy occupations' ('Moralizing', p.[2]).[22] A.R. Lockhart read to Sir Robert Hamilton's 1893 Royal Commission a brief legislative history of the island from 1775: modernisation ('advance') is linked with the relief of 'social and political disabilities' from the population of 'African descent', popular education, the emergence of a class of 'peasant free-holders', and restoration of fiscal responsibility through increasing the number of elected members of the Legislative Assembly in relation to government-nominated members. Speaking for the electives, he associated the arresting of progress with the 'hybrid constitution' of 1865, offered as an alternative to Crown Colony rule and designed to curb the increasing political power of the 'coloured' population.[23] Crown Colony rule was imposed in 1898, with the promise of a substantial grant for road-building to 'open up' virgin soil. The grant was used by Administrator Henry Hesketh Bell to build the Imperial Road. Davies called Crown Colony rule a *'coup d'état'* [sic], engineered by 'a conspiracy of the Government and the white section' of the people, 'mostly new comers from Europe' disturbed by a seeming '(dis)order' of 'Providence': finding 'nearly the whole mercantile body and the local proprietary composed of black and coloured men', instead of 'an upper crust of whites and a lower crust of subservient blacks' as in the 'gorgeous East'.[24] In 1899 Steber published in the *Dominica Guardian*, which had led the campaign against Crown Colony rule, 'The Real "White Man's Burden"', a parody of Rudyard Kipling's infamous poem, by Ernest H. Crosby, a white United States socialist. The first and last verses indicate the tone Crosby adopts in critiquing the imperialist project of 'civilizing savage hordes':

> Take up the White Man's Burden;
>   Send forth your sturdy sons,
> And load them down with whisky
>   And Testaments and guns.
> Throw in a few diseases
>   To spread in tropic climes,
> For there the healthy niggers
>   Are quite behind the times. . . .

> Take up the White Man's burden,
>   And if you write in verse,
> Flatter your Nation's vices
>   And strive to make them worse
> Then learn that if with pious words
>   You ornament each phrase,
> In a world of canting hypocrited [sic]
>   This kind of business pays.[25]

Crosby's use of the term 'niggers' to indicate racism accords with the practice of Steber and the elective members of the Assembly.[26]

To describe Dominica's beauty Nicholls and Watt use a vocabulary of the picturesque sublime and quote Gifford Palgrave's representation of the island within this compositional tradition. Palgrave is effusive: 'in the wild grandeur of its towering mountains, . . . in the majesty of its almost impenetrable forests; in the gorgeousness of its vegetation, the abruptness of its precipices, the calm of its lakes, the violence of its torrents, the sublimity of its waterfalls, it stands without a rival, not in the West Indies only, but, I should think, throughout the whole island catalogue of the Atlantic and Pacific combined.' Nicholls and Watt's epithets are generally formulaic: a plateau is 'magnificent', trees 'lofty', the island in 'many parts . . . indescribably rugged', volcanoes 'slumbering'. A shift to a 'heightened or intensified consciousness'[27]—a hallmark of the Romantic sublime—is effected by the transcendent prospect of the 'virgin soil' being 'mapped out in thriving plantations' and a latent anxiety that imperial capital may remain 'turned to the East': Dominica is then summed up as 'the richest, the loveliest, and the grandest island of the Carribbean [sic] Archipelago'. Andrew Wilton argues that the emergence of the sublime in landscape representation in the late eighteenth century was to enable the painter 'to accomplish the leap from the "local" and trivial to the grand and universal'.[28] The picturesque sublime and an Edenic discourse facilitate this kind of leap in Dominican autoethnography. Nicholls and Watt's language genders the soil and island feminine. It is 'loveliest', virgin and passive, waiting for the 'tide of wealth in men and money' which will reterritorialise a colonial plantation economy (Nicholls and Watt, p.[3]). In 'Acrostics', an anonymous poem published in the *Dominican* in 1880, the island's prosperity, ordained by 'Nature', is '[a]n Eden of old', the agent of lapse has been '[c]ruel man', and a 'hope sublime' of restored 'bliss' is contingent on fertile Dominica being 'made' its 'hidden treasure to unfold'(31 July, p.[3]). In these gendered discourses Dominica's richness or treasure is not widely enough known, waiting to be opened up, or hidden.

Hidden treasure is a common motif in Rhys's representations of Dominica; I do not have scope in this essay to discuss in detail Rhys's engagement with the discourse of capitalist invigoration to open up the land, an engagement which is entwined in complex and conflicted ways with the Imperial Road and Rhys's witness of change during her return to Dominica. The change is thematised in her writing as ingratitude and hostility towards white Creole people and as corruption. Concerned about the racist tone of 'The Imperial Road', Rhys's publishers reportedly refused it for *Sleep It Off Lady: Stories* (1976).[29] Rhys understands capitalist invigoration of turn-of-the-century Dominica as the policy of Henry Hesketh Bell, the Administrator from 1899 until 1905. In 'Pioneers, O Pioneers' and 'Fishy Waters', collected in *Sleep It Off Lady*, Rhys thematises the failure of the policy, as settlers have difficulty coping with the forest, racialised politics (illustrated by newspaper editorials and letters to the editor) and damaging gossip.[30] The unnamed female protagonist of 'Mixing Cocktails' (1927)[31] and Rochester in *Wide Sargasso Sea* contemplate the landscape through the historical romance of buried pirate treasure. Farewelling Dominica, Rochester explains the 'law of treasure': 'the finders never tell, because you see they'd only get one-third then', the law taking the rest. The desire for Antoinette which violates his masculine English reserve is then, through a process of association, constructed as the treasure he has found. He has persistently conflated Antoinette's un-Englishness with the tropical landscape. In his mind he proposes they behave '[l]ike the swaggering pirates', '[k]eep[ing] nothing back', before his 'sickening swing back to hate'. His hate is honed by the sense that he has been purchased with the Mason money, implying sexual enslavement. In Rochester's English home Antoinette's keepers try to contain her difference in a 'grey wrapper', a 'cardboard world',[32] metonymic of *Jane Eyre*. Antoinette's desire and otherness are emblematised in the red dress she worries they have hidden. She reports Rochester's comment that the dress makes her 'look intemperate and unchaste' (*Sargasso*, p.152); the words may also be read as his disgust with his former desire for her, for him a suffocating reversion to nature, coded in 'Obeah Night' through stock signifiers of blackness—'Obeah', 'dark', 'Angry', 'Blind fierce avenging', 'shameless', 'Hating and hated'.[33] Rhys alludes to the story of Ali Baba and the forty thieves in 'Temps Perdi' (1967); the treasure to which the expatriate white Creole protagonist wants the 'Open Sesame' on her return visit in 1936 is the ability to make sense of her experience.[34]

Froude invokes the picturesque sublime to represent the geography of Dominica, personifying the island as a beauty, once treasured as 'the choicest jewel in the necklace of the Antilles'. He engages intertextually with local discourses: capitalist invigoration, scientific systematisation, treasure and Eden. Nicholls, praised as a scientific agriculturalist and 'the only man in the island of really superior attainments', was one of Froude's key informants (pp.153, 165). Dominica is for Froude an available sexualised beauty 'insolent' and 'conscious' of her 'charms', scorned by the 'enterprising youth of England' who take 'their energy and their capital' elsewhere. The land is 'fertile as Adam's paradise, still waiting for the day when "the barren woman shall bear children"'. The scorn is returned as 'indifference' and 'scornful feeling towards English authority' (pp.169, 160, 171, 161, 173, 163). The local economy had declined to such an extent that the tax revenues could not support the public service— eulogised as the implementation by English authority of the '"latest discoveries of *political science*"' [my italics]—and the plantation system and its monuments were in a state of 'ruin', 'desolation' and 'neglect'. Froude is not comforted by the 'industry of the black peasantry': alongside the ruin and the demoralisation of the English whites a 'state of things more helplessly provoking was never seen' (pp.144, 173, 153, 159). 'Neglect' became during the nineteenth century, Pratt argues, 'the touchstone of a negative aesthetic that legitimated European interventionism'. Like Robert Proctor in his 1825 view of Chile cited by Pratt, Froude 'encodes' his 'letdown in terms of money and dominance' (Pratt, p.149). For him the local indifference and scorn were symptomatic of a degenerative 'drift' back to an uncapitalised barbarism: 'the island drifts along, without credit to borrow money and therefore escaping bankruptcy'; the general mood is one of 'torpid content' interrupted only by the agitations of the 'elected members'; the 'black boys . . . deserve a better fate than to be sent drifting before constitutional whirlwinds back into barbarism, because we, on whom their fate depends, are too ignorant or careless to provide them with a tolerable government'; the English whites (settlers and Creoles) 'have lost heart, and cease to struggle against the stream'; and the 'poor black', if 'denied the chance of developing under guidance the better qualities which are in him, . . . will drift back into a mangy cur' (pp.145, 158, 159, 161). Froude's remedy for 'drift' in this extremity of the English body politic which may 'mortify and drop off' (p.173) is intervention to abolish the measure of representative government in the island's constitution. As Trinidadian John Jacob Thomas points out in *Froudacity* (1889), the best-known piece of nineteenth-century British Caribbean autoethnography, Froude's large project is the thwarting of 'political aspiration in the Antilles' by recommending against elective local legislatures, or elective elements in those legislatures, in effect the 'exclusion of the Negro vote'. Thomas draws attention to Froude's 'one-sided course' of relying on '"Anglo-West Indian"' political and racial views to form his opinions.[35]

Thomas places his countering of Froude as the more enduring part of a wider 'Ethiopic West Indian' project of refuting negrophobia (p.56). In Dominica that project had been undertaken in print by William Davies, then leader of the Mulatto Ascendancy.[36] Locals reportedly mocked Froude's opinion of Nicholls by fabricating inflated market reports about the prices his scientifically cultivated produce was fetching.[37] Davies published in the *Dominica Dial*, evidently without copyright permission, Froude's chapters on Dominica, judging that the cost of the book would prohibit a wide local readership of the 'tissue of misstatements', 'wicked and impolitic' in its inflaming of past racial hatreds.[38] He posted to Froude the issues in which he editorialised against the book and Froude's informants, and in which the chapters were republished.[39] The *Dial* also featured a long review of Darnell Davis's pamphlet 'Mr Froude's Negrophobia, or Don Quixote as a Cook's Tourist' (published in Demerera) and reprinted a critique of Froude from the *Voice* (St Lucia).[40] Davies notes before publication of *The English in the West Indies* Froude's connection with Thomas Carlyle, anticipating 'an exaggerated and fanciful record . . . largely tinctured with a leaven of the "damned nigger" theory of civilization as propounded by the cynical sage of Chelsea'. After publication he concentrates his attack on Froude's interpretation of local history and on his informants, 'negrophobist whites sighing for a past which cannot be recalled', who are said to have 'poisoned his ear'.[41] Froude's hosts had been Captain John Spencer Churchill, the island's Administrator, and his wife, Edith, née Lockhart, later to become Rhys's uncle and aunt. Davies identified Froude's local guide, Mr F—, as Acton Don Lockhart, another uncle ('Rubbish on the West Indies' p.[3]). Rhys's parents, William and Minna Rees Williams, were part of the 'upper ten' in the Administrator's social circle at this time.[42] '[L]ost heart', Froude's naming of the malady of the English whites (numbering fewer than a hundred in a population of about 27,000), could even be a pun on Lockhart, especially as the phrase occurs in a paragraph describing tours with Mr F—.

Throughout the 1890s until the imposition of Crown Colony rule Nicholls, Acton Don Lockhart and William Rees Williams were political allies against the demands and influence of the elective members. Their political principles were on tense occasions cited by the electives using the term for racism—'nigger'—or through mordant comment on a Rees Williams speech mannerism: overuse of the epithet 'beastly', as in the phrase 'those *beastly* mulattos'.[43]

Rhys records racism against Papa Dom in the former way in her 1927 story 'Again the Antilles'; and in *Voyage in the Dark* English class, gender and ethnic prejudice against the white Creole protagonist Anna Morgan and loss of class and ethnic privilege are registered as bestialisation. In 'Again the Antilles' Papa Dom edits English settler Mr Hugh Musgrave's 'damn niggers' to 'the ignorant of another race and colour'. A dispute between the two, in which racial insults and preconceptions have been traded, ultimately turns on a knowledge of Chaucer (*Left Bank*, pp.96-97). Papa Dom's allusions to English literature and history are factually incorrect, and, while presenting the persistence of error humorously, Rhys does work to suggest within the story that a sense of superiority about this is racist. Rhys (and any highbrow reader with verbatim memory of the General Prologue to the *Canterbury Tales* in Middle English) wins the game of 'oneupmanship' the two play over their memory of Chaucer. The game is seemingly won by Musgrave, but Rhys calls on the knowingness of her audience to fault Musgrave. After the death of her father Anna Morgan is dispossessed of her inheritance by her English stepmother Hester, who is unwilling to sacrifice any of her own caste by making Anna an allowance from the proceeds of the sale of the family's Dominican estate. Hester suggests her husband made a bad investment; he had practised scientific agriculture with Anna's help.[44] In England Anna, expected in Dominica to be a lady, struggles to make a living as a chorus girl. Contemplating her own poverty and 'cheap' clothes through a conflated class and racial signifier with Dominican and English resonances before her affair with Walter Jeffries, Anna thinks of '[t]he ones without any money, the ones with beastly lives. Perhaps I'm going to be one of the ones with beastly lives. They swarm like woodlice when you push a stick into a woodlice-nest at home. And their faces are the colour of woodlice' (*Voyage*, p.23). Peter Stallybrass and Allon White chart the Victorian production of desire through the association of the working class and the colonial Irish with the bestial in *The Politics and Poetics of Transgression*, arguing that '[i]t was above all around the figure of the prostitute that the gaze and touch, the desires and contaminations, of the bourgeois male were articulated' and that the smell of the 'low' was a cause of particular anxiety, because smell 'had a pervasive and invisible presence difficult to regulate'.[45] Vincent Jeffries describes the affair Anna has had with his brother Walter as a 'rather beastly sort of love' which 'simply doesn't matter', when 'you get into a[n English] garden and smell the flowers'. She is objectified sexually by anonymous men as a 'fair baboon', 'swine' and 'bitch'. Anna's xenophobic flatmate Ethel, a masseuse who wanted Anna as manicurist to charm her clients, puts her in a room with 'white furniture, and over the bed the picture of the dog sitting up begging—*Loyal Heart*' (*Voyage*, pp.80, 126, 138, 127). After withdrawing her consent during one sexual encounter, Anna retaliates against the implications of the representation in this setting by smashing the picture.

Davies's contestation of Froude through the metaphor of the dichotomy between native and exotic botanical species, is particularly pertinent to Rhys's representations of white Creole culture, English attitudes towards the white Creole, and Dominican attitudes to white settlers. In nineteenth-century imperial discourse colonies were 'planted'.[46] Froude speaks of 'whites whom we planted as our representatives . . . drifting into ruin' (p.121). Taking his cues from this discourse, Froude's metaphoricity of ill-health, and the discourse of scientific systematisation, Davies distinguishes between native and exotic species to contest Froude's historical master narrative of drift. For Davies non-white Dominicans are the generality of the 'sons of the soil', and 'trade and the soil' are in their 'hands'.[47] 'The white man', he writes, 'is an exotic requiring at the best of times the forced conditions of the atmosphere of slavery and the high price of sugar to enjoy a sickly existence. What with the abolition of slavery, the competition of the beetroot [sic] industry, and the operation of the bounty, he has been going from bad to worse . . .' ('Rubbish on the West Indies', p.[3]). Here he is engaging in both a Darwinian discourse of the survival of the fittest and a European ethnographic discourse about the degeneration of the white race in the tropics. Davies naturalises the inevitability of both the decay of white political, economic and social privilege and the upward class mobility of the coloured and black population, and indigenises that population. In the nineteenth-century British Caribbean, Creole was the term used to describe people born in the region, but not of indigenous Carib or Arawak ancestry. Distinctions were made between white, coloured and negro or black Creoles. Froude explains his racial description of Edith Spencer Churchill: 'English Creole—that is, of pure English blood, but born in the island' (Froude, p.147). 'Creole of pure English descent she may be, but they are not English or European either', Rhys's Rochester thinks of Antoinette in *Wide Sargasso Sea* (p.56). Davies prescribes different remedies for indifference and the 'unprosperous condition' Froude diagnoses as drift: the black man's 'equality before the law, and equality in citizenship' for indifference; and trusting to the 'local experience' and financial responsibility of the 'representatives of the people' for drift ('Froude Localised', p.[2]).

In her representations of white Creole people Rhys usually 'writes back' to Davies's horticultural trope and uses the English response to native species to expose the racism of anxieties about 'purity' of 'blood' or 'descent'. I have discussed elsewhere Rhys's invocation of the trope in the Black Exercise Book and 'Temps Perdi'.[48] The gardens of the Dominican estates of local white families in Rhys's 'Mixing Cocktails', *Voyage in the Dark*, and *Wide Sargasso Sea*, include both *native and exotic* species of plants. The mixed gardens are metonymic of a syncretic merging of cultures, the local and the European. Rhys represents Englishness in the mix by the presence of roses. In 'The

Birthday', an unpublished story, Rhys indicates the syncretism by Phoebe's wearing of a rose behind her ear, a Creole custom. Her English aunt is disgusted, linking the custom with the taint of Spanish Creole blood in her sister-in-law's family.[49] Rhys's response in the 1970s to the black nationalism of the Rastafarian movement, as reported by David Plante, is registered through the rose trope: 'No roses in Dominica. Who got rid of them? I know. I know. Up the Dreads. Yeah, the dreads. They're in London, too, and they wear dark glasses. In Dominica they live in the forests. They're taking over'.[50] Her hostility is integral to her sense that an element of the syncretism of Dominican culture and its history is being uprooted. Anna Morgan's English stepmother Hester, a newcomer to Dominica, cannot bear the smell of the flowers—the mix gives her the 'creeps', one native species (the pop-flower) makes her faint. She pointedly has roses on her dining-table and is obsessed that Anna is 'growing up more like a nigger every day', linking her 'turning out badly' with contamination by the black servant Francine, the possibility of 'coloured' blood in and the '[u]nfortunate propensities' of her Creole family, and resistance to her own improving influence by mixing with Francine. Her disgust at Anna's relationship with Francine and Anna's creole culture becomes focused on Anna's 'awful sing-song' Caribbean accent in speaking English (*Voyage*, pp.71, 77, 61, 54, 56).

Rhys signifies the racialised difference of Anna Morgan and Antoinette Cosway Mason, expatriate white Creole women in England, in their sustaining corporeal memories of Dominica, in which the intensely pleasurable smell, spectacle and colour of native species figure strongly. Anna Morgan's origin, memories, and response to an English forest are the markers of non-English ethnicity. The chorus girls she tours with before her affair with Walter rechristen her 'the Hottentot' because she was born in a tropical place (p.12). Sander Gilman has shown that by the late nineteenth century the 'Hottentot' woman had become a European 'icon of pathologically corrupted sexuality' whose physiological features were incorporated into representations of prostitutes and promiscuous women.[51] Walter, Anna's first lover, whose terms of endearment are 'rum child, rum little devil', remarks that the 'tropics would be altogether too lush' for him. He encapsulates her difference in an epithet normally descriptive of vegetation, which implies uncontrolled fertility, excess in relation to his own acculturated sense of restraint, and drunkenness. Anna, by comparison, thinks the Savernake Forest, which Walter shows her, 'beautiful', '[b]ut something had happened to it. It was as if the wildness had gone out of it'. Maudie, an English friend from the chorus line, is disturbed by Anna's approving reading of a poem left in her Adelaide Road boarding-room by a former tenant in which London is described as a 'vile and stinking hole'; Maudie's discomfort is apparent in her complaints about the 'blasted pineapples' among other plant motifs in the 'very dirty' moulding around the walls—they make her feel the room 'isn't cosy' (pp.48, 46, 67, 41). As Cora Kaplan notes, anger is a highly racialised emotion.[52] Antoinette's red dress, glossed as making her 'look intemperate and unchaste' by Rochester, is the 'colour of flamboyant flowers' (of the tropical flame tree), and it gives off a scent—the 'smell of vetivert and frangipanni, of cinnamon and dust and lime trees when they are flowering. The smell of the sun and the smell of the rain'. Rhys implies that her otherness among the English is experiential, internalised as corporeal memory and a differently acculturated structure of desire and pleasure, and that the otherness is racialised as degeneracy. Frangipani wreaths are laid out for the bridal couple; Rochester steps on his without compunction, an action which implies his contempt for Antoinette's cultural difference. For Rochester at the Dominican estate Granbois Antoinette embodies the 'wild, untouched, above all untouched' land with its 'alien, disturbing, secret loveliness', and excess (especially of floral scent). At the core of both Antoinette and the land Rochester senses a mystery, a secret of otherness, which unsettles him: '"What I see is nothing—I want what it hides—that is not nothing"' (*Sargasso*, pp.152, 151, 73). To use an Irigarayan formulation, he is 'threatened by "castration", by anything he cannot see directly, anything he cannot perceive as like himself'.[53] Rhys figures his racial anxieties through his presumptions of a recoding of a European garden of rose and orange trees. He finds 'a large clear space' in the 'virgin' forest he personifies as 'hostile'. A priest's house is in ruin, the trees in its garden have grown wild. The place has, Rochester assumes, become a site for the practice of obeah. He becomes 'lost and afraid among' the 'enemy trees' of the forest which close over his head, while 'the undergrowth and creepers' catch at his legs. Rhys encodes his disorientation and sense of danger through a vertical hierarchy of the body in which the head represents rational, Christian self-command, and the plant emblems of the 'native' threaten to tangle the lower body, bringing him down (*Sargasso*, pp.86-87). Daniel Cosway, an Iago figure in Rhys's reinscription of *Othello* motifs,[54] plays on Rochester's racial prejudices and anxieties. The secret Rochester credulously wants to believe is a taint of promiscuity—'indiscriminate mingling'[55] he labels 'intemperance and unchastity'—inherited from a white Creole ancestry.

Rhys figures Anna's state after having been scorned and abandoned by Walter as drift. Her early numbness (indifferently, 'I didn't care any more') is troped as drowning; she survives. Veronica Marie Gregg writes of the sensation of drowning as 'an effect of Walter's rejection and his enabling contexts—imperial history and the interlocking formations of class, gender and racial hierarchies' (*Voyage*, p.84; Gregg, p.131). Having complained of illness to her next landlady, Anna sings a song she had heard performed in a Glasgow music-hall. The lyrics, which celebrate the pleasure of smoking, suggest a song about the New Woman or 'wild woman', another signifier of whom is sexual licence:

> Blow rings, rings
> > Delicate rings in the air;
> And drift, drift
> > —something—away from despair

Anna tries '[l]egions' and '[o]ceans' in place of 'something', and then associatively settles on the 'Caribbean Sea'. When Ethel confronts Anna with a long list of complaints (failure to live up to her expectations, disloyalty, going on about the dark and cold), working up to '"Why don't you clear out?"', Anna responds, '"I can't swim well enough, that's one reason"' (pp.84, 90, 124). At the novel's close Anna, delirious after a botched abortion, imagines herself crossing a racial boundary by dancing to the tune of 'There's a Brown Girl in a Ring' during Dominica Carnival. In the original version of the ending Rhys revised at the request of her publisher, Anna waits for 'blackness' to come. The publisher interpreted blackness as death, and Rhys then revised the ending to imply a repetition of the cycle. In the first and the published versions of the novel blackness acquires metaphorical and primitivist resonances, manichean possibilities for Anna, and catches up the negativity of her black nurse Meta's hostility, and of English prejudice.[56] Froude interpreted white Creole drift as symptomatic of the demoralising influence of the power of the elective members; Rhys pointedly links Anna's drift to dispossession; lack of marketable skills, credit to borrow money and emotional support; youthful romantic naivety in her affair with Walter; and the demoralising pressures of economic circumstance and English xenophobia, sexism and class prejudice.

Rochester provides his patronym to readers when (assuming an Adamic prerogative) he names Antoinette Bertha. The garden at Granbois contains a tree of life, but any regenerative possibilities in the relationship for both of them are closed off by Rochester's contempt. The novel's title implies on one level that this contempt is the wide Sargasso Sea which separates them and Antoinette from the place which sustains her, and represses the treasure Rochester has discovered, and its narratability in an English world of cardboard walls and a grey wrapper. Rochester interprets Antoinette's state as they prepare to leave Granbois as 'blank indifference', and acknowledges a hatred of the 'indifference' of the landscape, but '[a]bove all' a hatred of Antoinette: 'For she belonged to the magic and the loveliness. She had left me thirsty . . .' (*Sargasso*, pp.137, 141). The Sargasso Sea is a barren sea covered with floating, entrapping seaweed, a place of floating wrecks—a fitting emblem of drift, conceptualised as a product in Rochester and Antoinette's relationship of English xenophobia, compounded by class, racial and sexual anxieties. Rochester's mind projects barbarism and promiscuity on to place and people. Rhys diagnoses the 'unprosperous condition' of Coulibri Estate in Jamaica before it is recapitalised by Mr Mason's fortune as a product of difficult relations of labour and property under the transitionary apprenticeship system, demoralisation by the wait for English monies to compensate for loss of slave labour, xenophobia, and the hostilities attendant on social change and a racialised social hierarchy.

Rhys writes in her autobiographical narratives of growing up in Dominica of a sublime desire to sustain an oceanic identification with 'a very beautiful' land.[57] She reconfigures her drift and indifference motifs on a more personal level in representing the blockages to realisation of her desire for transcendence of the pain of rejection and of the real world. In the autobiographical narrative in the Black Exercise Book (1938) she figures the desire as a frustrated sublime heterosexual romance: 'To me it behind the bright colours the softness grace was something very wild austere sad entirely male I wanted to identify with it to lose myself in it. [B]ut it turned its head away indifferent. & [i]t broke my heart'. She 'work[s] off the worst' of her romantic malady 'by writing poems'; her aesthetic is one in which the words 'most often' used were 'pain, shame, sleep, sea & silence'.[58] She edited out the gendering of the land in 'Love', fragmented memories of landscape drawn from this narrative and dated 6-12-38.[59] The land's gesture of rejection and the romantic malady are rewritten as part of a fraught mother-daughter relationship in *Smile Please* (1979), her unfinished autobiography. 'Yes, she drifted away from me and when I tried to interest her she was indifferent', Rhys writes of Minna Rees Williams (p.43). Rhys suggests that as a child she then sought oceanic identification with black surrogate maternal figures—servants Ann Tewitt, Francine and Victoria—the landscape,[60] and finally the alternate world of the English book. All but the last replicate the primary indifference of Rhys's mother; and the English book, an adolescent refuge, is figuratively linked with the coldness and stillness of death Rhys persistently associates with a whiteness which demands sameness. Looking back, she interprets the desire to lose herself 'in the immense world of books' as an effort 'to blot out the real world which was so puzzling' to her with its complexities of sex, religion, racial politics and tension, and class, inflected by gender as the 'business about ladies and gentlemen' (*Smile Please*, p. 62).

Late nineteenth- and early twentieth-century Dominican autoethnographic discourses of nature and place are integral to Rhys's worlding as a Dominican. For her the materiality of gender, race, ethnicity, class, nation and desire was always already written or articulated in these discourses, and she engages and rewrites them, even as she transculturates from the position of the white Creole expatriate European literary and historical narratives, tropes and motifs. Dominican journalism and the autoethnographic textual strategies of particular journalists and authors are crucial intertexts of and models for Rhys's writing.

Notes

[1] 'Three Women's Texts and a Critique of Imperialism', *Critical Inquiry*, 12 (1985/86), 244, 249, 253, 244.
[2] 'The imperial unconscious? Representations of imperial discourse', *Critical Quarterly*, 32.3 (Autumn 1990), 39.
[3] *Imperial Eyes: Travel Writing and Transculturation* (London: Routledge, 1992), pp.6-7.
[4] J.A. Froude, *The English in the West Indies or, The Bow of Ulysses* (1888; rpt. New York: Negro Universities P, 1968), p.142.
[5] Rhys's textual strategy of rewriting '*European* tropes, forms, themes, myths and the ways in which these operate' [my italics] is widely acknowledged in postcolonial criticism. The theoretical implications of such strategies are drawn out by D. Brydon and H. Tiffin, *Decolonising Fictions* (Sydney: Dangaroo P, 1993). My quotation is from p.78. In V.M. Gregg's *Jean Rhys's Historical Imagination: Reading and Writing the Creole* (Chapel Hill: U of North Carolina P, 1995), in many ways an

exemplary situation of Rhys's writing in relation to European narrativisations of post-Emancipation Caribbean history and recent Caribbean rewriting and contestation of them, Dominica is an object of history or travel writing, not a site of cultural production and traffic.

[6] L. Febvre and H.-J. Martin, *The Coming of the Book: The Impact of Printing 1450-1800*, translated by D. Gerard, edited by G. Nowell-Smith and D. Wootton (London: NLB, 1976), pp.210-12; B. Anderson, *Imagined Communities: Reflections on the Origin and Spread of Nationalism* (rev. ed. London: Verso, 1991), pp.61-62.

[7] J.A. Lent, *Third World Mass Media and Their Search for Modernity: The Case of Commonwealth Caribbean, 1717-1976* (Lewisburg: Bucknell UP, 1977).

[8] He compiled and published the *Leeward Islands Almanac* during this period, and his editorships of newspapers also included an earlier stint with the *Dominican*, and the *Echo* (Trinidad), and later the *Leeward Islands Free Press* (1905-1908), and subeditorship of the *Chronicle* newspapers in Trinidad (before 1872).

[9] [A.R. Lockhart], editorial introduction, 'Dominica & Its Boiling Lake', by H.A.A. Nicholls and E. Watt, *Dominican*, 15 May 1880, pp.[2]-[3].

[10] [A.R. Lockhart], 'In Memoriam!', *Dominican*, 28 August 1880, p.[3]. Bringing to notice and making known are stock postures of Dominican autoethnographers and publishers towards their overseas audiences in the period.

[11] The 1914 edition of *A Text-book of Tropical Agriculture* lists the following distinctions: F.L.S., C.M.Z.S., Corresponding Member of the New York Academy of Sciences and of the Chamber of Agriculture of Basseterre, Guadelope, and Honorary Member of the Royal Agricultural and Commercial Society of British Guiana, and of the Central Agricultural Board of Trinidad. The book won a prize offered by the Jamaican government in 1890 for the best text-book of tropical agriculture. Nicholls was knighted in 1926 for his services to tropical medicine and agriculture. He is the historical original of 'Old Master' in P. Shand Allfrey's *The Orchid House* (1953; rpt. London: Virago, 1982).

[12] Evidence of W. Marie, *Dominica Guardian* (Special Edition), 22 December 1893, p.[3].

[13] *British Parliamentary Papers: West India Royal Commission. Appendix C. Volumes 3 and 4 (1898)*, Colonies. West Indies 8 (Shannon: Irish UP, 1971), pp.123, 126. Davies' evidence is reported on pp.127-29, Lockhart's on pp.135-36.

[14] A. Trollope, *The West Indies and the Spanish Main* (1859; rpt. London: Cass, 1968), p. 161.
[15] 'Indian Country' is usually termed the Carib Quarter. I discuss Rhys's representation of Carib Indians in 'The labyrinths of "a savage person—a real Carib": the Amerindian in Jean Rhys's fiction', *Journal of West Indian Literature*, 7.1 (May 1996), 82-96.
[16] H.L. Gates, Jr, *Figures in Black: Words, Signs, and the 'Racial' Self* (New York: Oxford UP, 1987), p. 6.
[17] The evidence of W. Marie, H. Le Blanc and F. Pinard is reported in special editions of the *Dominica Guardian*, 22 December 1893, p.[3]; 22 December 1893, p.[2]; 11 December 1893, p.[3].
[18] [A.T. Righton], obituary of Joseph Fadelle, *Dominican*, 17 September 1896, p.[2]. See also A.R. Lockhart's untitled reply to European racist remarks in the *Dominican*, 1 December 1877, p.[3].
[19] 'Moralizing', *Dominica Guardian*, 19 August 1893, p.[2]-[3].
[20] Reported in the 'Local' column, *Dominica Dial*, 24 March 1888, p.[2]; 14 April 1888, p.[3].
[21] 'Obeah Legislation', *Dominica Guardian*, 7 May 1904, p.[2]; 'Dominica' [pseudonym], 'Superstition', letter to the editor, *Dominica Guardian*, 14 May 1904, p.[2]; 'What Is Obeah?' *Dominica Guardian*, 5 November 1904, p.[3].
[22] Other examples of this mapping include 'A Public Nuisance', *Dominica Guardian*, 7 November 1894, p.[3], and 'Juvenile Lawlessness and the Compulsory Education Act', *Dominica Guardian*, 28 August 1901, p.[2].
[23] 'The Special Inquiry', *Dominica Guardian* (Special Edition), 29 November 1893, p.[2].
[24] 'The *Mot d'Ordre*', *Dominica Guardian*, 22 June 1898, p.[3].
[25] *Dominica Guardian*, 26 April 1899, p.[3]. The author's name given here, Earnest H. Crosby, may be a pun. A slightly revised version of the poem was published in Crosby's *Swords and Ploughshares* (London: Richards, 1903), pp. 33-5.
[26] See, for example, A.R. Lockhart, *Dominican*, 1 December 1877, p.[3].
[27] T. Weiskel, *The Romantic Sublime: Studies in the Structure and Psychology of Transcendence* (Baltimore: Johns Hopkins UP, 1976), p. 13.
[28] A. Wilton, *Turner and the Sublime* (London: British Museum, 1980), p. 20.
[29] Guide to the Jean Rhys Papers, Department of Special Collections, University of Tulsa, Oklahoma. The unpublished story is held among the papers.
[30] *Sleep It Off Lady: Stories* (1976; rpt. Harmondsworth: Penguin, 1979).

[31] *The Left Bank and Other Stories* (1927; rpt. Freeport: Books for Libraries P, 1970).
[32] *Wide Sargasso Sea* (1966; rpt. Harmondsworth: Penguin, 1968), pp. 139, 152, 148.
[33] 'Obeah Night', in *Jean Rhys: Letters 1931-66*, edited by F. Wyndham and D. Melly (1984; rpt. Harmondsworth: Penguin, 1985), pp. 264-65. For Rhys 'Obeah Night' was the key to Rochester's character; elements of the poem are dispersed through the novel.
[34] *Tales of the Wide Caribbean*, edited by K. Ramchand (London: Heinemann, n.d.), p. 161. For a detailed reading of the story see S.Thomas, 'The labyrinths of "a savage person—a real Carib"'.
[35] J.J. Thomas, *Froudacity: West Indian Fables by James Anthony Froude* (1889; rpt. London: New Beacon Books, 1969), pp.51, 73.
[36] Subscriptions from Trinidad, Grenada and Dominica helped subsidise Fisher Unwin's publication of *Froudacity* (D. Wood, 'Biographical Note', *Froudacity*, pp.20-21).
[37] [W. Davies], 'An Ungrateful Munchausen' [sic], *Dominica Dial*, 24 March 1888, p.[2].
[38] [W. Davies], 'Rubbish on the West Indies, or Froude's Long Bow', *Dominica Dial*, 19 March 1888, p.[3].
[39] [W. Davies], 'Mr Froude's Friends', *Dominica Dial*, 14 April 1888, p.[3].
[40] [W. Davies], 'Negrophobia: A Review', *Dominica Dial*, 10 November 1888, p.[3]; '"The English in the West Indies"', *Dominica Dial*, 5 May 1888, p.[4]. The *Dominica Dial* did not normally carry book reviews.
[41] [W. Davies], '1887: A Retrospect', *Dominica Dial*, 7 January 1888, p.[2]; 'Froude Localised', *Dominica Dial*, 17 March 1888, p.[2]; 'Rubbish on the West Indies', p.[3].
[42] 'The Queen's Jubilee', *Dominican*, 30 June 1887, p.[3].
[43] 'The Garrison on Parade', *Dominica Guardian* (Special Edition), 11 December 1893, p.[2]; 'The Saint; the Sawbones and the Speculator', *Dominica Guardian*, 27 July 1898, p.[3].
[44] Anna would help him sex his nutmeg trees when they first flowered: Rhys, *Voyage in the Dark* (1934; rpt. Harmondsworth: Penguin, 1969), p.62. Nicholls explains in *A Text-book of Tropical Agriculture*, p.181 that '[o]ne male to every eight or ten females is quite enough; and those male trees should be, if possible, on the windward side of the plantation, so that the pollen may be carried by the wind to the pistils'.
[45] *The Politics and Poetics of Transgression* (London: Methuen, 1986), pp.126-34, 137, 139.

[46] See for example Sir W. Molesworth's speech in the House of Commons on 25 July 1848, *Hansard*, 3rd series, 100 (3 July-9 August 1848), col. 829. Davies cites the speech in his evidence to the 1897 West India Royal Commission, p.127.
[47] [W. Davies], 'The Medical Question', *Dominica Dial*, 10 September 1887, p.[3]; 'Froude Localised', p.[2].
[48] S. Thomas, 'Jean Rhys, "grilled sole", and an experience of "mental seduction"', *NLR: Decolonising Literatures*, 28/29 (winter 1994/summer 1995), 65-84; see also S. Thomas, 'The labyrinths of "a savage person—a real Carib"'.
[49] 'The Birthday', Department of Special Collections, University of Tulsa, Tulsa, Oklahoma. The story seems to date from the late 1930s or early 1940s.
[50] D. Plante, 'Jean Rhys: A Remembrance', *Paris Review*, 76 (1979), 274.
[51] 'Black Bodies, White Bodies: Toward an Iconography of Female Sexuality in Late Nineteenth-Century Art, Medicine, and Literature', *Critical Inquiry*, 12 (1985/86), 239n.16.
[52] '"A heterogenous thing": Female Childhood and the Rise of Racial Thinking in Victorian England', in *Human, All Too Human*, edited by D.Fuss (London: Routledge, 1996), p.187.
[53] L. Irigaray, *Speculum of the Other Woman*, trans. Gillian C. Gill (Ithaca: Cornell UP, 1985), p. 138.
[54] Letter to Diana Athill, 28 April 1964, in Wyndham and Athill, p.269. Rochester, Rhys says, 'becomes as fierce as Heathcliff and as jealous as Othello'.
[55] '**promiscuous** . . . characterised by or involving indiscriminate mingling' (*Macquarie Dictionary*).
[56] J. Rees, '*Voyage in the Dark*. Part 1V (Original Version), in *The Gender of Modernism: A Critical Anthology*, edited by B.K. Scott (Bloomington: Indiana UP, 1990), p.389. For a discussion of 'blackness' in the novel see S. Thomas, 'The Equivoice of Caribbean Patois and Song: Jean Rhys's Representations of African Caribbean Racial Differences in *Smile Please* and *Voyage in the Dark*, in *Crossings: Essays in Inter-National Writing*, edited by J. Thieme (Amsterdam: Rodopi, in press).
[57] *Smile Please: An Unfinished Autobiography* (1979; rpt. Harmondsworth: Penguin, 1981), p. 81.
[58] Black Exercise Book, Jean Rhys Papers, McFarlin Library, Department of Special Collections, University of Tulsa, Oklahoma. Reproduced with the kind permission of Francis Wyndham and the McFarlin Library, University of Tulsa.

[59] 'Love', David Plante Papers, Department of Special Collections, University of Tulsa, Oklahoma.
[60] The land 'turned its head away, indifferent, and that broke my heart' (Rhys, *Smile Please*, p. 81).

13   Journalism and Victorian Fiction

Lloyd Davis

The careers of many of the best known Victorian novelists encompassed the periodical press as well as fiction. The journals they wrote for ranged from literary and political reviews to informative magazines and the daily press. Their involvement in this broad range of genres ensured that comments, references or depictions of one form in another often revealed close if not inside perspectives on publishing, authorship and texts.

These viewpoints are reflected in reviews and essays on literature and in literary depictions of periodicals. In each case pointed observations of the other genre are frequently made. Many nineteenth-century reviewers aimed not only to appraise texts but to decide their cultural value. John Woolford underlines the judgmental and opinionated approach of the 'adjectival criticism' which proliferated in the 1850s, with reviewers positioning themselves 'as the organs of public reaction to a new book'.[1] This trend continued, a noted case occurring a few decades later in responses to J.W. Cross's biography of George Eliot. Numerous reviews sought to relocate the author's life and work within 'acceptable standards for female behavior'; the goal was to redeem Eliot without precisely defending her'.[2] In these instances the periodical press tried to assume a kind of cultural authority over authors and works, judging themes, styles and lives.

Literary writers contested this authority, either by responding directly to critical verdicts in articles and prefaces—for instance, Hardy's preface to later editions of *Tess of the d'Urbervilles*—or by attacking or satirising the periodical press in their work. In the second case attacks might focus on the press's social influence and its style of coverage as much as on the issues it covered. The hapless journalist Gigadibs from 'Bishop Blougram's Apology' moves to Australia to evade the cleric's power and cynicism. It is as though Browning, anticipating the haughty reviews of his 1855 volume *Men and Women*, wants to show the limits of the journalistic mind and genre in depicting matters of church and state. Magazine articles are merely 'loose cards/Flung daily down, and not the same way twice'.[3] Trollope also repeatedly takes on what he saw 'as the tyrannical power of the modern newspaper',[4] most famously in *The Warden* and its sequel. In *Barchester Towers* he reproduces the grave self-image of the 'fourth estate' in sage predictions of who will be the new bishop and dean. But if the *Jupiter*, 'the only true source of infallibly correct information on all subjects' (p.7), is right the first time, it is astray in endorsing Mr Slope (pp.418-22). Dickens too might depict reporters as 'Interlopers' who disturb the distinction between public and personal spheres by 'intruding into the private worlds of others'.[5]

Writers such as Browning and Trollope seem to suggest that literary depictions of social issues uncover their ironies and complexities far more subtly than can the periodicals. Simon Frith notes that a parallel antagonism to press coverage developed in intellectual circles in the late-nineteenth century. The academy sought to promote and insulate itself 'in particular, from the philistines' literary representative, the journalist, the object of recurrent academic hostility'.[6] By then the contest for cultural authority had shifted ground; no longer was it between fiction or poetry and the periodical press but between different strands within the latter—the 'higher journalism' versus the newspapers. During the same period, as Christopher Kent explains, 'the later Victorian novel severed its links with periodicals, as if seeking greater control of its own form'.[7] The genres settled into a less interdependent relationship.

Despite this growing separation, mainly in terms of publishing arrangements but with effects for narrative structure and readership, depictions of periodicals and journalists are an interesting aspect of numerous novels from the mid-nineteenth century on in both Britain and America. In themselves the periodicals and their staff offer a rich new source of characters and dramatic situations to novelists. The journalist may be discerning or controversial, a detached observer or powerful intriguer in personal and social affairs. Increasing press coverage of personal and domestic issues highlighted their significance and relevance for fictional narrative. The implied audiences of the many different publications also served to mark existing groups and values and to identify and construct emerging areas of public concern. That is, journals and magazines helped novelists perceive pertinent issues, activities and participants. For example, an important corollary of David Doughan's claim that 'a whole industry was established in the Victorian period to aim magazines at women' is that the political, personal and economic interests of many different women's groups had become conspicuous and significant, inciting and demanding journalistic and literary representation.[8] Such texts were to affect women's thinking about their lives to varying degrees—in one view even producing the 'typical woman of the new time, the woman who has developed concurrently with journalistic enterprise'[9]—and so lead to further pressure on the topics and perspectives to be depicted.

In addition to subject matter, characterisation and readership, periodicals offered another kind of stimulus to novelists. They could be used to represent a distinct level of reporting or commentary on the narrative action. This level would be more or less detached from the personal interests of characters and voice a broader social response to events. It could also serve to indicate the cultural and historical contexts in which characters and events were located. At the same time periodical views within a narrative remained framed by the narrator's perspective. The accounts given by papers and journalists often emerge as misguided or motivated interpretations which the narration eventually supersedes. They seem to have a degree of authority, and other characters in the narrative may find them credible. Yet their limits and errors—as the examples from Browning, Trollope and Dickens suggest—actually work to reinforce the superiority of narratorial knowledge and positions. Where a journalist is a central figure in a novel, a usual premise in the characterisation remains his or her 'objective' view of things. One effect of the narrative may be progressively to undermine or question this premise.

One area where narrative viewpoints on the authority of periodicals can be especially revealing concerns the ethos or social character of journalism and journalists. While doubts about press morality and insight appear in many texts, some novels display a less righteous, socio-historical interest in the ethical impacts of the mushrooming periodical press. How was the press able to claim a central institutional role for itself? What kinds of roles or identities were journalists able to fashion for themselves? With its generic interest in characterisation and interaction, narrative fiction could explore these questions in detail. In such cases, a variety of responses to the new profession and its practitioners enter the novels. Issues of gender, class and politics, as well as religion, are linked to the functions and effects of the press.

Notwithstanding the proliferation of domestic, political and special-interest publications for women in the second half of the nineteenth century, the milieu of periodicals was often conspicuously masculine. This is apparent for writers and readers of both popular and elite journals. Raymond Williams has emphasised the importance of the widely read Sunday papers in the development of a new kind of metropolitan popular culture in Victorian England. He implies, however, that this culture was practically an all-male phenomenon: 'They [the Sunday papers] were bought in, not only by clubs and coffee-houses, but by such places as barbers' shops, where the working man's Sunday visit might often be his only opportunity to read a paper or listen to it being read'.[10] A similar conclusion pertains to the upper-class counterpart of the Sunday papers, the evening 'clubland' press. Its prevailing tone of male address (though not its full range of subject matter) may be characterised by the copy of the *St. James's Gazette* that Lord Henry Wotton leaves for Dorian Gray, with the article 'Inquest on an Actress' marked out.[11]

Lucy Brown has made the point that in comparison to other professions, Victorian journalism was 'exceptional and noteworthy in its employment of women'.[12] However women comprised only 13 per cent of writers in journals, and the contributions of many consisted of only a letter or two to the editor. By the mid-nineteenth century, as Carol Christ maintains, the dominant cultural idea concerning periodical authors was Carlyle's 'hero as man of letters': 'In this world of heroic masculinity, women have almost no place'.[13] Instead they were conceived as either readers, novelists (writing of private rather than public life), or translators, 'suited not to the *act* of original thought' (p.25). Authorship, editing and ownership of the periodicals were understood as community activities, conveying 'serious reports of public affairs, local and national' to a reader assumed to have 'a serious concern for the affairs of a world power' (Brown, p.111). Notwithstanding the myriad publications for women noted above, in many respects the periodical press, from proprietors to readers, was a man's world.

As the nineteenth century progressed this world came to occupy the position of a dominant social institution. Numerous factors were involved in this development, and many sections of the press underwent a change of social position and image. In broad terms, as Stuart Hall argues, 'the liberal middle-class press of the mid-nineteenth century was constructed on the back of the active destruction and marginalisation of indigenous radical and working-class press'.[14] This institutional change interacted with the lives and careers of individual journalists with various consequences. Firstly, more and more journalists came to share 'the "middle ground" of politics . . . with the representatives of the main parliamentary parties'.[15] Secondly, the orientation of the 'popular press' shifted from 'radical' to 'commercial' ends, with popular newspapers becoming 'a highly capitalised market product for a separated "mass" readership' (Williams, p.49).[16] Thirdly, according to James Curran, underlying these changes is a growing awareness that newspapers could function 'to secure the loyalty of the working class' and 'build support for the social order through the expansion of the capitalist press'.[17] The press became tied quite tightly to the political and economic status quo.

A corollary of this change in the press's institutional and ideological positions is the improving social status of journalists and editors themselves (though Gissing's *New Grub Street* reminds us that 'improvement' was not every writer's lot). Prior to the 1840s the press had a rather poor reputation, with journalists often considered as 'hacks' or 'demagogues'.[18] From this decade on, however, journalism and writing started to be considered more and more as a profession and even, in romantic terms, a vocation. They offered a path to relative prosperity and possible celebrity: 'At one extreme the newspaper would provide a route by which the intelligent self-taught working man could rise to a position of social weight and influence' (Brown, p.75). Though in England an individual 'author-function' can be traced back to the publication of Ben Jonson's *Works* in 1616, the possibility of writing as a full-time, relatively autonomous career is not realised till the later decades of the nineteenth century. In 1840 Carlyle explicitly observed that 'He [the heroic author] is new, I say; he has hardly lasted above a century in the world yet'.[19] Yet not for another forty years were conventions and laws instituted which offered opportunities for material security: the establishment of the royalty system and firm copyright legislation, the emergence of publishing trade journals, and the founding of viable writers' associations, such as the Incorporated Society of Authors started by Walter Besant in 1883.[20]

Hence not only published articles but the complex array of social and ethical factors intertwined with the press reflect many of the period's cultural concerns—questions of gender, individualism, business and work, politics and class relations. These factors all contribute to the representations of journalists and journalism in Victorian novels. They inform strategies of characterisation and plotting. Two famous texts which show the intersection of the press's ideological conditions with these narrative strategies are *David Copperfield* (1849-50) and *Middlemarch* (1871-72). References to journalism and writing are relatively small components of the two texts (more central to Dickens's novel than Eliot's), and in each case the contexts of authorship and the press tend to be implied rather than detailed. Nonetheless in both novels the conditions which enabled the periodical press to gain status and power are significant aspects of the depictions of writing and writers.

It is well known that as a young man Dickens had extensive experience as a court and parliamentary reporter for the *Mirror of Parliament*, *True Sun* and *Morning Chronicle* between 1829 and 1835. In the second part of this period he also started to publish stories and sketches. The shift to fiction brought renown and eventually remuneration, and so coincides with Dickens's elevation through the social ranks. His rise reflects personal and professional ambition, and is a kind of metonym for the improving position and influence of many writers and of the press in the mid-nineteenth century: 'Throughout his professional life as an author, Dickens was much concerned with the question of the literary man's status'.[21] Here 'status' is a loaded term, implying the quality and value of the writer's work as well as growing cultural authority and power.

David Copperfield recounts a similar advancement in authorship and authority, one seen to exemplify the rewards of the work ethic. As Pam Morris has written, the novel's 'moral plot structure . . . is to construct the narrator as triumphant hero of moral progress in his own life'.[22] Writing is central to this progress, a key sign of personal and social growth. Along with Thackeray's *The History of Pendennis*, Dickens's work is one of the first to place a writer's progress at the centre of prose narrative—a novel about 'the making of a novelist'[23]—adapting the motive of *The Prelude* to a different genre just as Wordsworth's poem was published.

Like Pip's first tracing of his name in his father's headstone at the opening of *Great Expectations*, David's early encounters with books and writing are somewhat equivocal—a secret escape from Murdstone discipline at Blunderstone, an integral part of Creakle discipline at Salem House. However, when he first considers writing professionally, it is part of his efforts at self-discipline and improvement after Aunt Betsey loses her estate. A humorous tone softly respects David's keenness to start shorthand and court reporting: '"Dear me," said Traddles, opening his eyes, "I had no idea you were such a determined character, Copperfield!" I don't know how he should have had, for it was new enough to me'.[24] These efforts are soon repaid with money and acclaim: 'I make a respectable income. I am in high repute for my accomplishment in all pertaining to the art' (pp.511-12). David then starts to publish 'a good many trifling pieces'; their financial reward is again underlined as proof of quality: 'I am regularly paid for them. Altogether, I am well off' (p.512). For David, literary value is tied to the market.

Later the narrator stresses that he cites his works only 'incidentally . . . as a part of my progress' (p.562). He is not trying to praise or defend them. Yet David's writing becomes intertwined with and reflects his responses to private experience. As his marriage to Dora falters, he becomes a singular figure, the brooding creator, 'returning from a solitary walk, thinking of the book I was then writing—for my success had steadily increased with my steady application, and I was engaged at that time upon my first work of fiction' (p.542). Writing is now a vocation, central to his self-image, compensating for personal and domestic dissatisfaction.

This writer's work is contrasted with the failing attempts of others: Mr Dick's unfinishable *Memorial*, Traddles's inability to learn shorthand, Dora's failed bookkeeping. Successful writing creates David's social identity and helps to order his personal life. In both cases, it affirms a sense of masculine selfhood. Male authorship and authority are nurtured at home and then projected into society: '"Please let me hold the pens," said Dora. "I want to have something to do with all those many hours when you are so industrious. May I hold the pens?" The remembrance of her pretty joy when I said yes, brings tears into my eyes. The next time I sat down to write, and regularly afterwards, she sat in her old place with a spare bundle of pens at her side' (p.529). The narrative closes with a perfect image of feminine aid for the working, writing man: 'My lamp burns low, and I have written far into the night; but the dear presence without which I were nothing, bears me company' (p.717).

Dickens's portrayal of David's development appears, then, to be influenced as much by the social currents which construct authorship in the mid-1800s as by his personal experience. The idea of writing as an heroic masculine pursuit motivates David's efforts and the support of Dora and Agnes. This conception of hard, diligent work reflects the altered position of publishing and writing as careers, as well as their part in promoting the benefits of social change introduced by the consolidation of capitalism after the 1840s. Finally, David's reiteration of the *value* of writing suggests the role of the periodical press both in advocating political and economic norms of the mid-Victorian period and as 'one of the earliest consumer mass markets to develop'.[25]

The narrator's ceaseless scrutiny of others (the half-veiled expressions of Annie Strong, Uriah Heep, Mr Wickfield or Rosa Dartle, for example) connotes a society in which *reporting* people's deeds has become a central activity.[26] It also manifests the influence of 'social-exploration' and 'documentary style' journalism on the novel. Those modes' assumptions of accurate observation and recounting helped form the basis of mid-Victorian narrative realism (Kent, pp.6-7, 12). These assumptions are taken up and developed by George Eliot. The complexity of Eliot's narrative positions—constantly shifting and questioning viewpoints—challenges the limits of individual observation and even the possibility of empiricism.[27] The aim of this challenge is to promote a kind of reflexive realism, in which 'an ethic of veracity and honesty in reporting' is maintained and practised.[28]

Eliot's narrative style critically regards expedient and superficial modes of reporting in both fiction and the periodical press. *Middlemarch* exemplifies this discriminating outlook. Set in the late 1820s to early 1830s, the novel is highly 'conscious of the national struggle for . . . Reform', and of the struggle over ways of representing political issues.[29] By considering this earlier period, Eliot can reflect on issues and representations of moment in the 1860s, including the second Reform Bill and debates over women's work, education and right to vote.[30] The novel's publication in 1871-72 also enables it to review the first decade of vastly increased numbers of periodicals published after the repeal of the 'taxes on knowledge'. The use of historical distance allows it to analyse the connections between periodical (and personal) accounts of social and political events and the later consequences of those events. These considerations come into particular focus in the depiction of Mr Brooke's ownership and Will Ladislaw's editorship of the *Pioneer*.

Edward Royle has asserted that a key aspect of nineteenth-century newspapers was that they frequently functioned as 'party organs' and 'propaganda'.[31] Similarly Lucy Brown points to the 'propensity of party organizations' to use papers 'to organize different sections of the voting public'. She also suggests that most owners had 'active public interests' and that 'sovereign powers of decision were exercised by the proprietors and not by the editors' (pp.57, 89-93).[32] In fact a number of proprietors and editors used the press as 'a means of gaining local political office or a seat in Parliament' (Jones, 'Local Journalism', p.65). The political intent of much local newspaper publishing is foregrounded in the Middlemarch press's coverage of the question of reform.

Brooke buys the *Pioneer* to support his attempt to enter parliament. He employs Will Ladislaw as editor and 'campaign adviser'. Though Will has mixed motives in accepting the position, he presents his choice to Dorothea as a firm decision to 'settle' on some task (p.367), and begins to study 'the political situation with as ardent an interest as he had ever given to poetic metres and medievalism' (p.461). Eliot portrays a wry version of a journalist's motives and of the influence an owner could exert over the editor. Though Brooke likes to feel he is in charge, Will is far ahead in terms of political insight and intellect. Not only is he able to evade and negotiate partisan pressures, but his task becomes 'To coach Mr Brooke' (p.498). He also tries to counter the opposition to Brooke's pro-reform stance in the *Trumpet*, the town's other paper. His success is proved by the personal attacks that the opposing editor Mr Keck starts to direct against him.

After Brooke's failure in addressing the Middlemarch electors, Will looks to a larger arena: '. . . political writing, political speaking, would get a higher value now public life was going to be wider and more national, and they might give him such distinction that he would not seem to be asking Dorothea to step down to him . . . He could speak and he could write' (p.507). Literacy translates to cultural and political capital, and Will anticipates the kind of social rise and personal fulfilment that David Copperfield experiences. Meanwhile Brooke, devoid of such skills, withdraws from the press and from campaigning. Eventually Will's abilities do lead to a public career. Like others during the century, he makes the transition from writing to politics: 'Will became an ardent public man, working well in those times when reforms were begun with a young hopefulness of immediate good which has been much checked in our days, and getting at last returned to Parliament by a constituency who paid his expenses' (p.836). The narrator's comparison to contemporary times conveys a scepticism about the effectiveness of reformist writing and action in the second half of the nineteenth century. It is a view which seems to reflect the institutional centrality and conservatism which the political press had attained.

Like *David Copperfield*, though with a more wryly questioning tone, *Middlemarch* presents journalism as a masculine activity. The press is an arena where various kinds of rivalries are waged, including conflicts between religions, politics, town and estate. Eliot's novel shares with Dickens's an awareness that Victorian journalism functions at the intersections among individual ambitions and desires, social problems and controversies, and ideological constructs which shape those desires and problems.

Gissing's *New Grub Street* also deals with a number of these issues. Published in 1891 it looks back to the emergence of the man of letters during the 1880s. Yet this retrospective view endows the purpose and effort of various characters with dark irony rather than with the optimism that guides David Copperfield's recollections or Will Ladislaw's move from the press to politics. Jasper Milvain embodies in their most expedient form the personal and social motives that drove Victorian journalism. In his own words he is 'the literary man of 1882 . . . Literature nowadays is a trade . . . your successful man of letters is your skilful tradesman. He thinks first and foremost of the markets . . . There's no question of the divine afflatus' (pp.8, 12); and the narrator concurs, 'Milvain . . . unmistakably the young man who cultivates the art of success' (p.216). Though they don't talk about it in such terms Copperfield and Ladislaw either share or benefit from this outlook.

The success of these figures is dramatically shadowed in Gissing's novel by the deaths of Edwin Reardon and Harold Biffen, whose beliefs in literary value and intellectual truth are the antithesis of Milvain's opinions and have none of the envy and rivalry which mark the older Alfred Yule's regressive outlook. But they cannot fit into the social, literary marketplace. Their nostalgia for a truly literate past is fatally anachronistic. In presenting this view Gissing interestingly rejects a number of conventions for characterising male writers. Reunion with his beloved does not save Reardon as it does Copperfield and Ladislaw; publication is of no help to Biffen. Milvain's knowing pronouncements about journalism and letters are ultimately confirmed not disproved, while the narrator conspicuously refuses to comment: 'So Amy first played, and then sang, and Jasper lay back in dreamy bliss' (p.425).

The Victorian periodical press provides an important framework and source for these and other novels. The circumstances and content of periodicals highlight events and issues which novelists experienced and wrote about. At the same time, their works comment on and interpret the significance of the press. The two kinds of texts are thus in dialogic relation, often addressing and responding to each other. Both are central signs and agents in the complex variety of Victorian culture and discourse.

Taken together the novels and the press show that this culture was not a settled state or fixed condition in which writers worked. Instead they expose its dynamic denseness as, to quote Dominick LaCapra, 'a context [which] has its own complex particularity that calls for detailed interpretation'. The intertextual links between Victorian periodicals and novels throw significant light on issues which include gender, politics, class and language. They also help to remind us that 'the very reconstruction of a "context" or a "reality" takes place on the basis of "textualized" remainders of the past',[33] and so underline the importance of textual analysis to historical and cultural studies.

Notes

[1] 'Periodicals and the Practice of Literary Criticism, 1855-64', in *The Victorian Periodical Press: Samplings and Soundings*, edited by J. Shattock and M. Wolff (Leicester: Leicester UP, 1982), pp.112-15.

[2] T. Mangum, 'George Eliot and the Journalists: Making the Mistress Moral', in *Victorian Scandals: Representations of Gender and Class*, edited by K.O. Garrigan (Athens: Ohio UP, 1992), pp. 163-66.

[3] 'Bishop Blougram's Apology', in *Selected Poetry of Browning*, edited by K.L. Knickerbocker (New York: Random, 1951), pp.988-89.

[4] R. Gilmour, Introduction, in *Barchester Towers* (1855; Harmondsworth: Penguin, 1985), p.xvii. Further references to *Barchester Towers* are from this edition.

[5] P. Thoms, 'Detection in *Bleak House*', *Nineteenth-Century Literature*, 50 (1995), 149. 'Interlopers' is the title of Chapter 33 of *Bleak House*.

[6] 'The Good, the Bad, and the Indifferent: Defending Popular Culture from the Populists', *Diacritics* (Winter 1991), 111.

[7] 'Victorian Periodicals and the Constructing of Victorian Reality', in *Victorian Periodicals: A Guide to Research*, edited by J. Don Vann and R.T. VanArsdel (New York: MLA, 1989), p.2.

[8] 'British Women's Serials', in *Victorian Periodical Press*, p.71.

[9] George Gissing, *New Grub Street* (1891; Boston: Houghton Mifflin, 1962), p.298. The narrator is commenting on Amy Reardon.

[10] 'The Press and Popular Culture: An Historical Perspective', in *Newspaper History: From the Seventeenth Century to the Present Day,*

edited by G. Boyce, J. Curran and P. Wingate (London: Constable, 1978), p.48.
[11] Oscar Wilde, *The Picture of Dorian Gray* (1891; London: Peerage, 1991), p.87.
[12] *Victorian News and Newspapers* (Oxford: Clarendon, 1985), p.77.
[13] '"The Hero as Man of Letters": Masculinity and Victorian Nonfiction Prose', in *Victorian Sages and Cultural Discourse: Renegotiating Gender and Power*, edited by T.E. Morgan (New Brunswick: Rutgers UP, 1990), p.20.
[14] 'Notes on Deconstructing the "Popular"', in *People's History and Socialist Theory*, edited by S. Raphael (London: Routledge, 1981), p.230.
[15] A. Jones, 'Local Journalism in Victorian Political Culture', in *Investigating Victorian Journalism*, edited by L. Brake, A. Jones and L. Madden (London: Macmillan, 1990), p.66.
[16] Cf J.H. Wiener, 'The Radical and Labor Press', in *Victorian Periodical Press*, pp.46-47, and A. Jones, 'The Image Makers: Journalists in Victorian Popular Culture', *Trivium*, 24 (1989), 37.
[17] J. Curran, 'The Press as an Agency of Social Control: An Historical Perspective', in *Newspaper History*, pp 55-58. There was resistance to this overwhelming trend; see A. Jones, 'Workmen's Advocates: Ideology and Class in a Mid-Victorian Labour Newspaper System', in *Victorian Periodical Press*, pp.297-316, and Wiener, pp.54-55.
[18] G. Boyce, 'The Fourth Estate: The Reappraisal of a Concept', in *Newspaper History*, p.20.
[19] Thomas Carlyle, 'The Hero as Man of Letters', in *Thomas Carlyle: Selected Writings*, edited by A. Shelston (Harmondsworth: Penguin, 1980), p.235.
[20] See R. A. Colby, 'Authorship and the Book Trade', in *Victorian Periodicals and Victorian Society*, edited by J. Don Vann and R.T. VanArsdel (Aldershot: Scolar, 1994), pp.143-61.
[21] K. Chittick, 'Dickens and Parliamentary Reporting in the 1830s', *Victorian Periodicals Review*, 21 (1988), 154.
[22] *Dickens's Class Consciousness: A Marginal View* (London: Macmillan, 1991), p.71.
[23] John Gross, *The Rise and Fall of the Man of Letters: Aspects of English Literary Life since 1800* (London: Weidenfeld, 1969), p.20.
[24] Charles Dickens, *David Copperfield* (1850; Oxford: Oxford UP, 1991), p.430.
[25] Scott Bennett, 'Revolutions in Thought: Serial Publication and the Mass Market for Reading', in *Victorian Periodical Press*, p.226.

[26] Cf Audrey Jaffe, *Vanishing Points: Dickens, Narrative, and the Subject of Omniscience* (Berkeley: U of California P, 1991), p.117.
[27] David Carroll, *George Eliot and the Conflict of Interpretations: A Reading of the Novels* (Cambridge: Cambridge UP, 1992), p.237.
[28] Simon Dentith, *George Eliot* (Brighton: Harvester, 1986), p.47.
[29] George Eliot, *Middlemarch* (1872; London: Penguin, 1994), p.459.
[30] Gillian Beer, *George Eliot* (Brighton: Harvester, 1986), pp.152-62.
[31] 'Newspapers and Periodicals in Historical Research', in *Investigating Victorian Journalism*, pp.54-55.
[32] Brown notes that journalists were usually expected to fall in behind the proprietor's and editor's views (pp. 87-88).
[33] *Rethinking Intellectual History: Texts, Contexts, Language* (Ithaca: Cornell UP, 1983), pp.16, 27.

14 P.D. Edwards: Victorianist

Margaret Harris

Australia's most eminent Victorianist retired as Darnell Professor of English at The University of Queensland on his sixty-fifth birthday, 2 March 1996. Peter Edwards is one of the handful of Australian literary scholars of his generation to be a top-ranking world expert in his field. In addition to his internationally recognised achievements in his discipline, he made a sustained contribution during his career to the academic profession in Australia and to the educational and cultural environment of his home state. His stature in his University, in which he held a Chair in English for twenty-seven years, is evident from the positions he held there, including a five-year term as Pro-Vice-Chancellor (Humanities) from 1985 to 1990. He served as a Member of the Board of Management, University of Queensland Press from 1982 to 1989, though his active association with the Press began well before that period and extended beyond it. It is then fitting that the University of Queensland Press should publish this volume in his honour. In the wider cultural life of his state Peter Edwards served for many years (1972-84) on the Board of the Queensland Theatre Company and held executive positions in civil liberties organisations such as the Committee against Censorship (1969-73).

By any standard, a distinguished career. Its particular distinctions, in addition to Peter Edward's prestige as a Trollopian, are his place in the vanguard of new developments in Victorian literary studies, his ability to anticipate intellectual trends, and the combination of critical acumen and scholarly erudition in his work, not least in its concentration on the development of such research tools as the *Victorian Fiction Research Guides*.

Over more than three decades Peter Edwards established a formidable international reputation for his work on the great

Victorian novelist Anthony Trollope, through his editions, articles, notes and books. His major study, *Anthony Trollope: His Art and Scope*, was described by a reviewer in the specialist journal *Victorian Studies* as 'quite simply the best book on Trollope ever written'.[1] His first extended treatment of Trollope was in his 1961 doctoral thesis, written at Birkbeck College, University of London, under the supervision of the legendary Geoffrey Tillotson. One of Peter's earliest publications, 'Anthony Trollope's "Australian" Novels',[2] staked out his claim to particular expertise in Trollope's writings about Australia, soon consolidated by his edition (with R. B. Joyce) of Trollope's travel book, *Australia*.[3] This splendid volume has an extensive introduction, together with textual notes and variants, explanatory annotation, and other editorial apparatus including Trollope's itinerary in Australia, his writing timetable for the book, and a list of his other writings about Australia. Subsequent publications included *Anthony Trollope's Son in Australia: the Life and Letters of F. J. A. Trollope*, and work on *Harry Heathcote of Gangoil*.[4]

The Edwards and Joyce *Australia* is the first full critical edition of any of Trollope's works: earlier 'editions' had been simply reprints, sometimes with an introductory essay, and occasionally—as in the Oxford Trollope—with light annotation. Moreover it has the additional authority provided by a collaboration between a literary scholar and an historian. Peter's recognition of the need for texts of Victorian works with appropriate editorial apparatus coincided with moves by Penguin to publish more fully annotated texts, and anticipated the revival of Oxford University Press's World's Classics series. It had a number of consequences for Peter's own career, issuing both in his own editions of works by Trollope and Mary Elizabeth Braddon,[5] and in the launch of the Victorian Texts series by the University of Queensland Press. One of the first titles in this series was Peter's own edition of *He Knew He Was Right*, the first true scholarly edition of any of Trollope's novels.

Peter Edwards published a short book on Trollope in Routledge's Profiles in Literature series in 1968. The brief for this series was to provide an introduction to a writer's career through extracts with commentary and analysis. Peter's deep knowledge of his author enabled an intriguing selection from a range of Trollope's fiction, illuminated by pithy and discerning commentary directed to the central proposition that 'Trollope's "realism" *is* the result of art—of sophisticated art'.[6]

Anthony Trollope is a companion piece to his *magnum opus*, the substantial and widely acclaimed critical study *Anthony Trollope: His Art and Scope*. There were other books on Trollope published at much the same time (for example, those by apRoberts, Halperin, Kendrick, Kincaid, Lansbury, McMaster, Pollard, Skilton, Tracy), but none with the ambition of accounting for Trollope's overall accomplishment as Edwards effectively does. I must admit that at the time of publication I thought the subtitle 'Art and Scope' a bit quaint, but twenty years on various senses of 'scope' resonate. The book has proved durable in its address to the reach and range of Trollope's work: so vast a body of work, and, as Edwards subtly shows, so various. In its broadest terms it reads Trollope in relation both to the theory and practice of fiction in his time, and also in relation to contemporary events and issues. The understanding of literary and topical contexts everywhere informs discussion of particular texts, discussion which is frequently marvellous in its succinctness and unerring in its articulation of the quiddities of Trollope's writing. David Skilton commented in his review that it is reasonable 'to ask that critics command a style which can be read alongside passages from the works they are studying without a sense of pain or incongruity. Edwards's clean, straightforward, cultivated prose never fails him' (p.119). I would add that his enjoyment of Trollope is communicated, with relish and intelligence, throughout *Anthony Trollope: His Art and Scope*.

A more recent book complements the interrogation of assumptions about Victorian realism in the Trollope studies. *Idyllic Realism from Mary Russell Mitford to Hardy* has not had the attention it deserves. It is an impressive demonstration of Edwards's range, discussing poets (Tennyson and Patmore) as well as novelists (those named in the title, and others including George Eliot, Elizabeth Gaskell—and, of course, Trollope) in a challenging and compelling argument that 'the Victorian realistic idyll . . . imitates and exploits a grander mode than its own in order to implicitly deny the basic presuppositions of that mode; it not merely turns potential tragedy and heroic passion into comedy but implicitly denies the existence of the tragedy and heroic passion, whether in art or in life.'[7] While *Idyllic Realism* thus continues the elucidation of the subversive aspects of much Victorian writing that characterises a great deal of Peter Edwards's work, I take the book to be a deliberate counter to the emphasis in much of his criticism on lurid and melodramatic Victorian sensation fiction. This was an interest prominent in his PhD thesis, 'Anthony Trollope and the Victorian Novel of "Sensation"', and developed in his inaugural lecture, *Some Mid-Victorian Thrillers: the Sensation Novel, Its Friends and Its Foes*,[8] which has been widely quoted especially with the revival of interest since the 1980s in the Gothic and in nineteenth-century popular writing—a striking instance of Edwards's ability to pick (or start) a trend.

Among the scholarly initiatives that give evidence of the particular characteristics of Peter Edwards's work, two monograph series for which he was responsible take pride of place. One of these was Victorian Texts (1973-82), unmatched as a series of critically edited works of particular importance. It included works by Clough, Meredith, Surtees, Thackeray and Trollope, and was perhaps ahead of its time in the extent and sophistication of its critical apparatus. The other is the much-cited *Victorian Fiction Research Guide* series (1979 to the present). There are now twenty-six titles in the series, including bibliographies of particular authors, indexes to periodical fiction, and a catalogue of the manuscript letters of G.A. Sala to Edmund Yates. Peter himself has contributed three titles to the series: *Edmund Yates, Frances Cashel Hoey,* and (with Andrew

Dowling) *The Edmund Yates Papers in The University of Queensland Library*. Both the Victorian Texts series and the *Victorian Fiction Research Guides* have in common the aim of providing scholarly tools for others, a feature also of Peter's various contributions to works of reference.

He was instrumental in the 1970s in the setting up of an interdisciplinary course in Victorian Studies at The University of Queensland and of a conference which burgeoned into the Australasian Victorian Studies Association, now a thriving organisation. He discerned the appropriate moment to set up such a specialist organisation, and through it has encouraged a generation of younger scholars. I have been just one beneficiary of his sage sometimes saturnine advice, and of his intellectual generosity.

Each contributor to this volume would have a tale to tell of Peter Edwards's ability to influence and inspire. Paul Crook's recollections provide an example. Their relationship goes back to postgraduate days in London and encounters at a well-known watering hole for expatriate Australians, the 'Surrey' in the Strand. As colleagues at The University of Queensland, they jointly taught a Victorian Studies honours seminar that explored the interaction between literature and politics from Disraeli to Gissing. In a tribute Paul Crook speaks of this seminar as full of 'intellectual adventures . . . We valued Peter not only for his deep knowledge of Victorian writers, publishing and journalism, but also for his quiet subtlety and ironic humour. To my mind, Peter represents the best tradition of literary scholarship, insisting upon the highest standards of exact research, analysis and expression, resisting postmodernist nihilism, never captive to the latest theoretical fashion. I wish him a full and rich retirement.'

Now that Peter is released from the more onerous demands of an academic position, there is time freed for reading and writing, as well as for the family to which he is devoted and which now encompasses grandchildren as well as his sons and daughter, and wife Ann. He may now indulge more fully his passions for opera and cricket and his pleasure in travel at home and abroad.

However, the qualities described by Paul Crook are still being exercised. His World's Classics edition of Mary Braddon's *Aurora Floyd* came out almost exactly at the time of his retirement. Since then, in addition to entries for the nineteenth-century volume of the *Cambridge Bibliography of English Literature 3* and the *New Dictionary of National Biography*, he has also completed a monograph, *Dickens's 'Young Men': Edmund Yates and George Augustus Sala and the World of Victorian Journalism*.[9] Research for this book was assisted by the award of the A. Bartlett Giametti Visiting Fellowship at the Beinecke Rare Book and Manuscript Library, Yale University, in 1995. Its publication marks the culmination of his investigation of figures in the world of Victorian letters of figures sometimes dismissed as 'minor', but whose significance Peter is incomparably positioned to expound. This inimitable work manifests mature, deep and detailed knowledge not only of Sala and Yates, but of the whole rich field of Victorian journalism. The present volume essays some exploration of other parts of this field and celebrates the achievements and influence of P. D. Edwards, Victorianist.

Notes

[1] St Lucia: U of Queensland P, 1977; rpt New York: St Martin's and Hassocks, Sussex: Harvester, 1978. Extracts have been reprinted in *World Literature Criticism, 1500 to the present*, edited by James P. Draper (Detroit: Gale, 1992), 6, pp.25-27. The review quoted is by David Skilton, *Victorian Studies*, 23.1 (1979), 117.

[2] *Southerly*, 25.3 (1965), 200-07. The previous year Edwards had published a review article on *Harry Heathcote of Gangoil* in *Australian Literary Studies*, 1 (1964), 208-12. He has published on other Australian topics, including Lennie Lower.

[3] 1873; St Lucia: U of Queensland P, 1967.

[4] St Lucia: U of Queensland P, 1982; introduction to the Arno Press edition of *Harry Heathcote* (New York: 1981) and World's Classics edition of this novel (Oxford: Oxford UP, 1992).

[5] For the World's Classics series (Oxford: Oxford UP), in addition to *Harry Heathcote of Gangoil*, the following works by Anthony Trollope are

edited by P.D. Edwards: *An Autobiography* (1883; 1980); *Framley Parsonage* (1861; 1980); *Rachel Ray* (1862; 1988). He also edited Mary Braddon, *Aurora Floyd* for World's Classics (1863; 1996); and in the Victorian Texts series, Trollope's *He Knew He Was Right* (1869; St Lucia: U of Queensland P, 1972).

[6] *Anthony Trollope* (London: Routledge & Kegan Paul, 1968), p.6.

[7] *Idyllic Realism from Mary Russell Mitford to Hardy* (London: Macmillan/New York: St Martin's, 1988), p.3.

[8] St Lucia: U of Queensland P, 1971.

[9] Aldershot: Ashgate, 1997.

Notes on Contributors

Virginia Blain is the co-editor of *The Feminist Companion to Literature in English*, has edited collections of essays and is the author of *Caroline Bowles Southey: The Making of a Woman Writer 1786-1854* (1998) and numerous articles on nineteenth-century women's poetry. At present she is preparing an annotated anthology of nineteenth-century women's poetry for Longmans.

Paul Crook is Professor of History at the University of Queensland, author of *American Democracy in English Politics* (1965), *Diplomacy during the American Civil War* (1975), *Benjamin Kidd: Portrait of a Social Darwinist* (1984), and *Darwinism, War and History* (1994). He is currently working on Darwinism and imperialism.

Lloyd Davis teaches English literature and cultural studies at the University of Queensland. He has written previously on sexuality in Victorian literature and has an essay on sexuality in Henry James's *The Sacred Fount* forthcoming in *Victorian Literature and Culture*.

Barbara Garlick teaches eighteenth- and nineteenth-century women's writing and modernism at the University of Queensland. She is currently working on a study of anarchist women writers of the 1890s.

Margaret Harris is Professor in English Literature and Head of Department at the University of Sydney. Her publications in Victorian literature include editions of George Meredith's notebooks (with Gillian Beer, 1984) and George Eliot's journals (with Judith Johnston, 1998).

Judith Johnston is a Teaching and Research Fellow at the University of Western Australia. Her recent publications include *Anna Jameson: Victorian, Feminist, Woman of Letters* (1997) and several articles on the Victorian writer Louisa Anne Meredith.

Christopher Kent is a Professor of History in the University of Saskatchewan. He is the author of *Brains and Numbers: Elitism, Comtism and Democracy in mid-Victorian England* (1978), and many articles on Victorian journalism.

Judy McKenzie is a freelance editor and researcher with a special interest in nineteenth-century journalism. She has edited the letters of George Augustus Sala to Edmund Yates, is the co-editor of *Australasian Victorian Studies Journal*, and is currently engaged on a government-sponsored study of the literature and ecology of South-east Queensland.

Joanne Shattock is Professor of Victorian Literature and Director of Victorian Studies at the University of Leicester. She is editor of the nineteenth-century volume of the *Cambridge Bibliography of English Literature*, third edition, and co-editor of *The Nineteenth Century*, a monograph series published by Scolar/Ashgate Press. She has published widely on Victorian journalism.

Michael Slater is Professor of Victorian Literature at Birkbeck College, University of London, and a former editor of *The Dickensian*. He is currently engaged on a four-volume edition of Dickens's journalism and a biography of Douglas Jerrold.

John Sutherland is Lord Northcliffe Professor of Modern English Literature at University College London and divides his time between there and Caltech. He is the author of many books and articles on Victorian literature and journalism.

Meg Tasker lectures in literature at the University of Ballarat. Her research interests include Victorian poetics and Bakhtin. She is currently working on a critical biography of Francis Adams. She was a student of Peter Edwards's and attributes her interest in Victorian literature to his influence and teaching.

Sue Thomas is a Senior Lecturer in English at La Trobe University, Melbourne. Currently she is completing a book tentatively titled *The Worlding of Jean Rhys*. She has published extensively on late nineteenth- and twentieth-century women's writing and feminist theory.

Chris Tiffin teaches at the University of Queensland. He has published a bibliography of Rosa Campbell Praed and is editor or co-editor of *South Pacific Images, South Pacific Stories, De-Scribing Empire,* and *The Praed Papers*. He is interested in Anglo-Australian literature, publishing history, and computer applications in the Humanities.

Index

A

à Beckett, Albert, 76, 78, 92, 93
à Beckett, Arthur William, 76, 78, 92, 93
à Beckett, Gilbert, 76, 78, 92, 93
Adams, Francis, 146, 155-170
Albert, Prince Consort, 25, 35
Albert Edward, Prince of Wales, 76, 81, 84, 85, 87, 89, 90, 94
Alfred, Prince, Duke of Edinburgh, 149
Allen, Grant, 112, 114, 122
amateurism, 1-18, 89, 90, 94
anonymity, 1-18, 59, 90, 100
Argosy, 102
Argus, 131, 137, 138, 140, 163, 168, 169
Arnold, Matthew, 91, 157, 164, 165, 168
Ashley, Evelyn, 79
Athenaeum, 18, 19, 22, 25, 26, 27, 34, 35, 36, 37, 58
Atlantic Monthly, 115
Aunt Judy's Magazine, 102
Austen, Jane, 102, 104, 105, 107
Austin, Alfred, 77, 92, 147
Austin, Sarah, 25, 34, 36
Australasian, 157, 160, 168, 169
Australia, 44, 129-140, 141-154, 155-170, 197, 212-218
autobiography, 1, 12, 48-50, 59, 62-64, 95, 100, 103, 106, 190
autoethnography, 171

B

Baden Powell, 25
Belgravia, 102
Bell, C.F. Moberly, 112-113, 119, 179
Bell, Henry Hesketh, 169, 177, 179
Bell, Mackenzie, 169
Besant, Walter, 202
biography, 35, 46-61, 62-74, 95, 102, 103, 105-107, 171, 190, 197
Black, William, 147
Blackwood, Alexander, 6, 13, 18
Blackwood, John, 6, 99-101
Blackwood, Robert, 6, 18
Blackwood, William, 1-18
Blackwood, William & Sons, 1-18, 95, 100, 101
Blackwood's Magazine, 1-18, 96, 97, 98, 99, 101, 102, 103, 107
'Bob Bandicoot', 151
Boer War, 113, 118, 139
Bohemia, 89
Bowles, Caroline Anne (see Southey
Bowles, Thomas Gibson, 77, 78, 79, 84, 90, 92
Braddon, Mary Elizabeth, 102, 147, 213, 218
Brisbane Courier (see also *Moreton Bay Courier*), 135, 140, 145, 153, 158, 160, 161, 162, 163, 164, 169
Brisbane Newspaper Company, 145, 147
British Empire (see also imperialism), 125, 138
British Royal Commission (Dominica 1893), 174
British Weekly, 118
Brontë, Charlotte, 5, 17, 58
Brougham, Lord, 24, 57

Brown, John, 81, 82, 93, 94
Browne, Reginald Spencer, 142, 153, 161, 169
Bulletin, 144, 162, 163, 169
Buzacott, Charles Hardie, 145, 146
Byron, George Gordon, 7, 52, 53
Byron, Lady Noel, 53

C

Cabinet Cyclopaedia, 25, 36
caddism, 86
Caine, Hall, 147
Canada, 21, 116
Carlyle, Jane, 35, 103
Carlyle, Thomas, 22, 35, 46, 47, 60, 91, 103, 159, 182, 201, 202, 210
Caudle, Mrs, 38-45
Chamberlain, Joseph, 113, 115, 118, 119, 120, 122, 170
Chambers's Journal, 110
Charterhouse asylum, 64-66
Chicago Chronicle, 116
Christian Socialists, 57
Churchill, Randolph, 111-122
civil service, 76, 88, 91, 110, 111, 114
Clarke, Marcus, 146, 168
Clarke, William, 114, 117, 122
Clay, Frederick, 77, 78, 92
Clough, Arthur Hugh, 215
Collier, William Price, 115
Collins, Wilkie, 147
colonialism, 129-139, 151
Contemporary Review, 100, 101, 103
copyright legislation, 202
Cornhill Magazine, 17, 101, 110
Cornwall, Barry (Bryan Procter), 53

Creole, 171-191
Crimean War, 64, 73
Cross, J.W., 95, 103, 104, 197
Cruikshank, George, 2, 10, 11

D

Daily Chronicle, 114
Daily Mail, 118
Daily News, 46, 48, 52, 58, 117, 118, 124, 127
Daily Telegraph (London), 86, 89, 118, 120, 124, 125, 127, 134, 150, 152, 159
Daily Telegraph (Sydney), 134, 140
Dalley, Bede (Colonial-Secretary), 131, 133, 134
Darling Downs Gazette, 162
Darwin, Charles, 109, 112, 122
Darwin, Francis, 113
Darwin, Leonard, 113
Darwinism, 60, 108, 120, 121, 122, 126, 185
Davies, Emily, 95
Davies, William, 173, 175, 177, 182, 184, 185, 192, 194, 195
De Quincey, Thomas, 48-51
Delany, Mary, 102
Dickens, Charles, 37, 38, 64, 72, 73, 74, 76, 90, 102, 134, 135, 159, 198, 199, 203, 205, 207, 210, 211
Dictionary of National Biography, 47, 92
Disraeli, Benjamin, 80
Dominica, 171-196
Dominica Dial, 173
Dominica Guardian, 173, 174, 193, 194
Dominican, 172, 173, 179, 192, 193

Doyle, Arthur Conan, 147

E

Echo (London), 116
Echo (Trinidad), 192
Edinburgh Review, 22, 95, 101, 103, 107
education, 30, 33, 36, 53, 56, 77, 90, 104, 105, 172, 177, 206
Eliot, George, 95, 98, 99, 103, 104, 106, 197, 203, 205, 207, 215
Encyclopaedia Britannica, 120
English Illustrated Magazine, 110, 112, 122
Escott, T.H.S., 67, 68, 74, 77, 79, 92, 93, 126, 140
Evans, George Essex, 39, 146

F

Fabianism, 114
Family Herald, 157, 168
Favenc, Ernest, 146
Figaro (Brisbane), 140
Figaro (London), 78
Flaxman, John, 23, 31
Foott, Mary Hannay, 146
Forbes, Archibald, 124-140
Fortnightly Review, 101, 121, 165
Forum, 115
Fox, W.J., 101
Franco-Prussian War, 127
Frederick William IV of Prussia, King, 58
Froude, James, 46, 103, 172, 175, 180, 181, 182, 184, 185, 189, 191, 194, 195
Fun, 78

G

Garrick Club, 89

Gaskell, Elizabeth, 215
Gatty, Margaret, 102
gentleman, 5, 6, 14, 15, 69, 75-77, 78, 80, 83, 85, 86, 88, 92, 93
George III, 32
Gibson, Thomas Milner, 77
Gissing, George, 202, 207, 208, 209
Gladstone, William Ewart, 80, 111, 136
Glasgow Herald, 118
Gloucester, Duchess of, 56
Glow-Worm, 78
Goethe, Johann Wolfgang von, 22, 23, 24, 28, 35, 36, 165
Goethe, Ottilie von, 23, 24, 35
goldfields, 151
Gordon, Adam Lindsay, 157, 168
Grand, Sarah, 40, 43, 45
Grossmith brothers, 39
Grub Street, 89, 202, 207, 209
Guilford, sixth Earl of, 68-72

H

Hardy, Thomas, 98, 107, 197
Harris, Frank, 165
Harte, Bret, 147
Hastings's Encyclopaedia of Religion and Ethics, 121
Hatton, Joseph, 147
Hemans, Felicia, 12, 16, 17, 28
Heney, Thomas, 160, 162, 168
Herschel, Sir John, 53
Hogg, James, 1, 15
Home Rule, 118
Hornet, 78
Horne, R.H., 25, 78
Household Words, 64, 66, 159
Howitt, Mary, 97
Howitt's Journal, 102
Hunt, Leigh, 25

Huxley, T.H., 109

I

Illustrated London News, 127, 128
illustration, 10, 14, 39, 81, 85, 93, 127
imperial mission, 126
imperialism, 113, 116, 121, 125, 126, 129, 130, 137-139, 184
Incorporated Society of Authors, 202
Iris, 78

J

James, Henry, 98
Jameson, Anna Brownell, 19-37, 55, 97, 103
Jane Eyre, 171, 180
Jerrold, Douglas, 38-45
Jewsbury, Geraldine, 97
jingoism, 114, 132, 133, 135, 136, 138
Jonson, Ben, 202
Jowett, Benjamin, 113
Joyce, James, 41, 45

K

Keene, Charles, 39
Kemble, Fanny, 103
Kidd, Benjamin, 108-123
Kipling, Rudyard, 147, 177
Kropotkin, Peter, 110

L

Labouchère, Henry, 84
Landon, Letitia, 16
Landor, Walter Savage, 52
Landseer, Edwin, 30, 33, 134-135
Lane, William, 161
Lang, John Dunmore, 142

Lardner, Dionysius, 19-22, 24, 25, 36
Laski, Harold, 121, 123
Lawson, Henry, 141
Leader, 168
Leech, John, 39
Leeds Mercury, 118
Lewes, G.H., 101
Liberal Unionists,, 113
Liberalism, 52, 117, 163
Linton, Eliza Lynn, 97
lions comiques, 87, 94
Littell's Living Age, 110
'Little Englandism', 117
Livingstone, Dr David, 127, 136, 137, 138
Lloyd George, David, 117
Lloyd, Arthur, 87
Lockhart, Alexander Rumsey, 172, 173, 175, 176, 192, 193
Longman's Magazine, 101, 110
Longmans, 1, 2, 5, 14, 64, 73
Loudon, J.C., 25
Lubbock, Sir John, 110
Lukin, Gresley, 145
Lyall, Edna, 147
Lytton, Edward Bulwer, 19

M

Macaulay, Thomas, 51, 60, 67
Macdonald, George, 147
MacKenzie, John Stuart, 113
Macmillan's Magazine, 23, 35, 39, 100, 101
Maitland, Frederick, 113
Manchester Daily Despatch, 118
Man in the Moon, The, 78
Maori Wars, 133
marriage, 2, 3, 13, 15, 19, 25, 35, 42, 43, 53, 55, 56, 204

Marshall, Francis Albert, 76-79, 92
Martineau, Harriet, 46-61, 97, 100, 101, 103
Mask, The, 78
Matrimonial Causes Act, 1857, 100
Maurice, F.D., 23
Mayhew, Henry, 39, 45
Mazzini, Joseph, 25
McKinley, President, 115
Melbourne Opera House, 132
Melbourne Punch, 132, 140
Melbourne Review, 157, 158, 168
Merriman, Henry Seton, 147
Meynell, Alice, 99
militarism, 121, 126, 127, 129, 136
Mill, John Stuart, 22, 91, 100, 106
Mills, John Saxon, 114, 118, 119, 122
Mirror of Parliament, 203
Mirth, 78
Mitford, Mary Russell, 15, 102, 104, 105, 107, 214, 215, 218
Moir, David, 10, 17
Moir, George, 99
Monthly Chronicle, 19-37
Monthly Repository, 60, 101
Moonshine, 78
Moore, Thomas, 25
Moreton Bay Courier (see also *Brisbane Courier*), 142, 143
Morgan, Matt, 76, 77, 78, 81, 85, 92
Morley, Henry, 64
Morning Chronicle, 39, 44, 203
Morning Post, 77, 93
Mrs Caudle's Curtain Lectures, 38-45
Mulready, William, 30

Murphy, Charlotte, 22, 23
Murphy, Denis, 21
music hall, 87, 91, 94, 138

N

National Gallery, London, 26
National Review, 118
nationalism, 19, 21, 31, 33, 186
New England Magazine, 116
New Liberal Review, 118
New Monthly Magazine, 16, 21, 26, 28, 36
New Republic, 121, 123
New York Herald, 127
Nicholls, Dr H.A. Alford, 173-180, 183, 192, 194
Nineteenth Century, 111, 119, 132, 140, 169
'Noctes Ambrosianae', 1, 15, 101
North American Review, 116
Northcliffe, Lord, 120

O

Obeah, 176, 180, 193, 194
obituaries, 22, 46-61, 146, 165
Observer (Brisbane), 142, 145
Observer (London), 121
Oliphant, Laurence, 79
Oliphant, Margaret, 59, 95-107, 147
Opie, Amelia, 56
Outlook (London), 120
Outlook (New York), 115, 116
Owen, Robert, 57, 58
Owl, 79, 88, 93

P

Pall Mall Gazette, 79, 93, 112, 113, 164, 166, 169
Palmerston, Lord, 79, 134

patriotism (see also nationalism), 130, 136, 138
Payn, James, 147
Penny Magazine, 34
Piozzi, Hester Thrale, 102
Poor Law, 91
Post Office, 69, 72, 88
Praed, Rosa Campbell, 146
Pre-Raphaelitism, 33
Private Eye, 85
professionalism, 3, 6, 9, 15, 202, 203
propaganda, 129, 136, 206
Public Opinion, 121
Punch, 38-45, 76, 78, 91, 92, 93
Punch and Judy, 78

Q

Queensland Worker, 162
Queenslander, 141-154
Quiz, 78

R

racism, 178, 183, 185, 186
Reform Act, 1867, 85
republicanism, 81, 162
Review of Reviews, 112, 122, 156, 157, 168, 169
Rhys, Jean, 171-196
Richardson, Dorothy, 41
Richter, J.P.F., 24
Righton, Augustus Theodore, 172
Robinson, John, 60, 61
Robinson, Mary, 161
Rossetti, Dante Gabriel, 157, 168
Rossetti, William Michael, 164
Ruskin, John, 30
Russo-Turkish War, 127

S

Sala, G.A., 89, 124-140, 159, 164

Saturday Review, 39, 43, 44, 77, 79, 169
Savage Club, 89
Schiller, Johann, 24
Scott, Walter, 28, 37, 49, 60, 97
Scribner's Magazine, 116
Shakespeare, William, 23, 35, 37
Shelley, Mary, 25, 36
Sidgwick, Henry, 113
signature, 3, 12, 14, 59, 71, 100, 116
Simcox, Edith, 98
Smyth, Mrs Amelia Gillespie, 12
snobbism, 83, 90
socialism, 114, 147, 162, 164
sociology, 47, 116, 120
Somerville, Mary, 54-55
Southey, Caroline Anne Bowles, 1-18
Southey, Robert, 1-3, 7, 9, 13, 14, 15, 16, 17, 18
special correspondents, 124-140
Spectator, 18, 25, 36, 101, 114, 117, 118
Spence, Catherine Helen, 146
Spencer, Herbert, 109, 120
St. James's Gazette, 101, 200
Standard, 77
Stanley, Henry Morton, 124-140
Stead, W.T., 112, 113, 114, 115, 156, 157, 164, 165, 166, 168, 169, 170
Stephen, Leslie, 94, 102
Stephens, James Brunton, 146, 155, 157-161, 165, 167
Stevenson, Robert Louis, 147
Strachey, Lytton, 46
suffragette movement, 121
Surtees, Robert Smith, 5, 17

T

Tait's Edinburgh Magazine, 26, 28
tariff reform, 114, 118, 119, 123
Taylor, William, 22
telegraph, 127, 141, 143, 153
Tennyson, Alfred, Lord, 77, 146, 157
Thackeray, William, 38, 39, 44, 64, 76, 79, 83, 89, 92, 94, 102, 134, 135, 203
theatre, 24, 38, 76, 78, 87, 89, 90, 91, 152
Thomas, John Jacob, 181, 182, 194
Thompson, Alfred, 76, 92, 93
Tieck, Ludwig, 23, 35
Times, 58, 60, 62-74, 112, 115, 118
Toby, 78
Tomahawk, 75-94
Toynbee, Arnold, 113
transportation, 116, 142
Trevelyan, Northcote, 69
Trollope, Anthony, 62-74, 76, 91, 102, 106, 150-152, 175, 193, 198, 199, 212-215, 217, 218
True Sun, 203
Truth, 74, 84
Turner, Joseph Mallord William, 30, 31, 193
Twain, Mark, 147

V

Vanity Fair, 84
Vauxhall Gardens, 38
Victoria, Queen, 19, 20, 25, 29, 30, 35, 36, 76, 81, 83, 85, 90, 93, 94
Victorian Review, 157, 168
Volunteer movement, 86

W

Warter, John, 2, 15, 16
Warung, Price, 146
Watt, Edmund, 173-176, 178, 179, 192
Weismann, August, 112
Wellington, Duke of, 24, 32, 134
West India Royal Commission, 1897, 175, 192, 195
Westminster Gazette, 118, 166, 169, 170
Westminster Review, 28, 99
Whitehead, Alfred North, 113
Wilde, Oscar, 161, 210
Wilkie, David, 29
Will 'o the Wisp, 78
women's franchise, 55, 91, 100, 106
women's magazines, 199
women's work, 26, 34, 103-105, 201, 206
Wood, Mrs Henry, 102, 147
Woolf, Virginia, 97, 99, 102, 106
Wordsworth, William, 1, 15, 18, 50, 133, 203
World (London), 85, 124
World (Melbourne), 140
World's Work, 117

Y

Yates, Edmund, 85, 89, 124, 139

Z

Zulu War, 127